PEOPLE AND PARLIAMENT
IN THE EUROPEAN UNION

People and Parliament in the European Union

Participation, Democracy, and Legitimacy

JEAN BLONDEL

RICHARD SINNOTT

and

PALLE SVENSSON

CLARENDON PRESS · OXFORD
1998

Oxford University Press, Great Clarendon Street, Oxford OX2 6DP

Oxford New York
Athens Auckland Bangkok Bogota Bombay Buenos Aires
Calcutta Cape Town Dar es Salaam Delhi Florence Hong Kong Istanbul
Karachi Kuala Lumpur Madras Madrid Melbourne Mexico City
Nairobi Paris Singapore Taipei Tokyo Toronto Warsaw
and associated companies in
Berlin Ibadan

Oxford is a registered trade mark of Oxford University Press

Published in the United States
by Oxford University Press Inc., New York

British Library Cataloguing in Publication Data
Data available

Library of Congress Cataloging in Publication Data
Blondel, Jean, 1929–
People and parliament in the European union : participation,
democracy, and legitimacy / Jean Blondel, Richard Sinnott, Palle Svensson.
Includes bibliographical references (p.).
1. Political participation—European Union countries. 2. Voting—
European Union countries. 3. Democracy—European Union countries.
4. Legitimacy of governments—European Union countries.
5. European Parliament—Elections. I. Sinnott, R. (Richard)
II. Svensson, Palle. III. Title.
JN40.B56 1998 323'.042'094—dc21 98–12093
ISBN 0–19–829308–9

1 3 5 7 9 10 8 6 4 2

Typeset by BookMan Services

Printed in Great Britain
on acid-free paper by
Bookcraft (Bath) Ltd, Midsomer Norton
Somerset

PREFACE

The genesis of this book lies in a number of related concerns. There was, first, the large amount of abstention at European Parliament elections, despite all that had been said about the need to introduce direct elections in order to put the European Community, now the European Union, on a sound democratic footing. There was, secondly, the curious discrepancy between these high abstention levels and the prevailing view according to which, except perhaps in one or two countries, people were positively disposed towards the integration process. There was, thirdly, dissatisfaction with the explanations given for the low turnout and, in particular, dissatisfaction with the view that it arose because European elections were, for the electorate, 'second-order' elections. Finally, there was the general problem of whether, or how, representative democratic processes can be transplanted from the national level, where they have taken root, to the more difficult terrain created by the increasing internationalization of governance.

One of us then decided to undertake a new, but limited study of abstention in the 1984 and 1989 European elections in Dublin (Sinnott and Whelan, 1992). However, the scope of that study was such that it became clear that only a comprehensive survey, covering all twelve member states, as they then were, could provide the evidence needed to improve our understanding of abstention. Subsequently, two of us were asked to participate in a major study of 'Beliefs in Government', sponsored by the European Science Foundation, which provided many occasions to look closely at existing survey data sources and to identify the gaps in what was available. These developments led to the decision to involve the European University Institute (EUI) in the project and to apply for research funding to both the European Commission and the European Parliament. Support was generously granted; we were thus able link into the Eurobarometer and to draft a set of new questions for the Eurobarometer survey that took place immediately after the 1994 European Parliament elections. The findings of this volume are based in large part on the analysis of the answers to these questions. The data have been archived at the

Zentralarchiv at the University of Cologne and can be obtained from there and from linked social science data archives.

The analysis and the preparation of the report took a substantial amount of time; this period could not have been compressed. It took the best part of a year for the data to be ready for analysis: it suffices to note that the responses to the newly introduced open-ended questions were in nine languages and that there were nearly 13,000 completed questionnaires. In this regard, we wish to thank most warmly the group of postgraduate students of the EUI who, in the autumn and winter of 1994–5, undertook the major operation of coding and translating the open-ended responses. The rest of 1995 was devoted to data analysis, and 1996 to the preparation of a series of drafts. A group of MEPs and officials of the Parliament and the Commission gave generously of their time to discuss the main findings of the study early in 1997: their helpful comments and criticisms greatly improved the final version of the volume, which was sent to the publisher in summer 1997. Oxford University Press edited the material and printed text, tables, and figures very expeditiously so that the book could appear in early summer 1998—in time to contribute to discussions likely to take place in preparation for the European Parliament elections in 1999.

Of course the context of the 1999 elections will be different from that of the elections of 1994. In the interval since our survey was carried out, the European Parliament has fully exploited the new powers given to it by the Maastricht Treaty, especially as regards its powers of legislative co-decision, of approval of the nomination of the Commission, and of holding committees of inquiry. It has also significantly developed its existing powers in regard to the budget, to oversight of Commission activities, and to the organization of debates, hearings, etc. It has been extensively involved—with the Commission—in a comprehensive campaign to inform public opinion on EU matters. Finally, the Amsterdam Treaty has again extended the powers of the European Parliament, notably by the extension of the scope of co-decision and by the requirement of Parliament's approval of the nomination of the President of the Commission. As a consequence of all of this, it seems likely that the image of the Parliament will have evolved considerably since 1994 and that this evolution may have an effect on participation in the European Parliament elections of 1999. A further consequence is that it will be vital to renew the study of the relationship between Europeans and their Parliament in the context of the 1999 elections.

The help given to us in carrying out the present study has been immense. To begin with, without the financial support given by the Commission and the Parliament, the project would simply not have been possible: we wish to thank all those, including President Jacques Delors, the late Emile Noel, former President of the EUI, the current President of the EUI, Patrick Masterson, and David Martin MEP, who played an active part in securing funding for the study. We also wish particularly to record our thanks to those MEPs and officials who participated in the Florence seminar or otherwise commented on our work in progress: Jens Peter Bonde MEP, John Cushnahan MEP, Sergio Guccione, Philippe Herzog MEP, Francis Jacobs, Bobby McDonagh, Anna Melich, Anna Michalski, Annemie Neyts-Uyttebroeck MEP, Dietmar Nickel, Robert Ramsay, Dermot Scott, Elisabeth Sweeney-Smith, Graham Watson MEP, and Martin Westlake.

We also benefited enormously at all stages of the project, ranging from the design of the research and of the questionnaire to the preparation of the final text, from the helpful comments and suggestions of our colleagues in political science and social research. Since much of this discussion took place during and on the margins of international conferences (the 1994 Madrid ECPR Joint Sessions, the 1994 Berlin IPSA meeting, the San Sebastian meeting of the European Election Study), it would be impossible to mention all those who contributed in this way individually; however, we must express our special thanks to Bruno Cautres, Pilar del Castillo, Mark Franklin, Patrick Honohan, Roger Jowell, Roger Jupp, Max Kaase, Richard Katz, Hans-Dieter Klingemann, Michael Marsh, Warren Miller, Colin Mills, Oskar Niedermayer, Karl-Heinz Reif, Steven Rosenstone, Hermann Schmitt, Jacques Thomassen, Anna Triandafyllidou, Dominique Vancraynest, Cees Van der Eijk, Bernhard Wessels, Brendan Whelan, and Lieven de Winter.

There is then the help given to us at the European University Institute and at University College Dublin (UCD). We wish to thank particularly, at the EUI, the President, Patrick Masterson, the Head of the Academic and Research Service, Andreas Frijdal, and the Head of the Schuman Centre, Yves Mény; we wish also to thank most warmly Robert Danziger of the Computing Centre, Eva Anduiza, then also attached to the Computing Centre, Monique Cavallari and Dervla Ramsay of the Schuman Centre, and Laura Olmastroni from Florence, who dedicated themselves to the project at various points of its development, and Rita Peero, Serena Scarselli, and Roberto Nocentini of the Academic Service, who dealt with great patience with the numerous administrative aspects of the project. At UCD, we wish to thank especially Dolores Burke, James McBride, Ricki Schoen, and Nessa Winston: their contribution to this research project has been immense, essential, and beyond the call of duty. We are also most grateful to Dominic Byatt and Sophie Ahmad of Oxford University Press, who supported the project from the start and saw to it that its publication was speedy and without problems. Finally we wish to say special thanks to Tess, Margaret, and Alissa for their toleration of the extra demands on our time and for their critical interest and encouragement throughout the project.

With such a range of indebtedness to be acknowledged, we must conclude by emphasizing that, whatever mistakes of fact and errors of judgement there are in this volume, these are, naturally, the mistakes and errors of the three of us and of the three of us alone.

Jean Blondel
Richard Sinnott
Palle Svensson

Florence, Dublin, and Aarhus
March 1998

CONTENTS

LIST OF FIGURES

LIST OF TABLES

1

Electoral Participation, Democracy, and Legitimacy in the European Union

INTRODUCTION

For more than two centuries, the struggle for democracy has been so much centred on the state that it is easy to assume that the achievement of 'the democratic state' is the answer to all problems relating to the control of political power. This assumption has perhaps been reinforced in the 1990s as a result of an understandable concentration on the question of fostering and 'consolidating' democracy in Russia and Central and Eastern Europe, on the one hand, and in Africa, Asia, and Latin America, on the other. Yet these efforts must not distract attention from another challenge to democracy, that which results from the reduction of democratic control and accountability arising from the transfer of decision-making power to the international or supranational level. An organization such as NATO has in effect reduced the autonomous power of individual states in the defence field; but the centralized power exercised through the international institution is not subject to control by any recognizable majority in the way in which defence decisions taken at a purely national level ultimately are. Yet it is in the case of the European Union that these issues are most acute: the major development of European integration has meant that accountability, democratic control, and legitimacy constitute a substantial problem for the Union; this book addresses a central aspect of the problem by focusing on participation in European Parliament elections and on the relationship between the citizens of the European Union and the process, practices, and institutions of European integration.

The four European Parliament elections that took place between 1979 and 1994 seem to confirm the doubts and the worries that have been voiced about democracy and legitimacy in the Union: turnout has always been low and it has even decreased between 1979 and 1994 from 66 per cent to 59 per cent.[1] In many of the member states there is a gap of some 20 to 40 percentage points between turnout at European and at national elections. Low turnout is presumed to both reflect and accentuate low levels of legitimacy and a democratic deficit. Yet, despite the fact that the problem is so central to the politics of the European Union, abstention at European Parliament elections has not been comprehensively examined. Furthermore, the nature of the relationship between abstention, the democratic deficit, and legitimacy has so far been given limited attention. One of the main aims of this book is to start to remedy this situation.

As a matter of fact, abstention remains in general understudied. It is known to be widespread in a number of liberal democratic countries, in the United States and Switzerland in particular: yet it has not given rise, as voting patterns have, to major analyses, except to an extent in the United States.[2] This relative lack of interest may be due to the fact that, at national elections, abstention is, in very many countries, quite limited and is regarded as having a limited effect only, namely that those who do not vote do not contribute to the electoral outcome. Yet, whether or not this is the main reason for the dearth of analyses at national level, it does not apply at the European level: the distribution of seats in the European Parliament may depend on those who vote only, but the overall legitimacy of the Parliament and of the whole European Union seems, at least prima facie, to be affected by the size of the turnout. The high abstention rates that have characterized the four direct elections to the European Parliament between 1979 and 1994 seem to indicate, as no mere opinion poll or attitude survey could, that many Europeans are rather lukewarm about the Union and that they are certainly not adequately democratically represented at the Union level. But the democratic problems of the European Community or Union are not new.

DEMOCRACY AND EUROPEAN INTEGRATION

As a matter of fact, from its inception, what can be defined loosely as the 'European project' has been troubled, even bedevilled by the twin

---

[1] These figures give too rosy a picture of turnout in European Parliament elections since they include turnout data from several countries where voting is compulsory. The point is discussed in detail in Chapter 2.

[2] The literature on turnout is considered later in this chapter.

problems of legitimacy and democracy: founders and successors alike have both seemed sure that they had the right vision for the future of Europe and been profoundly worried about whether they were being followed. Believing that they were, so to speak, in advance of their time, they organized the European Community in a rather elitist manner using tactics akin to those of Fabian socialism; yet, recognizing that the transformation of European political, social, and economic life which they were promoting could not be achieved outside a democratic framework, they introduced here and there fragments of responsive institutions which were indeed quickly recognized to be what they were, namely fragments. As Monnet himself put it: 'I thought it wrong to consult the peoples of Europe about the structure of a community of which they had no practical experience.' Later, in a notable understatement, he showed at least some consciousness of the democratic problems that were being stored up when he observed that there was 'still progress to be made' in ensuring that 'in their limited field the new institutions were thoroughly democratic' (quoted in Featherstone 1994: 157). Thus the European project started on the basis of an ambiguity, which has remained attached to the whole enterprise.

There was and continues to be a reason for this ambiguity: it is that the promoters of the 'European project' had and, to an extent, continue to have to fight against those who place an overriding value on the sovereignty of the state. This is not the place to examine who is right and who is wrong in this debate or whether the terms of the debate are sensible: what has only to be noted is that there always was an element of deception—a kind of elite conspiracy—in the actions of the promoters of the European project, as there is an element of deception in all Fabian tactics. The gradual push towards a united Europe was made slowly, partly by the back door, because the promoters of the idea, rightly or wrongly, believed that the supporters of state sovereignty were so strong that they could not be beaten in a straightforward, open battle. This meant that the promoters of the project could not clearly come down in favour of outright democracy, as they could not have done so without abandoning their backdoor tactics: what democratic element there would be would therefore be limited and fragmented. Indeed, not only would democratization have risked mobilizing latent opposition to integration, it would in and of itself have involved a significant leap forward in integration and a strengthening of the supranational dimension that would almost certainly have been resisted by a majority of the member states.

The Fabian tactics may have been correct from the point of view of the interests of the promoters of the project, although they had the inevitable consequence that the democratic component of the project would be relatively small. The result has been that the European Union has suffered and continues to suffer from a kind of complex with respect to this democratic component. As the powers of the Union expand, the complex has intensified and has become more and more closely linked to the issue of legitimacy: given that, in liberal democracies, legitimacy and democracy seem to go together, it is assumed that, were the Union to be more democratic, it would also gain markedly in legitimacy.

Naturally enough, the European Parliament is at the centre of such an argument: the European Parliament is of course regarded as the institution most likely to provide a democratic component to the European Union, although other institutions, especially the Council of Ministers and the national parliaments, could also contribute to such a development. On the basis of this expected role of the European Parliament, it also seemed logical to suggest that direct elections and an increase in the powers of the Parliament would automatically increase the legitimacy of the European Union and of the whole European project. The Tindemans Report articulated this expectation in 1975: 'direct elections . . . will give this assembly a new political authority and reinforce the democratic legitimacy of the whole European institutional apparatus' (Tindemans 1975).

The outcome has fallen well short of these ambitions: direct elections have not solved the legitimacy problem (Reif 1985: 3); nor did the gradual but considerable increase in the powers of the European Parliament since 1979 help markedly, if at all, in the process. The result in some quarters has been a profound sense of disappointment in the role of the Parliament and a good deal of pessimism regarding the prospects for democratizing the Union. Weiler, for instance, first states that there are 'formal and formidable gaps in parliamentary control' in the Union; he then further states that there is a net increase in the power of the executive branch of the member states that has resulted from Union governance; he concludes, perhaps without noting sufficiently that similar characteristics can be found in the parliamentary and electoral politics of several member states of the Union, that, 'in its present state, no one who votes in the European parliament elections has a strong sense at all of affecting critical policy choices at the European level and certainly not of confirming or rejecting European governance' (Weiler 1995: 4). Yet even these comments are, according to Weiler, merely a 'standard critique', as he argues that there are more fundamental problems, including the need for a shift in consciousness and identity to the European level if full legitimate political authority at the European level is to be vested in the people of Europe (Weiler 1995: 17), a comment that goes much beyond what anyone has attempted so far to realize in the European Union. Schmitter also argues that the challenge is immense, amounting to no less than the invention and implementation of 'new forms of ruler accountability, new rights and obligations for citizens and new channels for territorial and functional representation' (Schmitter 1996: 25).

We fully agree that there is more to democratizing the Euro-polity than upgrading the European Parliament and its representative processes. Shifts in consciousness and new or at least reinvigorated channels of representation may indeed by required. The point is that it is essential to analyse and understand the present consciousness and the use and non-use of the existing channels of representation before these challenges can be seriously contemplated. One key to such an understanding is a systematic analysis of turnout in European Parliament elections, an analysis that leads inescapably to the examination of a number of fundamental questions about the relationship between the European people and the European Union. Given that legitimacy and democracy are at the centre of the problem, we need in the first instance to be clear about what legitimacy means and about the relationship between legitimacy and democracy in the context of the Union: this is what we shall do in the coming section of this chapter. We shall then explore, in the second section, the extent to which the European Parliament can play a part and thus be expected to contribute to the legitimacy of the Union. As European electoral politics are often regarded as being a mere extension of national politics, we shall go on to examine the nature of the connections between them and see whether European elections can be regarded as being so dependent on national elections that they are, in reality, 'second-order elections'. This leads to a brief review of what we know about why people participate or abstain in national elections; the chapter concludes with some methodological considerations and an outline of the structure of the book.

LEGITIMACY AND DEMOCRACY
AT THE SUPRANATIONAL LEVEL

A problem which worries many integrationists is the alleged lack of legitimacy of the process of integration, particularly in a period when that process faces some far-reaching changes and challenges. Lack of legitimacy, in turn, is frequently regarded as being due, at least in part, to the 'democratic deficit' of the Union. There are serious doubts, however, as to whether either of these concepts can be applied directly and in this simple manner to the problem. We need therefore to examine them both successively and jointly in order to be able to see if, or more accurately in what way, they are indeed applicable to the European Union and to the European Parliament.

The concept of democracy has been discussed extensively and its various attributes have been elaborated at length;[3] in actual political life, however, the ideal democratic process has not been fully realized in any state or institution of any magnitude. In practice, democracy implies a representative form of government based on universal suffrage and fundamental political rights such as freedom of speech, assembly, association, etc. A key part is played by regular competitive elections and important elements include the responsiveness of elective institutions, the transparency of decision-making organs and of interest groups operating around them, and, in the last analysis, the accountability of political leaders. Such institutional configurations have developed in nation states; the issue is whether it is possible to extend them, with appropriate adaptations, to the supranational level.

The concept of legitimacy poses appreciably more problems, essentially because analyses and applications of the concept have not been sufficiently systematic. The starting point for an empirically applicable concept of legitimacy is support: the legitimacy of an institution stems from the support which individuals belonging to the group in question give to it. This means that legitimacy should not be viewed as a dichotomous, but as a continuous concept, since the amount of support can obviously vary: thus a state is not either legitimate or not legitimate, it is more or less legitimate.

A distinction is frequently made between affective and instru-

---

[3] For an introduction, see Held (1996).

mental support. In his analysis of support, Easton refers to a concept of 'diffuse support', which he describes as 'a reservoir of favourable attitudes or good will that helps members to accept or tolerate outputs to which they are opposed or the effect of which they see as damaging to their wants' (Easton 1965: 273): this type of support is fundamentally affective in character. Yet there can be, and often is, an instrumental element. Easton himself recognizes that, in the long run, diffuse support is not independent 'of the effects of daily outputs' (ibid.); whether this is 'in the long run' or not, the important point is that support, however diffuse, is linked to the evaluation which the individual makes of the organization. The reason why the support given by individuals to an institution is affective or instrumental has to do with the nature of the attitudes which individuals have in the particular case: they may 'like' what the institution is and does in a general manner and how it does it; they may, on the contrary, be concerned with some specific benefits which they can draw from the institution. In all situations, however, support ultimately depends on the distance between what individuals wish to see the institution doing and how this 'what' should be done, on the one hand, and what the institution is regarded as doing and how it is doing it, on the other: the shorter that distance, the greater the support.

Some have questioned the notion that legitimacy should be based on the support of individuals (Grafstein 1981a): yet there is no alternative to support as the basis of legitimacy,[4] although, as we shall see shortly, this support is more complex in character than is usually recognized. Moreover, support, which is an attitudinal concept, must be distinguished from system stability, which is often viewed as a consequence of support and legitimacy on the grounds that those who support a system are likely to maintain it. To the extent that opponents of a 'psychological approach' object to the link between support (and legitimacy) and system stability being viewed as automatic, they are correct: one should not infer (at any rate directly) behaviour (maintaining a system) from an attitude (which support is). The question whether system stability is connected to support and to legitimacy is an empirical one: as a matter of fact, there may be (and obviously is) system stability in the context of severe coercion;

---

[4] Commenting on Lipset's discussion of legitimacy, Barry asks whether legitimacy is a genuine intervening variable that helps to explain the support for a regime or 'is it merely a synonym for "support"?' He remarks: 'These may be separable concepts but it is difficult to see that "legitimacy" is carrying much weight here' (Barry 1978: 69).

conversely, some systems collapse despite the fact that they receive appreciable support. This question is not one into which we have to enter here, however, as our direct concern is with the support for and the legitimacy of the European Union, not with the further consequences of this support, except in the particular context of voting.

It follows from the fact that legitimacy stems from support that legitimacy has three general characteristics which render the concept complex. First, as support can and does vary over time, legitimacy also can and does vary over time; second, support is given by individuals to a variety of groups, institutions, or organizations; third, support is not given, normally at least and in particular in modern societies, as a 'blank cheque' and over all issues: even where it is broad, it remains bounded.

Let us examine these three points. The fact that support varies over time is manifest. As the support of each individual for the state, for instance, may vary and as the overall support for (and legitimacy of) the state is composed of the support of all the individual citizens, this support can be high or low; it could even be 'negative' when there is opposition to the state. Second, support relates, not just to the state, but to every group, institution, or organization. Although legitimacy is typically referred to in the context of the state, such a view is too narrow and appears to stem from the normative point that the state is considered to be 'above' other institutions. States are the objects of likes and dislikes on the part of those who belong to them: the same is true of the other groups or institutions to which individuals belong; indeed, likes and dislikes may be stronger vis-à-vis these bodies than vis-à-vis states, not just in traditional, but in modern societies as well. Some may support the village, community, or region in which they live more than they do the state. For these, the legitimacy of these communities is thus greater than is the legitimacy of the state. The idea of legitimacy is therefore applicable at the same time with reference to a number of groups and institutions in the same area or including the same people. Thus the idea of legitimacy applies to the European Union as well as to other groups and institutions and it applies to the European Union while also applying to the states of that Union.

Third, and indeed to an extent as a counterpart, legitimacy is not unbounded: it is more or less broad or more or less narrow, depending on the extent to which the support given to the group is broad or narrow. In some cases the support can be very broad, so broad that it sometimes seems to hover above, so to speak, the specific activities of the organization: this is typically said to be the case in the context of the state; but this can be true of other organizations; in some cases, on the contrary, the support is narrow, as will tend to occur with specialized groups and institutions. While the support of the state tends to be broad, at any rate in modern societies and especially in the West, even in this case the support does not cover every possible activity which the state is or may conceivably be involved in. As a matter of fact, what occurred in some Western countries in the 1980s has amounted to a reduction of the area of legitimacy of the state: this was the case with Thatcherism, which was based on a more limited vision of the scope of the actions which could be legitimately undertaken by the state. Similarly, support given to groups or institutions other than the state may be broad or narrow: the support given traditionally to families or local communities tended to be very broad and to cover almost every aspect of life; the support given to interest groups is markedly narrower. In short, support is related to the fields or areas in which individuals wish to see the group or institution being involved. Thus a trade union may have support when it focuses on matters relating to wages and working conditions or taxation and social welfare policy, but not when it deals with foreign affairs. Thus also, a state or a local authority or an international or supranational institution may receive support with respect to some matters and not to others.

One should not refer, therefore, strictly speaking, to the legitimacy of the state or of other bodies, as this legitimacy is circumscribed, even in the case of the state. It is based in part on what might be called a broad 'capital of support' due to habits, past experience, etc., as the Eastonian concept of 'diffuse support' emphasizes; it is also based on current developments, on actions and on expectations, as well as on the impressions which leaders convey (Weatherford 1987). Furthermore, all groups are legitimate with respect to certain fields: one should not refer to the legitimacy of the various levels of public bodies and in particular of the legitimacy of international or supranational bodies: one should refer to the areas of legitimacy of these bodies.

Such a conception provides a means of approaching realistically the question of legitimacy in the context of the European Union; there is, on the other hand, no satisfactory answer in the case of the European Union so long as legitimacy is viewed as being 'all or nothing'. The European Union is manifestly not legitimate in the sense that it receives the total support of all European citizens in every field or area; but it is also manifest that some European citizens support the European Union to some extent and that they may support its activities in some fields and not in others. Thus the legitimacy of the European Union is variable and is likely to be limited to some fields, as is indeed the legitimacy of any other institution or group.

Since legitimacy is based on support, the question of the relationship between legitimacy and democracy depends on the relationship between support and democracy, a relationship which is contingent, not axiomatic. Support can manifestly be given and is indeed very often given, in democratic societies, without any reference to democracy: citizens may support an institution because it acts efficiently even if they do not participate or are not asked to participate in it. Legitimacy and democracy are related if members support an institution only to the extent that they view it as democratic: the relationship between legitimacy and democracy is therefore at the level of beliefs and of beliefs that the institution has to be democratic if it is to be supported. The relationship between democracy and support at the supranational level is also contingent: it depends on the extent to which citizens believe that the Union needs to be democratic for them to support it, a belief that may, of course, be encouraged by fledgling democratic processes. This is obviously a matter in which the European Parliament can be expected to play a key role, if any element in the European Union is to play any role at all.

THE ROLE OF THE EUROPEAN PARLIAMENT

This analysis of legitimacy and of its relationship to democracy makes it possible to view both more realistically and more precisely the potential role of the European Parliament in fostering the legitimacy of the Union. The obvious starting point is the recognition that the European Parliament constitutes the representative-democratic element par excellence in the structure of the Union. It may not be the only democratic element: the governments that are represented on the Council of Ministers have a democratic base, albeit an indirect one, since they need to retain the support of the MPs in their respective countries to remain in office; the national parliaments are also involved, in a variety of ways, in monitoring and even to an extent controlling the activities of the Union; furthermore, a growing corpus of interest groups and organizations engage in an officially encouraged process of functional representation and contribute to democratic linkage in the policy process; but the European Parliament is the only body serving the whole Union which is directly elected. It has also been set up in order to constitute the democratic component, especially from the moment direct elections were introduced. To this extent at least and although we shall shortly have to qualify this point, the European Parliament can be regarded as the 'democratic pillar' of the Union.

While analysing legitimacy and the relationship between legitimacy and democracy, we noted two essential points. On the one hand, the legitimacy of an institution is always related to given fields or areas, even if these may be very wide; on the other, the legitimacy of an institution in a given field or area is enhanced by its democratic character if, but only if, there is a widespread belief that decision-making needs to be democratic with respect to that field or area. There are therefore four different ways in which the European Parliament may affect the legitimacy of the Union; they are summarized in Figure 1.1.

Prima facie, the European Parliament has a central role to play with respect to fields or areas which are in the top left quadrant of Figure 1.1, that is to say when the involvement of the Union in the decision-making process is accepted and the decision-making is felt to have to involve a representative democratic element. Meanwhile, the European Parliament has only a potential role in the areas which fall within the other three quadrants, because the involvement of the Union in the fields or areas concerned is not accepted, because the involvement of the Union, while accepted, is not regarded as having to be democratic, or indeed for a combination of both reasons. Movement from one quadrant to another may of course occur. But there is no universal, let alone inevitable, trend for fields or areas to move away from quadrants (2), (3), and (4) and towards quadrant (1): there can be moves in the other direction. This happens when some citizens no longer feel that the Union should be involved in a given field or area; negative views which they may have about the European Parliament may contribute to this development. Yet if fields or areas may move away from quadrant (1), they may also move into quadrant (1). The European Parliament may contribute to such movements: in regard to issues in quadrant (2), an increased role for the European Parliament depends on the Europeanization of issues; in regard to issues in quadrant (3), it depends on the democratization of issues; in

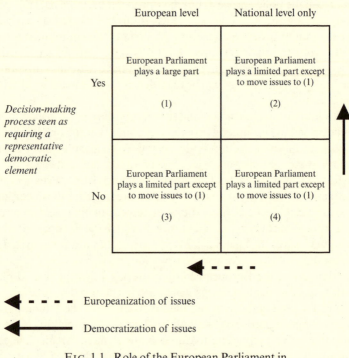

FIG. 1.1. Role of the European Parliament in
regard to the legitimacy of the EU

regard to issues in quadrant (4), it depends on both. Beginning with
the 1984 Draft Treaty on European Union and continuing through
the European Parliament's efforts to wield some influence in the
Inter-Governmental Conferences leading to the Maastricht Treaty
and to the Amsterdam Treaty, the Parliament has devoted considerable effort to bringing about precisely the movements depicted by the
arrows in Figure 1.1.

The reality is, however, more complex than that suggested in
Figure 1.1: the role of the European Parliament is further affected by
the perceptions that citizens have of the Parliament even with respect
to fields which are located in the top left-hand quadrant. For the
European Parliament to affect the support of citizens for the Union,
its characteristics and to begin with its very existence must be clearly

identified: if, for some citizens, the Parliament is not distinguishable from other institutions of the European Union, it cannot play any part at all in fostering the support of these citizens; it does not help to build support even in those fields or areas in which these citizens believe that action by the Union is appropriate and should be democratic. The first requirement is therefore that there be some appreciation of what the European Parliament is and what it is expected to achieve.

This is not the only way in which the role of the European Parliament can be more limited than expected, however. It can also be limited in two other ways. It can be limited if citizens recognize the distinct existence and role of the Parliament but pass negative judgements about it: they may for instance regard Euro-parliamentarians as not being effective or even as being concerned only with the material benefits which they can draw. Such negative views of the Parliament are unlikely, to say the least, to contribute to the legitimacy of the Union. Meanwhile, the effect that the European Parliament has on the legitimacy of the Union will also be limited if citizens believe its powers to be very small: ineffectiveness then stems not from failings of parliamentarians but from perceived institutional inadequacy.[5] In both cases, however, the result is the same: relatively negative views of citizens about what the Parliament is or does will reduce appreciably and at the limit even eliminate altogether any effect which the Parliament could have in fields or areas in which the involvement of the Union is accepted and is expected to be democratic. In short, the role of the European Parliament with respect to the legitimacy of the Union can be significant; but it is also complex. When we take account of the nature of elections to the Parliament, the complexity increases.

THE NATURE OF EUROPEAN ELECTIONS: *SUI GENERIS* OR 'SECOND ORDER'?

In order to understand abstention in European Parliament elections and its implications for the legitimacy of the Union, we need to

---

[5] The power of the Parliament has, of course, increased in successive stages since the first direct elections in 1979. This has occurred through more effective use of existing powers, through inter-institutional agreement, and through treaty revision. Public perceptions of the power of the Parliament will be dealt with in Chapter 6.

examine whether or to what extent European elections are conducted independently from other elections and in particular from those elections which are most popular and might be considered to be the 'engines' which pull the rest of the electoral machinery. In other words, the question is whether European elections are '*sui generis*' or whether they are 'second order' (Reif and Schmitt 1980: 3–44; Reif 1985: 1–36 and especially 7–10).

If European elections are 'second order', abstention at European elections has to be regarded as being merely the 'tip of an iceberg' or the more manifest form of the limited contribution of these elections; abstention thus becomes just one of a broader set of reasons which demonstrate that the European Parliament makes a limited contribution to the legitimacy of the Union. While those who abstain at European elections can be regarded as displaying little interest, at best, in the Union, the idea that these elections are 'second order' goes further: it suggests that those who vote do not do so because of the Union, but because of electoral considerations at other levels of government and in particular because of elections at the national level. At the limit, if all those who vote at European elections were to do so exclusively by reference to other levels of government and especially by reference to the national level, the European elections would have no effect whatsoever on the legitimacy of the Union:[6] the hopes and indeed expectations placed on the idea of direct elections to the European Parliament would be wholly unfounded.

The concept of 'second-order' elections has, however, a double meaning; both meanings contribute to reducing the part played by such elections, but to a different extent. One meaning relates to importance: elections are rated 'second order' because they are not (regarded as being) as important as others and, in the case of European elections, not as important as national elections. The other meaning relates to the relationship between the two sets of elections: in this interpretation, behaviour at the 'second-order' level of elections is conditioned by what electors want to do at the 'first-order' level: they may for instance want to punish the national government by voting for the opposition at the 'second-order' level, which may indeed be European or local. While of course the second meaning entails the

[6] Conversely the level of turnout would have no value whatsoever as an indicator of legitimacy.

first (the elections in question are less important, as otherwise they would be treated as valuable in their own right), the first meaning does not entail the second: at a 'less important election', electors may abstain, for instance; or they may vote in an 'automatic', 'expressive' manner for the same parties as they do at the 'first-order' elections and do so merely because this is the way they are accustomed to voting.

Reif (1985: 9) suggests that the consequences of second-order status are low turnout, good prospects for small and new parties, and a negative outcome for government parties. Behind these consequences are primarily four factors, namely the nature of the parties competing at these elections, the low salience of European issues, the limited extent to which parties compete against each other at the elections, and above all, the fact that, ultimately, these elections do not allocate power.

In the first place, party competition at European elections takes place by and large within the framework of each national unit rather than within the broader European context, since the effective party organizations are at the national level. 'Transnational' parties which do exist, even the Socialist and European People's parties, are scarcely more than loose arrangements primarily in existence to handle activities in the parliament and at most to coordinate some of the election campaign pronouncements (Reif 1985: 32–3; Bardi 1996): they do not direct or control in any way these campaigns let alone the activities of the national parties. Moreover, only the European Socialist party covers the whole of the Union: the European People's party does not, since Christian parties do not exist everywhere. The role of the other 'transnational' parties is even more limited: it tends to relate exclusively to minimal post-election parliamentary matters; several are even mere 'marriages of convenience'. On this basis, it is therefore fair to conclude that the European elections are fought by means of a series of parallel national campaigns whose actors scarcely relate to each other. This structural characteristic does not by itself make European elections 'second order', but it does give, prima facie, an advantage to national rather than to European considerations in these elections.

Second, European issues have little salience, except to the extent that they relate, or are presented by the parties as relating, to national questions. At the 1994 elections, for instance, efforts were made by some to give a European-wide profile to some questions such as the situation in former Yugoslavia or unemployment: the first of these matters was quickly shown to raise little interest while the second was not sufficiently orchestrated, for whatever reasons, and never had a real impact as a European-wide problem.

Third, this salience of European issues is probably rendered even lower because, by and large, the main parties have shown little desire or ability to compete against each other on European issues and at the European level. In each of the countries these parties have supported the European project: this is the case with the two largest 'federations', Socialist and European People's party, as well as with the third in size, the Liberal federation. Thus the Centre, the Centre-right, and the Centre-left on the European stage are occupied by parties all of which are broadly speaking in favour of what is going on in the Union; these parties group approximately three-quarters of the voting public. This combined support is a source of strength for the Union, to be sure: if it did not exist, the Union would simply not exist. Yet, while agreeing on the fundamentals of integration, these parties might be expected to be in sharp conflict over a number of issues affecting the Union as a whole: this would make European election campaigns lively and therefore attractive to follow. This is not the case in practice. In reality, the only genuine conflicts which emerge are due to parties at the extremes of the political spectrum, on both Right and Left; these criticize the Union on a variety of grounds. Paradoxically, while they may often attack the very notion of integration or at least the extension of the powers of the Union, these parties contribute indirectly to further integration as they bring about genuine competition; but they affect only some countries and a minority of the electors in these countries.

Fourth, European elections do not in fact allocate power. What power there is at the level of the Union is not affected by the result of the elections. This is in part because most of the power is concentrated in the hands of the Council of Ministers or the Commission, the latter being only peripherally subjected to the control of the Parliament while the former is not subjected to it at all. Power is not affected by the European elections also because the Parliament operates on the basis of a broad coalition between three main 'transnational' parties (Socialist, Christian, and Liberal) and there seems to be no way in which this coalition can lose its overwhelming majority in the foreseeable future.

The four characteristics which we have just described thus reduce substantially the 'European' framework within which European elections are fought: yet, even taken together, they do not by themselves result in European elections being 'second order' in either of the two meanings of the expression which have been described earlier. It does not automatically follow from these characteristics that they are 'second order' in the sense of being less important than other elections: what would make them 'second order' is if they were regarded by (a large proportion of) the electors in this way. Nor does it follow a fortiori from any or all of these four characteristics that European elections are 'second order' in the strong sense of there being a link between the two sets of elections and that link resulting in European elections being, so to speak, 'appendages' of national elections: in this respect, too, what counts is whether electors regard the two electoral arenas as linked. The question can therefore be settled only if the views of electors on the matter are investigated.

Moreover, for European elections to be truly 'second order', two further conditions, both of which concern the party system, have to be fulfilled for there to be a direct link between national and European elections and therefore for European elections to be 'appendages' of national elections. First, parties must be the same at both levels: this is often not the case in federal countries; this is not the case everywhere either in the European Union. Second, there must be a clear division between one or more government parties, one or more 'traditional' opposition parties, and/or one or more protest parties, so that electors can clearly express their dislike of the government by voting for the opposition or for one of the protest parties: this means that the political system has to be 'adversarial', at least to a moderate extent. In several European countries, such a condition does not obtain or does not fully obtain: where a broad coalition is almost always in power and, at the limit, when there is a permanent 'grand coalition', as is the case in Switzerland, but also occasionally in some countries of the Union, that is to say when the system is broadly 'consociational', it is difficult to see how one can use one's vote against the national government by voting for 'the' opposition at another level (Reif and Schmitt 1980; Reif 1985). Indeed, Reif notes (1985: 34) that the second-order model 'seems to apply more to political systems with a clearly bipolar structure . . .'.

However, whether a link can exist or not, the crucial element in determining whether an election is 'second order' is constituted by the perceptions of citizens, which of course can differ from one election to another as well as over time. It is therefore wrong to state that some elections are 'second order' on the basis of a general examination of the nature of the election: the only correct way to come to the conclusion that these elections are, indeed, 'second order' is by examining the reactions of citizens. At one extreme, European elections are 'second order' in the full sense of the word for those electors who vote at these elections but vote exclusively by reference to the national scene and preferably in relation to the national government. At the other extreme, European elections are not 'second order' at all for those electors who vote at these elections exclusively by reference to European considerations. While the second of these two categories is likely to be very small, the first may not be very large either; indeed, as was just pointed out, only if some conditions are fulfilled by the party system can European elections be 'second order' in the strong sense of the expression.

The large majority of citizens are therefore likely to be found in intermediate categories. These are numerous and include various forms of linkages between the national and European scenes. One of these types of linkages is constituted by the 'expressive' vote of the large numbers of citizens who vote at elections, whether European or other, because they are attached to a particular party: their vote is essentially an 'expression' of attachment to their party. This type of voting pattern may have been in decline since the 1960s in Western Europe, but it remains large. For such electors, it is in reality impossible to tell whether their vote at European elections is 'second order' or not: some or even all of them may subordinate European elections to national elections; but the fact that they vote at European elections for 'their' party is no manifestation of such a ranking.

The other category which is directly relevant to the understanding of the voting process at European elections is that of those who abstain at European elections only. These may indeed be the prototype of those citizens who regard European elections as less important than elections at other levels and particularly at national elections, but whether this is the motivation for their abstention is a matter that must be investigated. This is indeed why it is essential to examine in detail the characteristics and *raison d'être* of this Euro-specific abstention, a point to which we return in detail in Chapter 2 and later in the book. In the meantime, the different responses to national and European elections outlined above and their implications for the applicability of the second-order election model are summarized in Table 1.1.

TABLE 1.1. *Responses to national and European elections: implications for the second-order election model*

Action	Nature of response	Implications for the second-order model (SOEM) of European elections
Does not vote at all	Apoliticized, uninterested, opposed to all elections	No specific implications for SOEM
Votes at national elections only	Euro-elections may be less important, but this and other possible reasons for abstention must be investigated	May support weak version of SOEM but offers no support for strong version
Votes at both national and European elections referring to:		
(1) national considerations only	Votes in EP election on basis of preferences in first-order arena	Supports SOEM in both weak and strong versions
(2) parties by way of identification	'Expressive' vote. No necessary link between European and national elections	May support weak version of SOEM, but not necessarily strong version
(3) European considerations	Genuine Euro-vote	Not second order in either weak or strong sense

APPROACHES TO THE STUDY OF TURNOUT

We noted early in this chapter that turnout in European Parliament elections is low by the standard of turnout in national elections, the proportion of electors voting in these elections being only little more than half the registered electorate and having perceptibly decreased over the course of the four European elections. The difference with national elections is substantial as, in the twelve countries which belonged to the Union in 1994, the average turnout was about 80 per cent. But turnout in national elections also varies, even if these differences are smaller than they are at European elections between the same countries: over 90 per cent of the electors vote in Belgium while less than 70 per cent have done so in recent elections in Ireland. Thus, although, globally, citizens abstain substantially more at European elections than they do at national elections, they also vote more at European elections in some countries than they do at national elections in some others. The analysis of European election abstention would therefore appear to have to take into account the sources of differences in turnout in national elections.

With a few notable exceptions (Tingsten 1937; Lancelot 1968), the analysis of turnout in Western Europe remained underdeveloped for a long time: this traditional lack of interest was probably due in part to the fact that abstention was rarely considered to make a difference to the outcome; it may have been due in part to the fact that non-voting was consistently low in several European countries and was particularly low in the decades immediately following the Second World War. Rather than scrutinizing abstention, Europeans therefore tended to congratulate themselves on 'quasi-miraculous' levels of turnout, especially in the countries which had been politically reconstructed after the Second World War, Austria, Germany, and Italy; indeed, as the two countries in which voting had been compulsory for decades, Belgium and Luxembourg, did not have markedly higher rates of turnout than several other European countries, it seemed that a turnout of 90 to 95 per cent was the maximum attainable. An abstention rate of 10 per cent or even a little more was therefore not worthy of investigation.

Not all the countries which were to form part of the European Union enjoyed such a low abstention rate: while five of the original six countries of the Union had typically a very high turnout, turnout was often appreciably lower in France: in that country, relatively low abstention rates were occasionally registered at presidential elections, but, at parliamentary elections, turnout was typically in the 70 to 75 per cent range only. Moreover, the difference was even larger among the countries which were to join the Union later: Britain had experienced a turnout in the 80 per cent range in 1950 and 1951, but these records were never repeated afterwards and turnout in the low to mid-seventies became the norm. Similar or lower levels are found in Ireland and Spain, whereas 80 per cent or over typically voted in Denmark, Greece, and Portugal. Yet, despite these marked variations which clearly showed that abstention constituted 'a problem' in parts at least of Western Europe, political scientists have been slow to move away from the traditional belief that there was little to analyse in regard to abstention in national elections.

It is therefore in the United States that the matter has mostly been the subject of scholarly inquiry: indeed works on the subject were written as early as the 1920s (Merriam and Gosnell 1924; Gosnell 1930). It is perhaps not surprising that this should have been the case, given that turnout had been very low in America for decades and also given the fact that, also for decades,[7] political science has been more advanced in that country than elsewhere. Analyses of turnout in American political science were for long marked by two clearly differ-ent emphases: on the one hand, on the characteristics of individual electors as the source of explanation and, on the other, on structural and contextual factors. Individual factors comprise the attitudes, re-sources, skills, and characteristics of the individual elector; structural and contextual factors are typically the institutional arrangements for elections and certain features of the constitutional system and of the party system, including the ways in which political elites exploit these structures at any given time.[8]

Individual-level explanations are frequently socio-psychological in nature, emphasizing the attitudes and perceptions of electors, these tending in turn to be seen as shaped by the social conditions of voters, such as their class, race, religion, or gender. These explanations go back at least to Lazarsfeld and his collaborators in 1948 in *The People's Choice*, who argued that 'non-voters stayed away from the polls deliberately because they were unconcerned' (1948: 47). This

[7] Brody (1978) laid down a challenge to American political scientists by noting that what was then a sixteen-year decline in turnout in presidential elections had taken place despite the relaxation of restrictions on suffrage and in particular despite a sharp upturn in such relevant citizen resources as represented by educational attainment. Turnout has been almost equally low in Switzerland and it is a pity that more studies should not have been undertaken of Switzerland, as the problems and conditions of political life in that state resemble closely those of the European Union. The fact that Swiss electors are asked to go frequently to the polls (five times a year on average for federal matters alone) is typically given as one of the reasons for low turnout, though it is also pointed out that French-speaking Swiss, women, and manual workers are more likely to abstain (Sidjanski 1979: 105–11; Kerr 1987: 140–4; Powell 1982: 119; Jackman 1987: 409). In his analysis of the 'Problem of Switzerland's turnout', Sidjanski argues that it is based on a 'particular combination of negative and positive attitudes towards government and society' (Sidjanski 1979: 111).

[8] Franklin (1996) suggests a distinction between three theories of electoral parti-cipation: a theory based on individual resources, one based on political mobilization, and one based on what he calls instrumental motivation. He argues that the latter is superior because it subsumes the other two. However, as his discussion makes clear, his concept of instrumental motivation is closely linked to consideration of the impact of structures and institutions; it seems more parsimonious, therefore, to consider it as part of the established structural and contextual approach, an approach which also readily incorporates the mobilizing activities of political elites.

lack of concern has been found to be associated with various socio-economic characteristics and in particular with occupation or class and education, the latter having been stressed by Wolfinger and Rosenstone (1980: 79).

Structural explanations include the legal requirements under which contests take place, such as registration and compulsory voting and the electoral system *stricto sensu*. A number of mechanisms were indeed deliberately introduced to depress turnout among blacks, for instance, as well also among poor whites in the South and even else-where: this was the case in particular with literacy requirements, but the annual registration procedure was also partly enacted with the same end in mind (Powell 1986: 18–26; Jackman 1987: 405–23; Piven and Cloward 1988: 102 ff.). It has always been pointed out that such impediments did not exist in Europe; indeed, quite the contrary, com-pulsory voting is a mechanism designed to ensure that the turnout is the highest possible (Powell 1982: 113–22); but Crewe did also note the importance of certain structural factors in depressing turnout in Europe (Crewe 1981). Structural factors are also thought of, how-ever, as including political aspects, chief among which is the nature of the choice offered to electors by the party system and the degree to which that choice is connected to basic cleavages in the society (Crewe 1981 and Powell 1986).

It is not that those writers who emphasized individual factors ignored the structural context of voting; rather they incorporated the institutional effects into an explanation pitched at the individual level, as in the case of Wolfinger and Rosenstone who argued that 'The barriers imposed by restrictive laws seem to make little difference to the well educated but are a fairly formidable impediment to people with less interest and bureaucratic skill. To put it another way, the difference in turnout produced by variations in registration laws is an indication of the varying commitment and capacity to vote of different kinds of people' (Wolfinger and Rosenstone 1980: 80). The structuralists do the reverse: Jackman concludes that 'the odds . . . that citizens will vote vary with the structural conditions that they confront' (Jackman 1987: 419) and that 'high rates of turnout cannot be taken in themselves as evidence of participatory norms' (ibid.). Piven and Cloward go further and argue that the evidence 'strongly suggests that who votes and who does not vote has no inherent relationship to either variations in attitudes or socio-economic status' (Piven and Cloward 1988: 117) and that 'the socio-psychological model confounds causes and consequences' (ibid. 119). While it may be true that the better-off and the better educated are more able to manipulate institutions and that, therefore, institutional hurdles are important, it is difficult to follow them when they state, further down in the same paragraph that '[a]pathy and lack of political skill are a consequence, not a cause of the party structure and political culture that is sustained by legal and procedural barriers to electoral participation' (ibid.): it seems more sensible to view the process as two-way.

To say that the process is two-way is not to evade the issue. This can be made clear by approaching the matter from a broad rational choice perspective. The starting point for such an approach is not just that there are costs and benefits associated with voting but that 'turn-out is, for many people most of the time, a *low* cost, *low* benefit action. Turnout is a decision almost always made "at the margin". Small changes in costs and benefits alter the turnout decision for many citizens' (Aldrich 1993: 261, emphasis added). The limited benefits that normally accrue from the act of voting and the equally limited costs normally associated with it explain why turnout is affected by a plethora of variables, why the relationships between such variables and turnout tend to be moderate at best and why no one variable or even set of variables is decisive (ibid. 264). The notion of benefits must be understood quite broadly; it includes expected benefits resulting from the outcome of the election (which may or may not be dis-counted by some notion of the probability of affecting the outcome); however, it also includes intrinsic benefits derived from the act of voting itself and from the conformity of the act with norms of solidarity and civic obligation. Costs must also be broadly conceived; they relate to the voting decision, for example, the cost of acquiring information about the alternative parties or candidates, as well as to the physical act of voting, the latter being affected by such things as registration arrangements, opportunities for postal voting, the day on which polling takes place and by a myriad of individual situational factors.

The limited costs and benefits associated with voting mean that politicians can alter the balance of costs and benefits by the amount of effort and resources they put into the campaign. In putting in greater effort and resources, they increase the perceived benefits of voting by, for example, persuading the voters that party or candidate A or B is more attractive. They reduce the costs of voting by providing more information, by communicating more effectively, and by 'getting out the vote'. The result is increased turnout. An important point is that this change in the behaviour of the electorate is brought about without any change in the basic predispositions of the individual electors; the change occurs because of an interaction between political context and individual characteristics. Note also that the change in behaviour can occur without voters being particularly aware of the closeness of the contest. A close contest affects the behaviour of the candidates or parties which in turn alters the balance of (low) costs and (low) benefits that determines the elector's decision whether or not to vote. Aldrich develops these implications of the low-cost low-benefit assumption in discussing what he calls the strategic politicians hypothesis (ibid. 274). In similar vein, Rosentone and Hansen link the individual characteristics of the electors and the mobilizing efforts of politicians and political groups: 'Political participation arises from the interaction of citizens and political mobilizers. . . . Personal characteristics—resources, perceived rewards, interests, and benefits from taking part in politics—define every person's predisposition toward political activity. The strategic choices of political leaders—their determinations of who and when to mobilize—determine the shape of political participation in America' (1993: 36). However, the basic point can be extended beyond the actions of political elites to any aspect of the political or institutional structure or context that might affect turnout; seen in this fashion, it provides a means of thinking systematically about the interaction between context and individual motivation and action. Thus, it is not a matter of choosing between individual characteristics and structural factors as the sources of participation or abstention: these two interact with each other and do so in ways that can be teased out and analysed in the case of any particular election or type of election.

These considerations also suggest an important qualification to any assessment of the second-order election model. A distinction must be made between the applicability of the model to the perceptions and behaviour of political elites and the applicability of the model to the perceptions and behaviour of voters. In the present study it is the latter that counts and detailed evidence on this will be presented in Chapter 6; it is, however, worth considering at this stage the possibility that apparent second-order election effects (e.g. low turnout) may be due to strategic calculations in the minds of political elites and the actions that follow from them rather than to any complex perceptions and calculations regarding the relative power being allocated in different electoral arenas that the second-order election model assumes are made by the electorate. As emphasized above, whether and to what extent such perceptions exist and whether and to what extent they or quite different perceptions and calculations contribute to low turnout in European Parliament elections are matters to be empirically determined. They are also matters that have a fundamental bearing on both the understanding of the legitimacy of European integration and of the functioning of European democracy and on any expectations one might have as to how electorates would react to changes in the structural or political contexts of European Parliament elections. They are, in short, fundamental concerns of this book.

This review has focused on research conducted in the United States on the grounds that, in large part due to the severity of the problem of abstention, the matter has received most attention there. This is not to say that the problem has been entirely neglected in Europe; apart from the comparative research already noted, there has been a growing interest in research on turnout in Europe as such (Crepaz 1990; Lane and Ersson 1990; Flickinger and Studlar 1992; Anduiza 1995; Borg 1995; Oppenhuis 1995; Topf 1995; and the various country chapters in Font and Virós 1995). In any event, studies of turnout, whether American or European, comparative or single-country, have accumulated a substantial store of particular findings and some suggestive insights as to how these might be integrated into an overall explanation of turnout. It is not, however, the aim of the present book either to produce a synthesis of these ideas or to develop a grand theory of turnout; the aim is both narrower and wider: it is to analyse the nature and sources of low turnout in European Parliament elections drawing eclectically on the insights and methods deployed in previous research and to situate this problem in the context of the legitimacy of the European Union. The remaining task of this introductory chapter is to comment briefly on the methods employed in this study and to describe the structure of the book.

METHODOLOGY

There are two sources of evidence on turnout: the aggregate statistics of actual turnout contained in official reports and data collected by means of survey research based on representative samples of individual citizens. Although we shall use aggregate data in Chapter 2 to assist us in refining our definition of the problem of turnout in European Parliament elections, the main source of our evidence is a specially commissioned survey of representative national samples of the electorates in each of the member states of the European Union that was conducted as part of the post-election Eurobarometer of June–July 1994. The point on which survey data score most heavily over aggregate data is clear: 'The direct rather than the inferential linkage between individual social position and behaviour is the great advantage of survey research over ecological analysis' (Linz 1969: 102). Survey research enables one to bring attitudes and perceptions and individual socio-economic and demographic characteristics such as social class, education, age, family background, type of employment and employment status, group affiliations and involvement to bear directly on the problem.

This focus on the individual is, however, also a potential source of weakness. Two main problems arise. In the first place, data collected directly from individuals are only as good as the quality and range of questions asked. In analysing survey data, one sometimes wishes that the question had been formulated in a different way. Such considerations are challenges and limitations to be overcome or taken into account in interpretation rather than insuperable obstacles that jeopardize the entire enterprise. But one is also limited by the range of questions that can be inserted into a particular questionnaire or, as in this case, into a segment of a shared questionnaire. In order to overcome the consequential problem of the limited number of topics for which we could design and insert new Eurobarometer questions, we have relied on two sets of questions that are not specific to this study. One set consists of standard Eurobarometer questions that occur in every Eurobarometer and that were automatically included in the 1994 post-election Eurobarometer. The other set consists of questions on other topics that have been asked in previous Eurobarometers. In some parts of our study we draw on these data in order to fill out our account of attitudes to European integration and to the European Union. Of course, in drawing on both these sets of data, one risks exacerbating the quality of question problem, since one has no control over the formulation of these questions. The approach adopted here is to take a critical approach to these data and to use them judiciously in order to draw up as complete a picture as possible of the political culture of European integration.

The second potential source of difficulty with the survey approach

TABLE 1.2. *Excess of reported turnout over actual turnout, European Parliament elections 1994*

	BE	DK	FR	GE	GR	IR	IT	LU	NE	PO	SP	UK	EC12
Actual turnout	90.7	52.9	52.7	60.0	71.7	44.0	74.8	88.5	35.6	35.5	59.1	36.4	58.5
Reported turnout	91.0	70.0	66.0	76.0	94.0	60.0	89.0	96.0	54.0	55.0	75.0	51.0	72.0
Excess of reported turnout over actual turnout	0.3	17.1	13.3	16.0	22.3	16.0	14.2	7.5	18.4	19.5	15.9	14.6	13.5

Sources: Actual turnout: *European Election Results*, Strasbourg: The European Parliament, 1995. Reported turnout: EB (Eurobarometer) 41.1.

is that it is based entirely on the willingness and ability of those inter-
viewed to give accurate responses. At first sight, this might seem to be
a particularly acute issue in a study of turnout, as reports of turnout
based on survey data appear to overestimate the extent of participation. Over-reporting has been found in survey research both on
turnout in European Parliament elections (Schmitt and Mannheimer
1991: 34) and on turnout in general elections (Budge and Farlie 1976).
Despite a carefully crafted turnout question that sought to minimize
some of the potential sources of the exaggeration of turnout, the
problem persists in the present data set (see Table 1.2). It must be
emphasized that not all of the discrepancy between actual and
reported turnout in Table 1.2 is attributable to misinformation
provided by respondents. An individual-level comparison between
actual turnout based on the official records and turnout as reported
by respondents in the British Election Survey tested four potential
sources of the discrepancy—misreporting by respondents, response
bias in the sampling process, sampling difficulties arising from
residential mobility, and, finally, redundancy in the electoral register.
The authors concluded that misreporting accounted for one-quarter
of the discrepancy, response bias for another quarter, and that the
remainder was due, in indeterminate proportions, to the two other
factors mentioned (Swaddle and Heath 1989). While we do not know
to what extent this pattern is repeated in other countries and in the
context of the different sampling methodology used in the Eurobarometer, there is some reassurance in the fact that misreporting by
respondents may be as low as it appears from the British study. It
must be borne in mind, however, that the non-voters in this survey
may not include all non-voters.

STRUCTURE OF THE BOOK

The immediate focus of this book is abstention at European elections;
as we already noticed, the problem is more complex than it seems at
first, if only because of the large variations between high and low
turnout countries. Thus the coming chapter is devoted to a systematic
description of the contours of abstention in the European Union and
to an examination of the reasons those who abstained have given for
their (in)action. Chapter 3 explores attitudes to the European Union
and considers how far abstention is related to these attitudes. Chapter

4 then looks at the extent of citizens' interest in European politics, at their knowledge of European affairs, and at the relationships between evaluation, interest, knowledge, and participation. Chapter 5 turns to the European Parliament, examines the attitudes of citizens to that body, and assesses how far these attitudes to the Parliament appear related to voting and non-voting. Chapter 6 analyses the impact of party and candidate perceptions and campaign penetration on support, interest, and turnout. Chapter 7 then looks at differences between countries and in particular between groups of countries characterized by high, medium, and low turnout. The aim of Chapter 8 is to bring together the material considered up to that point in a systematic examination of the relationship between the three key aspects of the analysis, attitudes to the European Union, attitudes to the European Parliament, and electoral participation. Finally, the last chapter summarizes the findings and draws some conclusions and implications regarding the present and future role of the European Parliament and European elections in contributing to democratic legitimacy in the European Union.

2

The Extent and Nature of the Problem of Abstention in European Parliament Elections

INTRODUCTION

Abstention at European Parliament elections is far from uniform: it varies substantially from member state to member state; it varies over time; it varies within states; perhaps most importantly, it takes different forms. For instance, it may or may not be specific to European Parliament elections. Before attempting to look for some of the reasons which may account for these differences, we need to examine the variations more closely, identify the precise contours of abstention at European Parliament elections, and clarify the nature of the questions which need to be answered.

VARIATIONS IN RATES OF ABSTENTION BETWEEN AND WITHIN COUNTRIES

Turnout in European Parliament elections is low and falling—average turnout across the member states was 65.9 per cent in 1979, 63.8 in 1984, 62.8 in 1989, and 58.5 in 1994. These averages mask a wide range and extraordinarily low rates of turnout in some countries. In 1994 turnout was an abysmal 36 per cent in the Netherlands, in Portugal, and in the United Kingdom (see Table 2.1). At the other end of the scale, it was 90.7 per cent in Belgium and 88.5 in Luxembourg. Even leaving aside these extremes, there were wide variations between the remaining countries: from 74.8 in Italy and 71.7 in Greece to just under 53 per cent in Denmark and France and 44 per cent in Ireland. Only Germany (60 per cent) and Spain (59.1 per cent) showed little or no deviation from the European average.

TABLE 2.1. *Turnout in European and national elections, 1979–1994 (%)*

| Country | European elections | | | | | | Last national election | Mean turnout in | | Difference between mean turnout in European and national elections |
	1979	1981	1984	1987	1989	1994		European elections 1979–94	National elections 1979–94	
Belgium	91.4		92.2		90.7	90.7	92.7	91.3	93.6	-2.3
Denmark	47.8		52.3		46.2	52.9	82.2	49.8	85.3	-35.5
France	60.7		56.7		48.7	52.7	85.8	54.7	85.0	-30.3
Germany	65.7		56.8		62.3	60.0	77.8	61.2	84.8	-23.6
Greece		78.6	77.2		79.9	71.7	81.5	76.9	82.2	-5.4
Ireland	63.6		47.6		68.3	44.0	68.5	55.9	72.2	-16.3
Italy	84.9		83.4		81.0	74.8	86.1	81.0	88.0	-7.0
Luxembourg	88.9		88.8		87.4	88.5	88.5	88.4	88.4	0.0
Netherlands	57.8		50.6		47.2	35.6	78.3	47.8	83.0	-35.2
Portugal	n.a.		n.a.	72.6	51.2	35.5	68.2	53.1	78.0	-24.9
Spain	n.a.		n.a.	68.9	54.6	59.1	77.2	60.9	73.7	-12.8
UK	32.3		32.6		36.2	36.4	77.7	34.4	75.6	-41.2
Mean—all member states	65.9		63.8		62.8	58.5	80.4	62.9	82.5	-19.5
Mean—states without compulsory voting and without concurrent European and national elections	54.7		49.4		49.5	47.0	77.0	52.2	79.7	-27.5

Note: EP turnout figures are from *European Election Results* (Strasbourg: European Parliament, 1995). National turnout figures for the period 1979–89 are based on data in Mackie and Rose 1991 and, for the period 1990–4, on data in *Electoral Studies*. The latter source does not include invalid votes. This gives rise to some problems in comparing average turnout in national elections over the whole period to turnout in the most recent national election. French national election turnout is for Presidential elections.

Gross differences in European Parliament turnout between countries are only the most obvious and, in some ways, the least interesting variations. For one thing they partly reflect higher or lower levels of turnout in national elections (see Table 2.1). This can be taken into account by examining variations in the *difference* between turnout in national and European elections in each country. The discrepancy between average turnout in European Parliament elections and average turnout in general elections is a startling 41 percentage points in the United Kingdom, 35.2 points in the Netherlands, and 35 points in Denmark (see the right-hand column of Table 2.1). It is somewhat smaller but still very substantial in Germany (23.6 points), Portugal (24.9), France (30), and Ireland (16.3). This way of looking at the matter gets close to the nub of the problem: what has to be explained is the *gap* between turnout in European Parliament elections and turnout in national elections.

It is not just, however, that turnout varies between countries and between national and European elections in individual countries; European Parliament election turnout itself varies *within* countries. Figure 2.1 presents a map of turnout in the European Parliament elections of 1994. The advantage of the cartographical presentation over the way in which the data are presented in Table 2.1 is that it takes us inside each individual state, showing the main variations from region to region. It is immediately apparent that there are very substantial differences in turnout between different regions in Germany, Spain, Italy, and Greece and that considerable interregional differences also occur in several of the other member states.

Variation in turnout in Spain and Germany spans four scale intervals (from the forties to the seventies). In Spain, lowest turnout is found in western Galicia, in the interior of the Basque country, and in the Balearic Islands. Turnout is moderate (50 to 59 per cent) in the remainder of north-western Spain and over the whole of the northeast, including both Catalonia and Aragon. There is also a moderate level of turnout in the larger Madrid area (*Comunidad de Madrid*). The areas of high turnout (60 to 69 per cent) comprise essentially the interior and southern Spain, with turnout rising to over 70 per cent in two provinces in Andalusia (Cordoba and Jaén). In Germany, lower turnout is found in a band running from Schleswig-Holstein in the north, through Hessen and down into Bavaria. Turnout is considerably higher in the south-west, in Baden-Württemberg and especially in Rhineland-Palatinate and the Saarland. It is higher also in almost all of the *Länder* of former East Germany, the exception being Brandenburg and Berlin; indeed turnout in Thuringia and Saxony was at the same level as the Rhineland-Palatinate and the Saarland.

The contrast in Greece is mainly on an east–west axis: turnout is highest in Central Macedonia, and very high in Thessaly, Central Greece, and the Athens region; it is very much lower in the western areas of Epirus, western Greece, and Peloponnese. In Italy, predictably enough, the main contrast is between north and south, though the situation is more complicated than a simple north–south dichotomy would allow. The highest turnout (over 80 per cent) is found in the area from Umbria, north through Tuscany, Emilia-Romagna, and into Lombardy. In contrast, right across the south (Campania, Apulia, Basilicata, and Calabria) turnout is, on average, 20 percentage points lower. Middling levels of turnout, middling, that is, by Italian standards, are found in the centre and on the edges: in Lazio and Marche, in Piedmont, Liguria, Trentino-Alto Adige and Friuli-Venezia Giulia in the north and in the islands.

Although the other member states tend to show less dramatic regional contrasts, there are discernible differences which help to refine one's sense of what needs to be explained. Why is turnout in the Dublin region lower than in the rest of Ireland, while in Denmark low turnout tends to occur in the more peripheral areas (North Jutland, Viborg, and Ribe)? The British pattern also contrasts with the Danish one in so far as higher turnout is found in some though not in all areas of the periphery: higher turnout is found in Wales, in the south-west, in Cumbria in the north-west, and in the south of Scotland; however, turnout in the north of Scotland remains more akin to that in the rest of Britain and higher turnout is found in a few areas in the south-east. Note should also be taken of the extremely low rates of turnout in the Merseyside and Greater Manchester areas, in South Yorkshire, and in parts of Birmingham and east London. The contrast in France is limited in scale but territorially extensive, distinguishing several large and contiguous geographical areas from the rest of France. Areas of higher turnout (50 to 59 per cent) are found across the south and in a zone stretching from the south through central France, north through the Paris region, and on to the Belgian border. Lower turnout occurs to the west and east of the central rib, the only exception being Franche-Comté. In the remaining three countries (Belgium, the

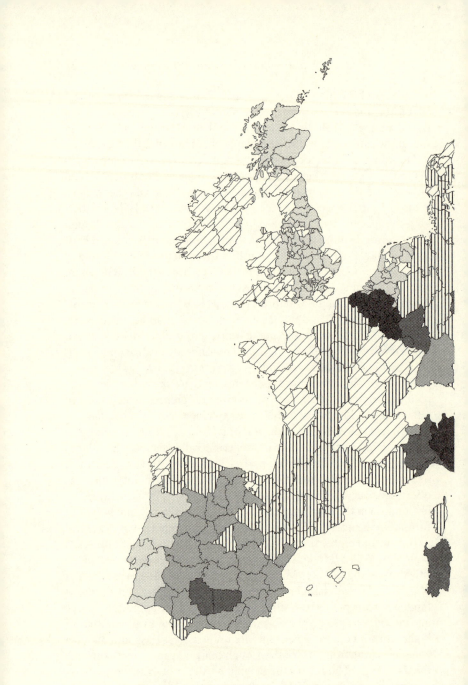

FIG. 2.1. Percentage turnout in European Parliament elections 1994, sub-national breakdown

Source: *Europe Elections 1994* (European Parliament: DG for Information and Public Relations, June 1994), national data archives, and national newspapers.

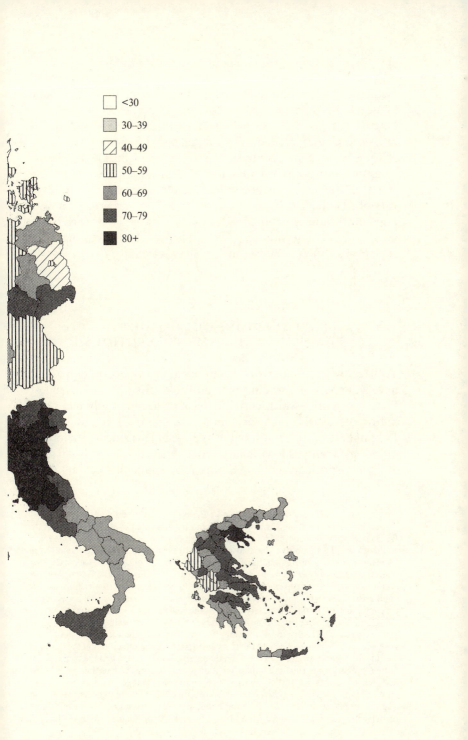

☐	<30
▨	30–39
▨	40–49
⊞	50–59
▨	60–69
▨	70–79
■	80+

Netherlands, and Portugal), spatial variation in turnout is quite limited. In Belgium turnout is uniformly high (80 per cent plus); in the Netherlands it is, with the single exception of the older industrial area of Overijssel, uniformly low; in Portugal also it is uniformly low.[1]

These intra-country contrasts confirm the emerging picture of wide variations in European Parliament election turnout: variations by country, over time, by subnational region and, most importantly, variations in the *gap* between turnout in European Parliament elections and turnout in national elections. All these variations need to be taken into account in attempting to uncover the factors that may explain abstention at European Parliament elections.

EXPLANATIONS OF TURNOUT IN EUROPEAN PARLIAMENT ELECTIONS

To begin with, a number of institutional characteristics appear to have an impact on turnout. First, as Table 2.1 shows, it is manifest that, in countries which currently have or have recently had compulsory or quasi-compulsory voting (Belgium, Greece, Italy, and Luxembourg),[2] voters turn out at European Parliament elections in much larger proportions than in other countries. In addition, and also not surprisingly, holding European and national elections at the

---

[1] Portugal illustrates the point made at the outset of this discussion of regional contrasts: the degree of uniformity within a country is affected by the very broad scale that is necessary to encompass the pan-European differences involved and by the size of the geographical subdivisions that can be portrayed on a Union-wide map. As it happens, the five main regional divisions in Portugal run on an east–west axis; this makes comparisons between east and west impossible (see Figure 2.1). When we go to a more detailed geographical breakdown (and a finer scale or discrimination), such a comparison is possible and it shows that the main contrast does in fact lie between the east and the west, or more precisely, between the coastal areas and the interior.

[2] Compulsory voting was abolished in Italy in the 1993 electoral law (law 277/1993). Prior to that, the penalty for not voting was publication of the list of names of non-voters in the *albo communale* and the recording of the fact of abstention in the citizen's 'certificate of good conduct'. In the present analysis Italy is included in the compulsory voting category on the basis that the obligation to vote remains part of the constitution and that there was very little publicity surrounding the change in this aspect of the electoral law; it seems probable, in other words, that voting is still regarded as at least quasi-compulsory in Italy. On the other hand, however, turnout at European Parliament elections in Italy declined from 81 per cent in 1989 to 74.8 per cent in 1994.

same time increases European Parliament election turnout. Ireland provides an illustration of this point. When the European Parliament election was combined with a national election in 1989, turnout in the European Parliament election increased by 20 percentage points; on the other hand, when the next European Parliament elections in Ireland did not coincide with any other contest, it fell to 44 per cent.[3] A third factor seemingly affecting rates of turnout is that in some countries (Denmark, Ireland, the Netherlands, and the United Kingdom) voting takes place on a weekday while in other countries it takes place on a Sunday; the data in Table 2.1 suggest that voting on a weekday is associated with lower turnout, a notable exception being Portugal in 1994, where, despite Sunday voting, turnout was among the lowest in the Union. The last institutional influence that is often cited is provided by differences in the type of electoral system, as it would seem that, *ceteris paribus*, turnout tends to be higher in countries that use some system of proportional representation than where the majority system is adopted. Britain is the only country in this last category, all the other member states having some form of proportional representation in use at European Parliament elections; the average turnout in Britain in the four elections to the European Parliament election is the lowest of all the countries.[4]

Cartographical analysis permits one further inference about institutional effects beyond those made on the basis of the data in Table 2.1: concurrent *local or regional* elections can raise the level of turnout in particular areas within a given country. In 1994 regional elections occurred in three *Länder* of former East Germany, the exceptions being Brandenburg and Berlin; they also occurred in Andalusia in southern Spain. The effects on turnout are reflected in the maps for Germany and Spain, though it is also apparent that some other regions of both countries had a turnout as high as in the areas where there were concomitant regional elections. The local election effect is confirmed by the Irish experience: concomitant local elections were held in Ireland in 1979; turnout at the 1979 European Parliament election (63.6) matched that normally found in Irish local elections, whereas in the European Parliament elections in which

[3] Luxembourg was the only country to hold European and national elections on the same day in 1994.

[4] The effect of proportional representation and other 'macro' factors on turnout in national elections is examined in Crewe 1981: 239–57; see also Blais and Carty 1990, and Lane and Ersson 1990).

there was no coincidence with another election (1984 and 1994), turnout was in the mid-forties.

Thus a number of institutional factors (compulsory voting, concurrent national or local/regional elections, Sunday voting, and, perhaps, proportional representation) seem to increase turnout at European Parliament elections. Yet, with very few exceptions, these institutional factors do not vary between national and European elections. Consequently, though these factors may help to explain differences between countries, they simply cannot explain what was identified above as the crucial puzzle: the large gaps between turnout at national elections and turnout at European elections that obtain in most of the states of the European Union (see right-hand column of Table 2.1). Nor, with the exception of the concurrent local or regional election factor, do they help to account for the differences in European Parliament election turnout at subnational level that are evident in the map in Figure 2.1. In any event, the explanation of variations in turnout in terms of compulsory voting and concomitant national elections is close to being tautological. If there are laws that state that people must vote, most people will vote. Similarly, since turnout at national elections is consistently and substantially higher than turnout in European Parliament elections, holding the two events on the same day will increase European Parliament election turnout. Thus, while on the basis of the gross differences in rates of turnout between countries, these institutional factors seem to affect turnout, they also leave much to be explained.[5] Chapter 1 looked briefly at the literature on turnout and some of the suggestions

[5] It should also perhaps be noted that compulsory voting and concomitant national elections are unsatisfactory explanations in a practical sense since their introduction as measures to boost turnout at European Parliament elections is inconceivable. Compulsory voting has in fact been dropped in Italy (for both national and European elections) and the notion of setting out to herd European electorates to the polls for European Parliament elections in countries that do not already have compulsory voting is outlandish. It would of course not be outlandish if turning out to vote at elections of all types were made compulsory. However, despite the fact that a strong argument for a comprehensive legal requirement to at least turn up at the polling place for elections at all levels was made in the 1996 Presidential Address to the American Political Science Association (Lijphart 1997), such a development remains unlikely. In regard to concomitant national elections, with the exception of Luxembourg, these occur randomly and rarely and cannot be manufactured to order; no more than compulsory voting, such an arrangement is simply not available as a means of solving the practical problem. The possibility of making European Parliament elections concurrent with regional or local elections may be more realistic but it would run the risk of the European election being swamped by local issues.

that occur in that literature will be taken up again as the analysis proceeds. In addition, however, a number of explanations have been put forward in the literature that deals specifically with European Parliament election turnout. The problem is that there are marked differences in the explanations that have been given.

On the basis of an analysis *of intention to vote* at the 1979 European Parliament election, Inglehart and Rabier pointed to three factors which, they claimed, are conducive to turnout: cognitive mobilization (a combination of frequency of discussion of politics and attempting to persuade others of the merits of one's own strongly held opinions), awareness of the campaign and, finally, pro-European attitudes. They acknowledged that these influences were interrelated but held the view that pro-European attitudes in particular had a positive effect (Inglehart and Rabier 1979: 488–9). Analysing the same 1979 European Parliament election, Blumler and Fox looked at the impact on *reported* turnout of two of these factors (campaign interest and exposure and pro-European attitudes) plus three additional variables: party loyalty, education, and age. On the basis of a multivariate analysis, they concluded that all five factors were influential but that the impact of pro-European attitudes tended to be indirect rather than direct (Blumler and Fox 1982; see also Blumler 1984).

Analysing turnout by country and including data from both the 1984 and 1989 European Parliament elections, Niedermayer examined the effect of positive attitudes to the European Community while controlling for the effect of two of the institutional variables mentioned above: compulsory voting and concomitant national elections. His conclusion was that 'for both elections analyzed, a (moderately) positive relationship exists between the individual member states' electorates' pro-European attitudes and turnout, even controlled for compulsory voting and national/European elections coincidence. The results . . . confirm the hypothesis that turnout in European elections has something to do with the "Europeanness" of the individual member states' (Niedermayer 1990: 49).

In striking contrast to these findings is the bleak conclusion reached by Schmitt and Mannheimer in their individual-level analysis of the data from the 1989 European Parliament Elections Survey: 'it may be that electoral participation to a large degree is caused by non-systematic—and that means specific to one's individual situation or idiosyncratic—factors, which are beyond the reach of large scale survey research' and that 'despite all our efforts, participation in the

European elections of 1989 has hardly been explained. Why is it that some people participate while others abstain? We do not know much about it' (Schmitt and Mannheimer 1991: 50).

The most recent research takes a more optimistic view of the possibility of finding an explanation for abstention. Following an elaborate multivariate analysis, Franklin, van der Eijk, and Oppenhuis give pride of place to institutional factors: 'In summary: turnout is high in political systems where voting is compulsory or where votes are translated into seats with a high degree of proportionality . . . Sunday voting helps, but more important is . . . the question of whether political power is at stake (indicated in our data by the presence of concurrent national elections) . . . Where such contextual characteristics leave any room for individual variation, the quality of communications between parties and voters makes up the bulk of the difference. The three variables involved are political interest, campaign mobilization and the appeal of the most attractive party' (Franklin et al. 1996a: 328–9). Attitudes and orientations towards the European Community or Union are emphatically dismissed: 'Particularly noteworthy is the fact that EC-related attitudes, preferences and orientations play no significant role in the explanation of electoral participation in European elections, in contrast to the findings of some earlier, less elaborate studies' (ibid. 322). This latter finding is rather puzzling. Can it really be that attitudes to Europe—what people know and think and feel (or do not know and think and feel) about the European Union and its institutions—play no significant part in determining whether or not they vote in a European Parliament election?

Given the conflict between these interpretations and given that, as argued earlier, institutional explanations leave many questions unanswered, one has to conclude that there are gaps to be filled if turnout and abstention in European Parliament elections are to be understood. The first step to take is to distinguish between different types of abstention.

ABSTENTION IN EUROPEAN PARLIAMENT ELECTIONS: A BASIC DISTINCTION

At the outset of this chapter, attention was drawn to several variations in types of abstention, citing in particular abstention that is specific to European Parliament elections. The time has come to make a further vital distinction between different kinds of Euro-specific abstention based on responses to one of the open-ended questions that was designed specifically to probe more deeply into the nature of this kind of abstention. Respondents who had indicated that they had not voted in the European Parliament election were asked the open-ended question: 'What was the main reason why you did not vote in that election?' They were then further asked 'Which other reasons?', with the interviewer being instructed to 'probe until the respondent says none'. While one must be wary of rationalizations in responses to a question of this sort, there is a large difference in the nature and significance of not turning out to vote between the respondent who said 'I was in Canada on business at the time' and the one who said she had not voted because 'I didn't feel any of the candidates represented my views. We had very little literature in the post. I just feel that we know so little about the MEPs there is no point in voting. We are not armchair politicians; we like to know what is going on.' There is yet a larger difference between these two and the one who said 'I don't vote for anything, not even local councils. I haven't voted since I came out of the forces. I don't particularly follow any party . . .'. These three responses are taken from the British sample but the varieties of motivation they exhibit are found across the member states.

On the basis of such data, a distinction can be drawn between those who *could* not vote, irrespective of their interest in or commitment to European integration or their sense of civic duty, and those who *would* not vote, presumably because of something in their attitude to politics or to Europe or to parties and politicians or whatever. Thus one can distinguish between those who abstain in a European Parliament election for some *circumstantial* or involuntary reason (absence from home, illness or disability, pressure of work, registration problems, etc.) and those who can be described as *voluntary* or even deliberate abstainers, namely those who did not vote because they felt they were uninformed about, or uninterested in, or were critical of the European Union, or were uninterested in or distrustful of politics, for any reason. Obviously, the distinction is not entirely clear-cut. On the one hand, those who abstain for circumstantial reasons hold a variety of attitudes and perceptions and certain levels of knowledge and interest and, in the case of any individual circumstantial abstainer, if these attitudes or perceptions had been different, he or she might have

TABLE 2.2. *Types of participation and abstention, European Parliament elections, 1994*

	Voted in national election	Did not vote in national election
Voted in European election	National and European voters 72%	Euro-specific voters 3%
Did not vote in European election for circumstantial reasons	Circumstantial Euro-specific abstainers 7%	Circumstantial Euro-and-national abstainers 3%
Did not vote in European election for voluntary reasons	Voluntary Euro-specific abstainers 10%	Voluntary Euro-and-national abstainers 5%

Source: EB 41.1 (N=11,473).

overcome the inhibiting circumstances and voted. On the other hand, those who gave a voluntary reason for abstention may also have been constrained by circumstances that lower the likelihood of voting. While this qualification needs to be borne in mind and will become apparent as the analysis proceeds, the evidence is that people can be readily categorized in this way.[6] Combining this distinction with that between those who voted in the European election, those who abstained in the European election but voted in the last national election, and those who abstained in both produces the sixfold typology of participation and abstention that is illustrated in Table 2.2.

Our main interest lies in the contrast between those who voted at the European Parliament election (row one of the table) and the four

---

[6] The validity of the distinction and of our measure of it is supported by an analysis of the results of a question on the main reason for not voting that was used in the 1989 European election survey. The 1989 question was a closed question which presented a card to the respondent with nine precoded response categories and allowed for just a single response. Two of the categories refer, at a fairly general level, to forms of circumstantial abstention. Given the different methodologies involved, one would not necessarily expect identical results from the two questions. It is therefore reassuring that the level of circumstantial abstention found in 1989 is quite similar to the level reported in Table 2.3 (1989: 43 per cent circumstantial). While, for reasons that will shortly become apparent, we would argue that the open-ended question is a more effective means of probing the sources of abstention, our confidence in the open-ended question is reinforced by this comparison. We are grateful to Michael Marsh for suggesting it. The 1989 data has been used to analyse turnout in Ireland, distinguishing between 'non-voters by accident' and 'non-voters by design' (see Marsh 1991).

types in the lower two rows of the table,[7] namely, circumstantial Euro-specific abstainers[8] (7 per cent), circumstantial Euro-and-national abstainers (3 per cent), voluntary Euro-specific abstainers (10 per cent), and voluntary Euro-and-national abstainers (5 per cent).[9] Distinguishing between these various kinds of abstainers should throw considerable light on the problem of explaining turnout and abstention in European Parliament elections and, in particular, on the problem of the relationship between European attitudes and voting or not voting. Before proceeding to these problems, however, it is worth considering in some detail the reasons given for abstention in European Parliament elections, in order to clarify the circumstantial–voluntary distinction, in order to further classify voters within each of these categories, and in order to see how the overt reasons for abstention are affected by the arrangements for European Parliament elections that obtain in the different member states.

CIRCUMSTANTIAL ABSTENTION

The main reasons for circumstantial abstention are work and time pressure (26 per cent), being away from home (21 per cent), illness, disability, and old age (17 per cent), and registration or voting card problems (18 per cent). Although one might expect some variation due to different levels of participation in the workforce, in principle circumstantial factors that affect turnout should not vary markedly from country to country, that is, one would not expect people in one country to be much sicker or busier or more frequently absent from home, etc. than people in another. Yet the overall rate of circumstantial abstention varies appreciably between member states

[7] Because the classification in Table 2.2 is based in part on participation or abstention in the last national election, respondents who were too young to vote in that election have been omitted. Likewise the small number of respondents who gave no reason for abstention in the European Parliament are omitted.

[8] Circumstantial abstainers are those who only mentioned circumstantial reasons. Those who mention a circumstantial and a voluntary reason are categorized as voluntary abstainers.

[9] In order to avoid the constant repetition of the awkward phrases 'circumstantial Euro-and-national abstainers' and 'voluntary Euro-and-national abstainers', these groups will sometimes be referred to in the text as circumstantial double abstainers and voluntary double abstainers respectively. It must be remembered, however, that their circumstantial or voluntary reason applies only to their European abstention.

(see Table 2.3), and these variations form quite clear-cut patterns. First, circumstantial abstention is substantially higher in Belgium, Greece, Italy, and Luxembourg, i.e. in the four countries which have or have recently had compulsory voting regimes. This is so because voters in a compulsory voting regime do not need to be interested in or informed about or committed to politics in order to be motivated to vote (though supporters of compulsory voting argue that participation may increase interest, knowledge, and commitment (Lijphart 1997: 10)). For the most part, they turn out regardless of these kinds of political motivation. Consequently, when they abstain, they tend do so because of circumstances. As Table 2.3 shows, 60 per cent of those who did not vote in the European Parliament elections in the four compulsory voting countries cited purely circumstantial reasons;[10] the corresponding figure in the non-compulsory voting countries was 35 per cent.

Second, there are marked differences in the kinds of circumstantial reasons given in different countries. For example, the circumstantial reasons cited in the compulsory voting countries tended to be quite specific: the main ones were illness (30 per cent), registration and voting card problems (24 per cent), and being away from home (16 per cent)[11] (see Table 2.4). In contrast, in non-compulsory voting countries the main circumstantial reason for abstention was the vaguer category of 'too busy, no time, pressure of work' (27 per cent); this reason was cited by only 9 per cent in compulsory voting countries. Similarly, illness and registration problems appear as reasons for not voting noticeably less frequently in non-compulsory voting countries (illness being 15 percentage points lower and registration problems

---

[10] Among the compulsory voting countries, voluntary abstention is highest in the Italian case, an indication perhaps of the effect of the formal ending of compulsion in Italy in 1993, or of a weakening of the norm of obligatory voting in Italy's changing political system, or of both. Though the number of respondents in this category in the Italian case is small (46), it is worth noting that more than two-fifths of them cited lack of political trust as their reason for not voting in the European Parliament election of 1994. This proportion was well above that of most other countries and, as we shall see shortly, was exceeded only in Spain where a majority of voluntary abstainers mentioned this reason.

[11] There is one major variation between the four countries concerned in this pattern of responses, namely the very high frequency of occurrence of registration and or polling card problems in Greece (66 per cent of all circumstantial abstainers). This may account for the fact that in Greece the combination of circumstantial abstention in the European election with abstention in the last national election is also exceptionally high; presumably the registration difficulties apply to both.

TABLE 2.3. *Type of reason given for abstention in European Parliament elections, by country (%)*

	Non-compulsory											Compulsory					EC12
	DK	FR	GB	GE (W)	GE (E)	IR	NE	NI	PO	SP	Tot	BE	GR	IT	LU	Tot	
Neither	14	7	9	12	9	5	20	7	4	12	10	5	2	7	0	5	9
Circumstantial	35	36	42	27	19	36	28	40	44	35	35	64	96	55	74	60	37
Voluntary	44	43	44	54	63	53	47	43	46	48	48	25	0	35	26	32	46
Both	7	14	6	7	9	7	6	9	6	5	8	6	2	4	0	3	7
N	282	324	499	262	182	364	434	109	414	231	3,101	64	52	110	19	246	3,347

Source: EB 41.1.

TABLE 2.4. *Circumstantial reasons for abstention by compulsory voting requirement*

	Countries without compulsory voting	Countries with compulsory voting	Total
Too busy/no time/work	27	9	26
Away from home	22	16	21
Registration/voting card problems	15	24	18
Sick/disabled/elderly	15	30	17
On holiday	9	7	9
Family responsibility	6	3	7
Involved in leisure activity	2	0	3
Other circumstantial reasons	7	15	8
N	1,343	174	1,517

Notes: Entries are percentages. Due to multiple responses, percentages add to more than 100.

Source: EB 41.1.

9 points lower). In short, what counts as a circumstance preventing an individual from voting is affected by the rules governing participation, that is, by the existence or non-existence of a formal requirement to vote.

Circumstantial reasons also vary as between countries that vote on a Sunday and those that vote on a weekday (Table 2.5). The most prominent circumstantial reason for abstention across all non-compulsory voting countries is pressure of work, being too busy, or simply 'having no time'; this accounts for 27 per cent of circumstantial abstention in these countries. However, abstention due to time pressure is particularly high in Denmark (47 per cent of circumstantial abstainers), the Netherlands (42 per cent), Ireland (42 per cent), and Northern Ireland (43 per cent), all of which vote on a Thursday. In Britain, circumstantial abstention is less dominated by this factor but, even there, it is cited more frequently than in any of the Sunday voting countries (see Table 2.5). Overall, the time/too busy factor accounts for 38 per cent of circumstantial abstention in countries that voted on a weekday compared to 27 per cent in countries that voted on a Sunday; this is, it would seem, ample confirmation that Sunday voting facilitates turnout.

One must, however, also take note of the fact that one in five circumstantial abstainers in countries that vote on a Sunday could

TABLE 2.5. *Circumstantial reasons for abstention by country and Sunday versus weekday voting (non-compulsory voting countries only)*

	Weekday-voting countries						Sunday-voting countries						All
	DK	GB	IR	NE	NI	Tot	FR	GE (W)	GE (E)	PO	SP	Tot	
Sick/disabled/elderly	13	15	12	10	19	13	13	18	25	20	17	16	15
Away from home	20	16	25	9	9	17	24	25	21	38	23	24	22
On holiday	5	11	9	13	19	11	5	10	0	7	7	7	9
Too busy/no time/work	47	28	42	42	43	38	25	25	19	13	17	23	27
Involved in leisure activity	0	0	1	3	0	0	4	12	0	3	1	5	2
Family responsibility	9	6	6	6	6	6	8	4	8	2	7	6	6
Registration/voting card problems	2	23	13	11	15	14	25	6	17	15	20	18	15
Other circumstantial reasons	13	5	2	14	0	7	9	4	14	5	9	8	7
N	129	240	156	152	54	731	170	91	52	207	92	612	1,343

Notes: Entries are percentages. Due to multiple responses, percentages add to more than 100.

Source: EB 41.1.

find no time or were too busy to vote; the proportion was as high as one in four in West Germany and in France. In the German and French cases, one should probably add in the 12 per cent and 4 per cent who did not vote on the Sunday in question because of 'leisure activities'. Furthermore, the evidence in Table 2.5 suggests that Sunday voting may increase abstention due to absence from home: more than one-quarter of all circumstantial abstainers in Sunday voting countries cited this reason compared to one-sixth in the non-compulsory countries.[12] Adding together those in Sunday-voting countries who abstain because of lack of time or because of absence from home or because of leisure activities indicates that, although turnout as a whole tends to be higher in these countries and although Sunday voting as such contributes to this higher rate, it can also inhibit participation in various ways; this is true in particular in West Germany, France, and Portugal. Portugal in 1994 was a special case but West Germany and France were not. It may therefore be worth illustrating with examples from these countries some of the ways in which Sunday voting can reduce participation. The problem is that the European Parliament must compete for the time and attention of its potential voters and weekend voting may tip the balance in the wrong direction: 'I didn't have any interest in giving up my plans for the weekend. I don't think that the European Parliament is that important.'[13] Moreover, it is not just a matter of those who are in a position to say 'We were away for the weekend';[14] for some, Sunday is the only day of rest: 'I don't have any time: Sunday is my only rest day.'[15] For others, a particular Sunday may carry specific obligations ('I didn't have time, it was the day my son had his first communion'[16])

[12] The highest proportion saying they did not vote because they were not at home was in Portugal. This figure helps to explain the exceptionally low turnout in Portugal in 1994 that was pointed out in the discussion of Table 2.1 above. In Portugal, Sunday 12 June 1994 occurred between two major holidays—Friday 10 June was Portugal Day and the prominent Roman Catholic feastday of Corpus Christi fell on Thursday 16 June. Of itself, the occurrence of Portugal Day on the Friday would have encouraged many Portuguese to take a long weekend with the consequent high probability of missing out on voting on the Sunday. The occurrence of another holiday on the following Thursday increased the likelihood of absence from home by providing the opportunity to take a week-long holiday at the expense of only three working days.

[13] 'Ich hatte kein Interesse dafür, meine Wochenendplanung aufzugeben. Ich glaube nicht dass das Europaparlament so wichtig ist.'

[14] 'On est parti en week-end.'

[15] 'Je n'ai pas le temps. Le dimanche c'est mon seul jour de repos.'

[16] 'Je n'ai pas eu le temps, c'était la communion de mon fils.'

or specific counter-attractions ('Because the weather was finally nice, I went off with my boyfriend'[17]).

The argument is not that these people, or any or all of those shown in Table 2.5 to be in such situations, would definitely have voted on a weekday. Indeed the *Fräulein* who headed off with her boyfriend to enjoy the good weather was in two minds about how she would vote anyway ('Hätte aber nicht gewusst, wen ich da wählen sollte') and this might have been enough to cause her to abstain. The point is that, in these cases, Sunday voting lowered the probability of participation. Clearly, the widely held belief that Sunday voting facilitates turnout while weekday voting inhibits it is a considerable oversimplification.

Two more minor participation-inhibiting factors that are reflected in the circumstantial reasons for abstention merit brief consideration —registration and voting card requirements and the timing of the elections in mid-June. Registration procedures and requirements are a major preoccupation of research on turnout in the United States (Rosenstone and Wolfinger 1978); they are often assumed to be negligible factors in Europe. The data in Table 2.5 suggest that they are not negligible. Fifteen per cent of circumstantial abstainers in non-compulsory voting countries refer to registration or voting card problems; these problems are most widespread in France (25 per cent), Britain (23 per cent), and Spain (20 per cent). As a proportion of the total electorate, these groups of non-voters are quite small. Nonetheless, it would seem to be worth investigating the procedures and requirements related to registration and voting cards in different countries to see if they can be modified to facilitate greater participation.

On the matter of the timing of the elections in mid-June, one should note that 9 per cent of circumstantial abstainers in non-compulsory voting countries specifically said that they did not vote because they were on holiday. The figure ranged from 5 per cent in Denmark to 13 per cent in the Netherlands. These are minimum estimates of the number who did not vote because of absence on holiday, as it is highly probable that some holiday-makers were included in the category of people who simply indicated that they were absent from home without specifying the reason for this absence. Commercial research has shown that, while July to September is still the peak holiday period, only 41 per cent of holidays abroad are now taken in these

---

17 'Weil endlich mal schönes Wetter war, bin ich mit meinem Freund ausgeflogen.'

months. The period April to June accounts for 31 per cent of holidays abroad; almost certainly the majority of these are concentrated in June.[18] Coupled with the evidence that being on holiday prevented a small but noticeable number of people from voting, this suggests that, while June elections may fit the parliamentary calendar well, they may not represent the best timing in terms of maximizing turnout.

VOLUNTARY ABSTENTION

Four main reasons are given for voluntary abstention in European Parliament elections—lack of interest, distrust of or dissatisfaction with politics and politicians, lack of knowledge, and dissatisfaction with the European Parliament electoral process (including 'vote has no consequences'). Taking the eight non-compulsory voting countries as a whole, lack of interest is the foremost reason, being referred to by two out of every five voluntary abstainers (see Table 2.6). It is a very prominent reason for abstention in Ireland (62 per cent) and somewhat less so but still quite prominent in Portugal (49 per cent), France (48 per cent), and West Germany (47 per cent). At the other end of the scale, it accounts for relatively fewer voluntary abstainers in Spain (30 per cent), Denmark (33 per cent), former East Germany (34 per cent), and Britain (34 per cent). Not surprisingly, perhaps, the responses tended simply to declare lack of interest, without any further elaboration and, in most cases, it is not possible to infer from these responses alone whether this was lack of interest in European politics or in politics in general.[19] There was one notable exception to this lack of specificity: in France, 48 per cent of those who cited lack of interest as a reason for not voting referred specifically to lack of interest in the European Parliament elections. This amounts to about one-quarter of all French abstainers and 5 per cent of the French electorate and is part of a pattern of negative French responses to the European Parliament election itself which will be examined in more detail below.

The second most prominent voluntary reason, though a good way behind lack of interest, was dissatisfaction with or lack of trust in

[18] Source: Euromonitor, 1993.
[19] This issue is taken up in Chapter 4 when other measures of interest in politics and in Europe have been introduced.

TABLE 2.6. *Voluntary reasons for abstention by country (non-compulsory voting countries only)*

	DK	FR	GB	GE (W)	GE (E)	IR	NE	NI	PO	SP	All non-compulsory countries
Lack of interest	33	48	34	47	34	62	42	52	49	30	43
Political distrust or dissatisfaction	14	34	17	30	27	37	16	17	25	61	27
Lack of knowledge	39	24	40	16	21	18	26	7	23	10	24
Vote has no consequences	17	7	16	17	14	10	7	21	3	8	11
Opposed to EU	10	8	7	14	23	1	11	3	3	2	8
Dissatisfaction with EP electoral system	6	26	7	2	2	9	2	9	9	5	8
Dissatisfaction with EP as an institution	6	2	2	8	2	6	6	0	2	2	4
Rarely or never votes	2	4	8	4	2	2	3	10	2	3	4
EU not relevant or has no effect	1	5	4	3	2	7	6	0	3	6	4
N	155	187	255	169	133	220	239	58	215	124	1,755

Notes: Entries are percentages. Due to multiple responses, percentages add to more than 100.

Source: EB 41.1.

politicians or politics or both (27 per cent). Given that such a feeling is likely to be rooted in people's immediate experience of politics, one would expect it to vary between countries; so it does, from the low of 14 to 17 per cent in Denmark, the Netherlands, and Britain, to 37 per cent in Ireland and 61 per cent in Spain; it should be noted that virtually no Spanish responses of this type referred to European politicians whereas one-quarter of the Irish responses did.

The third most prominent reason was a declared lack of knowledge, in fact, at 24 per cent, it is more or less equal to distrust. Though more specific than lack of interest, one still cannot be sure in most cases whether it is a matter of lack of knowledge of European politics or of politics in general; a German response was typical: 'What one doesn't understand, one can't vote for.'[20] French respondents were again the exception: almost half of the French respondents who said they did not vote because they had not enough knowledge were quite specific, referring to lack of knowledge of the Euro-candidates and what they stood for.

The last of the four main voluntary reasons for not voting was dissatisfaction with the European Parliament electoral process. Specific dissatisfaction with the electoral system was expressed by 8 per cent of voluntary abstainers across the eight countries. Once again, French voluntary abstainers were distinctive, expressing the highest level of dissatisfaction (26 per cent). In addition to general complaints about too many lists and having to vote for unknown quantities ('to give a blank cheque to someone I don't know'/'I don't have much interest in voting for unknown people'[21]), there were quite explicit French criticisms of the list system as such: 'I feel that to vote only for a party is not right. There should have been several persons from the different parties. I find that better than only a party vote.'[22] Taken together with the already noted French lack of interest in the European Parliament elections as such, these responses suggest that the view that there is a straightforward positive association between the proportionality of the electoral system and turnout needs to be qualified by reference to the negative effects that the passage from a

[20] 'Von was man nichts versteht, kann man auch nicht waehlen.'

[21] 'donner des chèques en blanc à quelqu'un que je ne connais pas'/ 'Pas beaucoup d'intérêt pour moi à élire des gens inconnus.'

[22] 'Je trouve que voter juste pour un parti politique, cela n'est pas normal. Il aurait dû y avoir plusieurs personnes de différents partis. Je trouve cela un peu plus juste que rien qu'un parti politique.'

candidate-based non-proportional electoral system for National Assembly elections to a list-based proportional system for European Parliament elections would appear to have had in the French case. It also implies that turnout considerations should be borne in mind in any further discussions of a common electoral system for European Parliament elections. In considering the impact of different electoral systems on turnout, it is also worth noting that British abstainers are among the least likely to express dissatisfaction with their (plurality) electoral system and they are not any more likely to complain that their vote has no consequence than are abstainers in several countries which practise a variety of forms of proportional representation (see Table 2.6).

WHAT THE DISTINCTION SHOWS (AND DOES NOT SHOW) ABOUT THE CAUSES OF ABSTENTION

How much light has the distinction between voluntary and circumstantial abstention cast on the problem of turnout? In the first place, we now know that two-fifths of those who abstained in the European Parliament elections gave a purely circumstantial reason for doing so. The main inhibiting circumstances cited were work or time pressure, absence from home, illness or other disability, and registration or voting card problems. In the past, such factors have been regarded as being beyond the reach of survey research or, if within its reach, as random and therefore negligible. The evidence presented above indicates quite clearly that circumstantial reasons can be teased out and that they are far from random. Leaving aside the fact that both the incidence and the nature of the circumstances that lead to non-voting are affected by whether or not there is compulsory voting, they are also affected by whether voting is on a Sunday or on a weekday, by the timing of the elections in mid-June and by country-specific registration requirements and procedures. In other words, the fact that 40 per cent of European Parliament election abstention can be related to 'circumstances' does not absolve those who decide on the institutional arrangements for these elections of a share of the responsibility for low turnout: more measures could be taken to encourage participation, measures that do not involve even thinking about the unthinkable of compulsory voting for European Parliament elections.

Apart from the impact of circumstances, some of which is non-random and subject therefore to policy intervention, 60 per cent of abstainers saw their abstention as 'voluntary'. Lack of interest was the dominant voluntary reason given; this was followed by political distrust or dissatisfaction, lack of knowledge, and dissatisfaction with the European Parliament electoral system. This is not the whole story, however. First, without a much longer and more penetrating series of questions, respondents are unlikely to be sufficiently specific regarding their reasons for abstention. Thus we do not know whether a particular response, such as 'not enough knowledge' or 'not interested', relates to European politics or to politics in general; this lack of specificity has a particular bearing on the issue of the extent to which attitudes to Europe play a role in determining whether an individual will vote or abstain in a European Parliament election. With two exceptions (French negative reactions to the European Parliament elections and dissatisfaction with the European Parliament electoral system), the European categories in the coding scheme picked up relatively few responses—opposition to the EU was given as a reason by only 8 per cent of abstainers, dissatisfaction with the EU as an institution by 4 per cent, and perception of the EU as irrelevant by 3 per cent. This might seem to lend weight to the view, described above as puzzling, that EU-related attitudes and prefer-ences do not affect turnout in European Parliament elections. The evidence from the open-ended questions, however, is not precise enough to warrant such an inference. If a respondent says, 'I'm just not interested' and does not provide any elaboration, without further research one simply does not know whether this is an attitude to the election, to Europe, or to politics in general.

Second, even with the most elaborate prompting, most respond-ents would not be able to give a comprehensive list of the reasons for their abstention, if only because one reason leads to another and the first that comes to mind may not be the most important. Yet there is a third and more fundamental reason why the account of the sources of voluntary abstention which has just been given is incomplete: respondents may not be in the best position to account for their action or, in this case, inaction; they may not even be aware of the causes of their abstention. These considerations highlight the need to explore the attitudes and motivations of both voters and abstainers; this exploration begins with an analysis of attitudes to integration in Chapter 3.

3

Legitimacy and Participation

INTRODUCTION

When one compares the abstention figures at European and national elections, one cannot avoid the prima-facie conclusion that the legitimacy of the Union is rather low and, in particular, that it is appreciably lower than that enjoyed by the member states. Admittedly, not all this abstention is a mark of low legitimacy: the distinction introduced in Chapter 2 between circumstantial and voluntary abstention makes it clear that a substantial proportion of those who did not vote were unavoidably absent from the polls; but the distinction also shows that, for another group of abstainers, the decision not to vote was more or less deliberate. Moreover, not all voters can be assumed to feel close to the Union, since some, whatever their views, were legally obliged to go to the polls, while others voted for parties opposed to the integration process, and yet others always vote out of habit and not because they wish to express a positive feeling about the Union. The link between the legitimacy of the Union, on the one hand, and participation in the European Parliament elections, on the other, is therefore neither direct nor straightforward.

To investigate the extent and nature of this link, one must begin with legitimacy and examine how much support for or opposition to the European Union there is among the citizens, since, as noted in Chapter 1, the legitimacy of an institution arises from the support which people give to it. We also noted in Chapter 1 that legitimacy was not an all-or-nothing affair: the same applies to support. As legitimacy, support is more or less marked; it can be non-existent and can even be 'negative' where there is opposition; as legitimacy, support varies over time, both individually and in the aggregate; and, as legitimacy, support varies in breadth since it relates to either a wider or a more limited set of policy fields. To obtain a realistic picture of the extent of support and to see more clearly where support is lacking and where there is opposition, therefore, it is not sufficient simply to ask citizens whether they support the European Union or not. Support has many facets: one can support the main aims of a body but not like many of its specific activities; one can, on the contrary, be favourable to certain activities but be lukewarm towards its overall aims. Thus, to be realistically monitored, support for the European Union must be assessed by means of a variety of questions, ranging from general views about the integration process to specific points about particular directions which this process is taking or might take.

This chapter is therefore concerned with a description of the attitudes of European citizens to the European Union. It looks first at general measures of support for integration and at the extent to which European citizens identify with Europe. The chapter then follows up the idea that support and legitimacy vary by issue and by sector by analysing the extent of satisfaction or dissatisfaction with the scope of the policies that the Union pursues or might be intending to pursue. This leads to an examination of attitudes to the idea of a United States of Europe; our analysis of evaluations of the Union concludes by refocusing on the present and asking to what extent people feel the Union to be democratic. In the final section of the chapter, these assessments are related to patterns of voting and abstention to see whether there is any evidence of a link between attitudes and turnout and, if there is, whether this evidence varies in strength depending on the aspect of EU legitimacy that is being addressed. Overall conclusions about the influence of these attitudes on participation will have to wait, however, until Chapter 8, where the relative importance of these factors is examined alongside that of others—such as political interest and knowledge, attitudes to the European Parliament, and the role of parties, candidates, and the election campaign.

SUPPORT FOR EUROPEAN INTEGRATION

The analysis of attitudes to the European Union does not start from a *tabula rasa*. Some aspects of support have been monitored for a number of years, thanks to a battery of questions regularly asked of respondents in the six-monthly surveys of the Eurobarometer. Before embarking on an analysis of the answers given to the questions that are specific to this study, we need therefore to return to these standard questions, see what has been the pattern of response and examine the extent to which there have been variations over time. This will enable us also to place the findings of the current study in perspective.[1]

In recent decades, there has been a degree of satisfaction in some pro-integration circles about the extent of support which there appeared to be for the process of integration. Thus, Pinder has argued that 'despite a modest shift . . . since 1989, there is still predominant endorsement' (Pinder 1994: 496). Such views have not been shared by all commentators, admittedly: a number of analysts have pointed to relatively weak or apparently superficial attitudes characterizing many citizens, although this has tended to be said mainly by those who have analysed the extent to which there exists a sense of identification with Europe among the citizens (Duchesne and Frognier 1995: 193–226). Be that as it may, a close examination of the findings of the Eurobarometer surveys suggests that the interpretation to be given to the evidence concerning attitudes to European integration is not simple.

Attitudes towards the Union have been mainly monitored by means of four questions which have been used regularly in the Eurobarometer surveys. These questions are generally referred to as the 'unification indicator', the 'membership indicator', the 'benefits indicator', and the 'dissolution indicator'. Respectively, they tap: (1) support for European unification ('very much for', 'to some extent for', 'to some extent against', 'very much against'), (2) how membership of the European Union is regarded ('a good thing', 'neither good nor bad', 'a bad thing'), (3) feelings about the effect of the European Union on the country ('benefited', 'did not benefit'), and (4) attitudes if the Community or Union were to be scrapped ('very sorry', 'indifferent', 'relieved').[2]

Straightforward and unequivocal conclusions are difficult to draw from the answers to these questions. For one thing, as Niedermayer points out, two of the questions do not allow for a 'middle' position (the 'unification' indicator and the 'benefit' indicator): those who are uncertain may therefore find it difficult to answer;[3] moreover, there is

---

[1] As well as the questions designed specifically for this study, EB 41.1 included some standard Eurobarometer questions. This means that we can trace the development over time of the attitudes measured by these indicators and relate these attitudes to the new variables which are the main focus of this study. The full set of questions from EB 41.1 used in the present study are reproduced in the Appendix.

[2] This last question—the dissolution indicator—was dropped in 1995.

[3] Respondents can and indeed do state that they are unable to reply to some or all

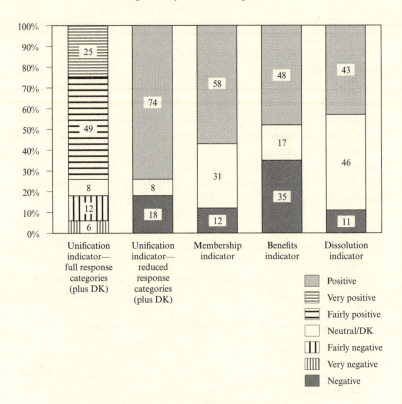

FIG. 3.1. Attitudes to the European Union
on four 'standard' Eurobarometer indicators
(unification, membership, benefits, and dissolution), 1994
Source: EB 41.1.

an asymmetry in the positive and negative response categories in some of the questions (Niedermayer 1995: 54–6). These and other aspects of the variation in the phrasing of the questions give rise to apparently quite different estimates of support for integration in our survey: as measured by the unification indicator, such support in June–July 1994 was 16 percentage points higher than support as measured by the membership indicator, which was, in turn, 15 percentage points higher than that shown by the dissolution indicator

of the four questions; the point is that uncertainty or neutrality is handled differently by the different questions.

(see Figure 3.1). The reason is partly that the different questions are measuring different things and partly that they are measuring the same thing more or less satisfactorily.

The 'unification' indicator, may seem to suggest that commitment to integration is strong; in reality much of the support it measures appears to be rather superficial. The question measures a vague integrationist aspiration ('efforts being made to unify Western Europe') and the combination of its ordinal response format and the absence of an explicit neutral category tends to boost rather artificially the more positive answer or the positive answer which is nearest to the middle position. Although at least 70 per cent of respondents state that they support the process of unification, a majority of these is consistently found among those who declare that they support unification 'to some extent', not among those who support it 'very much': in the present survey, for instance, while 25 per cent of the respondents declared themselves 'very much' in favour of efforts to unify Western Europe, 49 per cent declared themselves to be in favour 'to some extent' (see the left-hand column of Figure 3.1). Thus it may not be altogether as important as it seems at first sight that only 12 per cent declared themselves 'to some extent' against the process of unification and 6 per cent 'very much' against it, while 8 per cent gave no reply: what is probably more important is that a near-majority of the respondents stated that they were in favour 'to some extent' only, thereby 'hedging their bets', so to speak, and displaying little real commitment. Moreover, the percentage of strongly favourable answers has diminished from about one-third in the mid-1980s to only a quarter by 1994 (see Figure 3.2), while the percentage of don't knows also declined and that of opponents increased (from 5 per cent in 1970 to 19 per cent in 1994). There is little in these findings to justify the view that support for integration is strong.

The 'membership' indicator measures a concrete overall evaluation of the fact of belonging to the Union, where the basic choice is between good and bad but where the starkness of this choice is softened by a neutral category ('neither good nor bad'). The responses it elicits suggest that support is substantial but far from overwhelming: in the summer of 1994, a majority of respondents (58 per cent) declared that their country's membership was a good thing, while 31 per cent gave an indifferent or don't know response and 12 per cent were opposed (see Figure 3.1). Responses to this question provide a useful measure of trends in support for integration since 1973. The modest majority

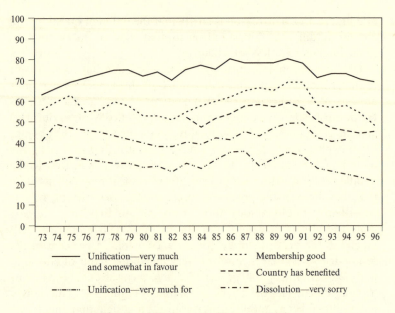

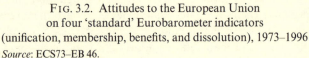

FIG. 3.2. Attitudes to the European Union
on four 'standard' Eurobarometer indicators
(unification, membership, benefits, and dissolution), 1973–1996
Source: ECS73–EB 46.

of the early to mid-1990s is the culmination of a process of decline
that began in the autumn of 1991, accelerated in 1992, and has failed
to show any signs of recovery (see Figure 3.2). It can also be seen from
Figure 3.2 that support for integration had entered a valley period in
the early 1980s, after which it then grew consistently for almost ten
years. The current trough appears to be of longer duration and is presumably attributable to the politicization of integration issues arising
from the combination of the Single Market programme entering its
final stages and the controversies surrounding the Maastricht Treaty
and the proposals for monetary union. While future developments in
the process of European integration are difficult to predict, we can be
fairly certain that the politicization of EU issues will continue and that
there will be continued pressure on public support for integration.[4]

---

[4] The underlying process of politicization was anticipated a long time ago by the
revisionist school of neo-functionalist integration theory: as integration makes inroads

The 'benefits' indicator also provides only limited cause for optimism for supporters of European integration as, in the present survey, the difference between the proportion of those who stated that their country had benefited and the proportion who stated that it had not was only 13 percentage points, with those stating that their country benefited having ranged between 40 and 50 per cent for a long time (see Figure 3.2). Furthermore, only in five countries, all of them small or medium-sized (Ireland, Greece, Luxembourg, Portugal, and the Netherlands), was the positive difference truly large (40 to 50 per cent or more): it was around 25 per cent in Italy and Belgium and even smaller in Germany and France; finally, the proportion of negative answers was larger than that of positive answers in Britain and Spain. It may be, however, that the benefits indicator is less useful as a direct measure of support for integration, as it deals with the respondent's *perceptions* of whether or not his or her country has benefited from membership of the Community or Union rather than with the respondent's *evaluation* of the Community or the country's membership of it. The significance of this distinction is illustrated by the fact that only 23 per cent of those Germans who thought that Germany had not benefited from being a member were themselves opposed to German membership of the Union.

If the benefits indicator needs to be discounted somewhat, the same cannot be said of the final of the four indicators, 'dissolution'. This question posits the hypothetical situation of the dissolution or 'scrapping' of the Community or Union and asks respondents if they would be very sorry, indifferent, or very relieved as a result.[5] Although sometimes criticized for being not just hypothetical but unrealistically hypothetical, its value is that it gets at intensity of support in a more decisive way than the unification indicator. As such it gives proponents of European integration even more cause for worry. According to our data, only just over two-fifths of the respondents would be very sorry if they were told tomorrow that the European Union had been scrapped (see Figure 3.1 above). The proportion of those who would

on the basic functions of states, public opinion becomes politicized, leading to fundamental problems for the integration project if the politicization is premature, i.e. if it occurs before support for integration had become deep-rooted and well structured. For a review of the role attributed to public opinion in the various stages of the evolution of integration theory see Sinnott (1995*a*).

[5] The original negative category in this question was 'relieved'; the 'very' was added in 1993.

be very relieved if such a dissolution were to take place may be small (11 per cent overall but double that figure in Britain and Denmark), but 37 per cent said they would be indifferent if this were to happen and a further 9 per cent gave a don't know response. Thus, nearly half the respondents appear not to care whether the Union exists or not and, as of the mid-1990s, opponents, indifferents, and don't knows constitute a majority.

In summary, an examination of the answers to the four questions indicates that, as was suggested earlier, the bulk of those who say that they are in favour of efforts to unify Western Europe are in reality rather uncommitted; the only 'real' supporters seem to be those who state that they support the Union 'very much' or, at most, the two-fifths who would be very sorry in the event of a dissolution of the Union. This throws some doubt on the conclusions which are typically drawn from the 'membership' indicator: it is difficult to believe that there is real support for integration among all the 55 to 60 per cent or so who respond positively to this question.[6] Moreover, if one considers all four indicators jointly over time, one notices a substantial decline in support since 1991, a decline that is almost certainly related to the fact that integration has reached a more intrusive and demanding stage. Finally, what the large swathe of indifference to a hypothetical break-up of the Union reveals is that sentiments vis-à-vis the existence of the Union are, to say the least, not deep. It may be that few are truly against European integration; yet many are probably so 'indifferent' that while they state that, yes, they accept the process of unification or the fact of membership as a good thing, they do not really attach much weight to the whole matter.

STRENGTH OF EUROPEAN IDENTITY

If the four indicators that we have just examined only provide a limited guide to the extent of support for and opposition to the European Union, it is important to attempt to find out how citizens relate to Europe in other ways, including especially the extent to which they have a sense of European identity. Two authors who have examined

---

6 It should also be noted that estimates of support for the Union may be exaggerated because a positive answer may be widely regarded as, in the jargon of survey research, the socially desirable response.

this question, Duchesne and Frognier, have concluded, in a somewhat pessimistic manner, that there was probably not as yet a European identity. In a section entitled 'Too soon to speak of a European identity?', they note that '. . . [the] sense of European identity is far weaker than four other measures of attitudes to European integration' (1995: 221), these being the measures obtained from the four indicators examined above. They also state: 'As an economic, political, and administrative construction, Europe evidently elicits evaluative attitudes, but not a real community of belonging of the kind experienced in nation states' (ibid. 223).

The analysis conducted by these authors was based on two types of questions which appeared successively in the Eurobarometer. During the early period, respondents were asked to specify what were their first and second choices among five types of identities, local, regional, state, European, and worldwide; since the 1980s they were asked to state whether they felt 'often, sometimes, or never' citizens of Europe as well as of their own country. Both questions were rather unsatisfactory: the first was unsatisfactory because the reference to three identities other than those of the nation state and Europe made it impossible to ascertain precisely the extent and weight of the European identity; the second was unsatisfactory because it did not give respondents sufficient opportunity to indicate degrees of European identity, other than by reference to a temporal dimension (often, sometimes, never).

Accordingly, in the present survey respondents were asked to express their sentiments in a somewhat different manner. They were asked whether, as well as thinking of themselves as [French or Irish or Danish . . . or Flemish or Catalan or whatever . . .], they thought of themselves also as European. To give respondents an adequate range of choice within which to express their feeling on this matter, they were offered the opportunity to answer on a ten-point scale. The two extreme points on the scale corresponded, on the one hand, to a purely national identity (respondents having no sense at all of being European) and, on the other, to a genuinely combined European and national identity if respondents thought of themselves as 'very much' European in addition to having a sense of national identity.

Rather than taking the bell-like shape of the 'normal distribution', the responses to this question assume an odd shape on the scale: they peak near the middle all right; but then, rather than tailing off at both ends, the proportions increase at the extreme points on the scale (see

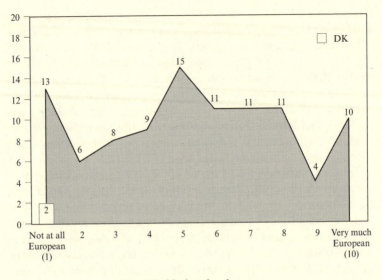

FIG. 3.3. National-only versus
combined European and national identity, 1994
Source: EB 41.1.

Figure 3.3). The impression is more of a sombrero, albeit a rather battered one, than of a bell. The evidence thus indicates some degree of polarization on this issue between the 13 per cent (or 19 per cent if we include points one and two in this extreme category) on the not at all European side and 10 per cent (14 if we include points nine and ten) on the very much European side. In between these extremes, 32 per cent place themselves at points three, four, or five and an almost identical proportion (33 per cent) place themselves at points five, six, or seven. Overall, therefore, the distribution is fairly evenly balanced between the two halves of the scale, with 51 per cent either at or leaning towards the non-European side and 47 per cent at or towards the European side; there were 2 per cent don't knows.[7]

This evidence suggests that some of the conclusions relating to the

---

[7] The extremely low level of don't knows might be seen to suggest that the middle points of the scale may have acted as a surrogate don't know category and attracted respondents who had really no opinion on the matter. However, an analysis of the rate of don't knows given in other questions by respondents at each point on the identity scale does not indicate any significant increase in a tendency to give a don't know response in these middle categories.

identification of citizens with Europe may be overpessimistic to the extent that they suggest that this identification does not exist (Duchesne and Frognier 1995: 221–3). That last conclusion was drawn because, as Duchesne and Frognier submit, Europe seems not (at least not yet) to generate the kind of emotional feelings typically associated with the concept of identity in the strong sense of the word (ibid.). The existing evidence does not in fact permit us to be definitive about whether or not emotional feelings underpin people's sense of being European; what we can say is that a substantial number of respondents declared themselves attached to Europe as well as to their nation but that the extent of this attachment varied markedly. These variations confirm the conclusion drawn on the basis of considering the four indicators with which this chapter opened, namely, that Euro-enthusiasm is a minority pursuit and that there is a very large middle segment of European citizens who are neither strongly pro-Europe nor strongly anti-Europe but, while they may lean one way or the other, are on the whole rather uncommitted. However, the evidence also confirms the point, made in Chapter 1, that legitimacy can be enjoyed simultaneously by different bodies and that, consequently, the legitimacy enjoyed by each of these bodies is typically 'partial'. Chapter 1 went on to make the further point that legitimacy is not just shared: it is, in principle, bounded in the sense of being specific to particular policy sectors and even to specific issues.

A BOUNDED LEGITIMACY?

Attitudes to policy issues are normally thought of as preferences regarding policy outcomes: for or against privatization, for or against a minimum wage, for or against stricter immigration controls, etc. There is a prior preference, however, that, in most political systems, is not contested and may not even be explicit, namely the preference regarding how, and in particular, at what level, policy issues are to be decided. This is the very stuff of legitimacy. In established unitary political systems this preference is implicit; in established federal political systems it is explicit but usually not contested; in a political system such as the European Union that is being constructed by bringing together pre-existing states, the preference is both explicit and contested. In short, in order to have a full picture of the legitimacy of this system-under-construction, one needs to know what are the preferences regarding the allocation of decision-making power and over which issues. While the legitimacy of the scope of decision-making undertaken by any political body or institution may be 'bounded', i.e. it may vary from one area of policy to another, this is particularly important in the case of the European Union since, even before the debate on subsidiarity, it was clear that the question of the allocation of policy responsibilities between the states and the Union was one of the key issues in European integration. Accordingly, an examination of public reactions to the scope and extent of involvement of the European Union in the making of policy should help to clarify the real nature of the support for or opposition to the Union and thereby the character and extent of its legitimacy.

Given what has just been said about the centrality of this matter to the integration process, it is not surprising that the Eurobarometer has fielded questions on it over a long number of years. The wording of the questions has varied considerably; the main version current since 1989 has been as follows: 'Some people believe that certain areas of policy should be decided by the [national] government, while other areas should be decided jointly within the European Community. Which of the following areas of policy do you think should be decided by the [national] government, and which should be decided jointly within the European Community?' The distribution of responses to this question over a series of policy areas as of December 1995 is shown in Table 3.1. The evidence indicates a remarkable range of variation in support for European decision-making, from a high of over 75 per cent on such issues as policy towards the developing world and the fight against drugs to the mere one-third or less who are willing to accept a European role in decision-making on health and social welfare, on cultural policy, and on education. While it is impossible to draw clear-cut distinctions between sets of issues in a ranking of the kind displayed in Table 3.1, broadly speaking, one can delineate three groups of issues: (*a*) issues on which European decision-making seems to be *widely regarded as legitimate* (60 per cent or more support for European decision-making); (*b*) those which produce a *moderate degree of Euro-legitimacy* (between 50 and 59 per cent supporting European decision-making); and (*c*) those in relation to which European involvement is *widely regarded as illegitimate* (those issues on which less than half the public say that decisions should be made at the European level). On the basis of the data in

TABLE 3.1. *Preference regarding European versus national responsibility for decision-making by issue, 1996 (%)*

	Policy should be decided by		
	European Union	National government	DK
High Euro-legitimacy			
The fight against drugs	77	19	4
Cooperation with developing countries	77	17	6
Equality for men and women	71	24	5
Trade with countries outside the EU	71	22	7
Scientific and technological research	70	25	5
Foreign policy towards countries outside the EU	70	22	8
Protection of the environment	66	30	4
Currency	62	33	5
Supporting regions with economic difficulties	61	32	7
Competition policy	60	28	12
Moderate Euro-legitimacy			
Immigration policy	57	37	6
The fight against unemployment	57	39	4
Fishing policy	56	35	9
Rules for political asylum	55	37	8
Defence	52	44	4
Consumer policy	51	43	6
Agriculture	50	45	5
Rates of VAT	49	42	9
Low Euro-legitimacy			
Health and safety of workers	44	52	4
Workers' rights vis-à-vis their employers	42	53	5
Basic rules for broadcasting and press	39	54	7
Health and social welfare	36	59	5
Cultural policy	34	60	6
Education	29	68	3

Source: EB 45.

Table 3.1, the first group would run from policy towards the developing world (77 per cent for Europeanization) down to and including competition policy (60 per cent in favour of Europeanization); the moderate group extends from immigration policy (57 per cent) to agriculture (50 per cent) and the group of issues with low Euro-legitimacy ranges from health and safety of workers (44 per cent) to education (29 per cent).

All of this would seem to suggest that the public recognizes the bounded character of the legitimacy of European integration, with widespread acceptance of European policy-making in some areas and fairly minimal acceptance in others. In fact, however, the problem of the legitimacy of European decision-making is much more complex than is suggested by the evidence in Table 3.1. This is so for three reasons: first, the distribution of support for European decision-making on certain issues varies substantially from member state to member state; secondly, public support for European decision-making must be understood in the context of the claims to European policy-responsibility staked out on behalf of the European institutions and in the context of the nature of the policy issues involved;[8] thirdly, we now know that data such as those in Table 3.1 present an oversimplified picture of public opinion in this area. This emerges from the consideration of new evidence derived from a question inserted in EB 41.1 as part of the present study.

The standard Eurobarometer question on preferences regarding the attribution of policy responsibility produces remarkably low levels of don't know (an average of 6 per cent across the twenty-four items in Table 3.1). This might seem to suggest that virtually the entire mass public in Europe has a considered view on the application of the principle of subsidiarity across a very wide range of issues. Suspicious of this finding, the present survey approached the matter in a more exploratory way. Respondents were asked three questions. First, did they feel that the scope and extent of the issues decided on by the Union was too large, too small, or about right? Second, they were asked whether their assessment of this matter was based on a general feeling about the European Union or on consideration of specific issues. Finally, respondents who stated that their reaction was based on specific issues were asked which issues they had in mind. The precise wording of the main question was: 'There has been a lot of discussion recently about the European Union (European Community). Some people say that too many issues are decided by the European Union (European Community), others say that more issues should be decided by the European Union (European Community). Which of the following statements comes closest to your view?' The card handed to the respondents included the three obvious responses (too

---

[8] Claims to policy-making responsibility by European institutions give rise to *exogenous* internationalization (or Europeanization) of issues; the nature of the issue (whether dealing with the issue actually requires European-level decision-making) gives rise to *endogenous* internationalization; public opinion gives rise to *attributed* internationalization. The relationship between these three modes of internationalization of issues is discussed in Sinnott (1995*b*).

many, about right, more should be decided at EU level) plus the option 'I haven't really thought about it'.

The answers to these questions suggest that the salience of this dimension of legitimacy is very low: many people simply do not have an attitude on the matter and, for the bulk of those who do have a view, their view reflects their general feeling towards the European Union rather than any specific judgements about particular issues or policy sectors. In addition to the 10 per cent who gave a don't know response, 26 per cent chose the option of 'I haven't really thought about it'; most of the remainder (46 per cent of the sample) said that their opinion was based on a general feeling rather than on specific issues; only 17 per cent indicated that they had specific issues in mind when answering the question and went on to specify a particular issue or set of issues (Table 3.2). Among this minority, agriculture was the issue that was mentioned most frequently, followed by economic issues of one sort or another and by issues having to do with the way in which the EU is governed (the role of various institutions, the need for transparency, criticisms of bureaucracy, etc.). As Table 3.2 indicates, however, the proportions making reference to any one of these policy or issue areas are tiny: for example, 3 per cent of the sample in the case of agriculture and 3 per cent in the case of economic issues.

TABLE 3.2. *Type of response to question on preference regarding scope of EU decision-making*

	%
Don't know/haven't thought about it	36
General feeling	46
Specific issues in mind	17
Of which	
Agriculture	3
Economic issues	3
Governance	3
Education and culture	2
International relations	2
Other issues	2
Environment	1
Social and health	1
N	12,478

Source: EB 41.1.

TABLE 3.3. *Preferences regarding scope of EU decision-making, by type of response*

| | All respondents | Type of opinion expressed and issue mentioned | | | |
| | | General feeling | Specific issues in mind | Specific issues mentioned | |
				International relations	Social and health
Don't know/haven't thought about it	36	—	—	—	—
More on some issues, less on others	9	13	19	28	18
More issues should be decided at EU level	18	26	32	52	50
Number about right	18	33	13	11	15
Too many issues	19	28	36	10	18
N	12,478	5,771	2,172	242	96
% of total N	100	46	17	2	1

Source: EB 41.1.

Accepting that attitudes in this area are relatively unformed, the question still arises as to what are the preferences of European citizens regarding the overall allocation of policy responsibility? Across the body of European citizens as a whole, 36 per cent have, as we have seen, no opinion. Most of the remainder are rather evenly spread over the other three options presented to respondents: 18 per cent want more issues decided at EU level, 18 per cent think the number of issues decided at EU level is about right, and 19 per cent believe that too many issues are decided by the EU (Table 3.3). A small minority of discerning citizens (9 per cent) replied to the question by saying that on some issues there should be more EU decision-making and on some issues there should be less (this response was not included on the card handed to the respondents). In short, only 36 per cent take an unambiguously pro-integration stance on this question, that is those who are satisfied with the current level of EU decision-making and those who would like more. One may perhaps add to this the 9 per cent who think there should be more EU decision-making on some issues and less on others, thus bringing maximum support for European policy-making to 45 per cent. The remainder are either oblivious of the issue or are opposed to even the current scope of EU decision-making.

and issues mentioned (%)

Education and culture	Economic	Agriculture	Environment	Governance	Other
—	—	—	—	—	—
22	18	17	15	19	18
46	34	14	23	25	35
13	21	10	16	11	8
19	28	58	47	45	39
228	387	434	204	346	213
2	3	3	2	3	2

The basis on which people make up their mind in this area is related to their preference: those for whom it is a matter of a general feeling about the EU are more likely to endorse the status quo; those who think in terms of specific issues tend to be polarized—32 per cent favouring more EU decision-making and 36 per cent seeking less EU involvement (see Table 3.3). For the minority which thinks in terms of specific issues, support for EU decision-making varies depending on the issue that preoccupies them: those who mention international relations problems, education and cultural issues, and social welfare and health tend to think that the EU should be doing more; those who refer to agriculture, the environment, and governance issues tend to believe that the EU should have less decision-making power. It must be added, however, that these are very small proportions of the total sample; the vast majority either have only a vague and general view of the matter or no view at all.

In assessing the scope of EU legitimacy, therefore, two findings must be taken into account. The first is that, if respondents are pushed by the formulation of the question to take a view on the scope of EU decision-making, they will do so and the aggregate response varies across a wide range of issues from highly positive to quite negative. The second finding provides, however, a vital qualification to any conclusion one might draw from these data: for very large numbers of citizens, the problem either does not arise or arises only in a vague and general way. While in principle the legitimacy of EU decision-making may be bounded, in practice this sophisticated perception does not percolate down to the mass of people on whose behalf the decisions are being made. In short, the real constraint on this aspect of EU legitimacy is not opposition but ignorance and apathy.[9]

In order to fill out this picture of attitudes to European integration, one needs to deal with attitudes to possible institutional developments in the Union. It was not, however, possible within the compass of this study to analyse attitudes towards every specific detail of the institutional changes that have been or are being contemplated for the Union; nor was it necessary. Instead, respondents were asked about one possible long-term outcome of this process of institutional development, namely, the 'development of a United States of Europe'.

SUPPORT FOR THE DEVELOPMENT OF A UNITED STATES OF EUROPE

Preferences regarding the development of a United States of Europe were measured on a ten-point scale ranging from total opposition (a 'very bad idea') to full support (a 'very good idea'). The results reveal an element of polarization, not unlike that encountered on the European identity scale: 19 per cent regard the possibility as a 'very bad idea' (points one and two on the scale) and 15 per cent regard it as a 'very good idea' (points nine and ten). Note that the strongly anti- and strongly pro-integration views are more nearly equal in size on this measure than on any of the four traditional indicators of attitude to integration; in fact, on this measure, strong opponents outnumber strong supporters by a small margin. If one were to include point three on the negative side and point eight on the positive side, the supporters and opponents of this version of integration are perfectly balanced: 27 to 26 per cent; in fact, no matter what the cut-off points used there is a symmetry between opposition and support. By revealing more opposition and less support than that revealed by questions

---

9 We shall return to the question of knowledge of the scope of EU decision-making in Chapter 4.

that refer to the current state of integration, the question regarding the possible development of a United States of Europe indicates the outer limits of the legitimacy of European integration.

In order to explore fully the implications of these long-term preferences for legitimacy, it is not sufficient just to note the levels of support for and opposition to the development of a United States of Europe. Integration is a process and the legitimacy of integration is likely to be affected not just by the preferences that citizens may have regarding the final outcome of the process but also by whether or not they are satisfied with how that process is being conducted and with whether their own views are represented or not in it. The main actors in the process of institutional development are the member states as they negotiate with each other in a recurring series of intergovernmental conferences. Since each member state has veto power in regard to the decisions of such conferences, what is particularly important from the point of view of the individual citizen is the position adopted by his or her own government. The same United States of Europe scale was, therefore, used to assess how citizens see their government's position; in particular, do citizens see their government as pursuing a broad policy that is in line with their own preferences or do they consider that their government is adopting a more integrationist or a less integrationist stance than themselves?[10] The wording of this part of the question, which followed immediately on the question regarding preferences vis-à-vis a United States of Europe, was: 'And where would you place the view of the [national] government on this same scale?'

The results show considerable discrepancies between citizens and governments on the question of the development of a United States of Europe. The extent of the lag can be measured by subtracting each respondent's score on one scale from his or her score on the other. The results show that only 27 per cent are in agreement with their government on this matter and that 23 per cent are more in favour of progress towards a United States of Europe than they see their governments to be. However 31 per cent regard their government as being too much in favour of such a development and a further 19 per cent either do not know where they themselves stand or where their

---

[10] Obviously the positions of individual governments will vary enormously; equally obviously it is not possible to go into such variations here. What matters from our point of view is the *relative* distance, if any, between the *preference* of the respondents and their *perceptions* of the position of their national government.

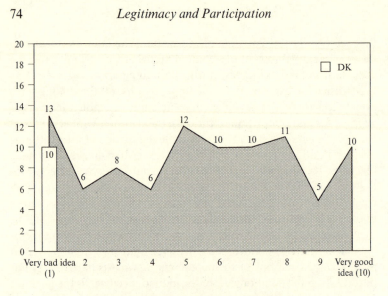

FIG. 3.4. Preference regarding the possible
development of a United States of Europe, 1994
Source: EB 41.1.

government stands or both. Looked at from the point of view of the
legitimacy a federal version of the objective of 'an ever closer union':
one-half are either happy to follow their government's lead or even
prepared to press ahead more decisively; but the other half are either
opposed to what they see as their government's commitment to this
idea or are in a state of confusion about the matter.

SATISFACTION WITH THE
WORKING OF DEMOCRACY

It has been claimed generally, one might say almost universally, both
by politicians and by academics, that one of the problems facing the
European Union is its 'democratic deficit', this 'deficit' being often
regarded as one of the key reasons why the Union only enjoys a
questionable legitimacy. However, to detect whether such a deficit is
perceptible to the mass public and, if so, whether it is felt to be large,
it is not sufficient to ask only how satisfied respondents are with the
way democracy works in the Union. Since asking about the 'deficit'

which is felt to exist is actually asking both an absolute and a relative question, an element of comparison must be introduced. Such an element can be provided by finding out also from respondents how satisfied or dissatisfied they are about the way democracy works in their own country. One can then assess the size of the 'democratic deficit' by measuring both the degree of satisfaction with democracy in the European Union and the gap between the assessment which citizens make about the way democracy works in the Union and the assessment which they make about the way it works in their own country.

The Eurobarometer has asked a variety of questions on satisfaction with democracy in the European Union in recent years, including a pair of questions in which respondents were asked to assess successively the way in which they felt that democracy works in their country and the way it works in the Union. This pair of questions was included as part of the standard Eurobarometer segment of the survey on which this study is based.[11] These assessments of democracy turned out to be both remarkable in absolute terms and quite closely associated with each other. First, it is remarkable that so many respondents should state that they are satisfied with the way democracy works in the Union, given what is commonly said about the 'democratic deficit'. Only 4 per cent stated that they were 'very satisfied' with the way democracy worked in the Union, admittedly, but 39 per cent said that they were 'fairly satisfied', as against 35 per cent who said that they were 'not very satisfied', 12 per cent who said that they were 'not satisfied at all', and 11 per cent who did not know. What is notable about this is that so many respondents should have regarded themselves as satisfied with the way democracy works in the Union, even if most of these are only 'fairly' satisfied and that only a small minority take the view that the democratic deficit is a major problem (i.e. the 12 per cent who are not at all satisfied with the working of democracy in the Union). What is also remarkable is that the distribution of the answers relating to democracy in the Union is so close to the distribution of answers relating to democracy in the country of the respondent. Marginally more respondents are 'very' satisfied with the way democracy works in their own country (7 per cent against 4 per cent), admittedly; but there are also more

---

[11] For a review of other Eurobarometer questions on assessments of democracy in the EU see Niedermayer and Sinnott (1995).

respondents who are 'not at all satisfied' with the level of democracy in their own country (17 per cent against 12 per cent). Perhaps the main difference relates to 'don't knows': only under 2 per cent of the respondents are unable to answer regarding the level of democracy in their own country while, as we have seen, 11 per cent are unable to answer with respect to the Union. Overall, however, the differences in the distributions of the two assessments are slight (see Figure 3.5). One can indeed be more precise about the relativities between the assessment of democracy at both levels: subtracting the 'score' given to democracy in the respondent's country from the 'score' given to democracy in the European Union reveals that 52 per cent of respondents gave an identical score to both, 13 per cent regard Europe as somewhat less democratic (a difference of 1 between the scores) and a mere 4 per cent regard it as much less democratic (a difference of 2 or more between the scores).[12] If we see the democratic deficit in relative terms, this evidence suggests that it is not widely perceived by European citizens.

Admittedly, the fact that there is such a close parallelism in the distribution of the answers to the two questions raises some questions about the interpretation to be given to these data. It is not entirely clear what respondents had in mind when replying. They may have stated what, in their opinion, is the reality; but it seems possible, perhaps likely, that at least a proportion of them, having a limited knowledge of how the Union functions, answered positively about the way democracy works in the Union simply by adopting broadly the same line as the one they adopt for their own country. It is even possible that some respondents may have interpreted the question as asking about how democracy works in the other countries of the European Union. Since the question on national democracy was asked immediately before the question on democracy in the Union, it would be surprising if answers to the latter were not in some cases 'contaminated' by the answers to the former. It would therefore be exaggerated to emphasize strongly the positive views which respondents adopted with respect to democracy in the Union and to draw too definite a conclusion about the 'democratic deficit' from these

---

12 There are substantial differences across countries in the both the absolute and relative assessment of democracy, as was to be expected: these differences reflect both the relative unease about the Union characterizing British and Danish respondents and relative unease about national democracy in some other countries. Assessments of democracy in the EU in the different member states are considered in Chapter 7.

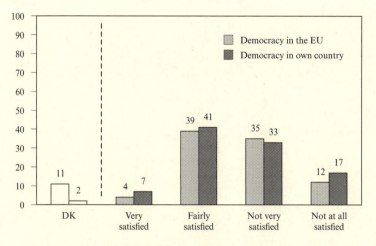

FIG. 3.5. Satisfaction with the way democracy works in the
European Union and in the respondent's own country, 1994
Source: EB 41.1.

answers.[13] Yet, one inference can reasonably be drawn: this is that the
view which is almost universal among 'elite circles' according to
which there is a large 'democratic deficit' in the Union that does not
exist in the member states does not appear to be shared by large
numbers of European citizens, either because they do not know what
the situation really is or because they do not believe that democracy
works very well in their own country.

The various dimensions of legitimacy that have been considered
here—general attitudes to European integration, sense of European
identity, attitudes (or, as we have seen, in many cases non-attitudes)
to the scope of EU decision-making, attitudes to long-term institutional developments, and assessment of the functioning of democracy
in the European Union—are all interrelated. While it would be
impractical to attempt to trace all these interconnections, two merit
special attention, namely the relationship between attitudes to the
scope of EU policy-making and to the functioning of democracy in
the European Union, on the one hand, and overall assessments of

---

[13] For a more extended discussion of the qualifications that need to be attached to
these data and for a comparison with other Eurobarometer evidence on the democratic
deficit, see Niedermayer and Sinnott 1995: 283–6 and especially 285–6.

TABLE 3.4. *Attitude towards a hypothetical dissolution of the EU by attitude towards the scope of EU decision-making (%)*

Attitude towards EU dissolution	Attitude towards the number of issues decided by the EU					
	Too few	About right	More on some, less on others	Too many—general feeling	Too many—specific issues	Don't know/haven't thought about it
Very sorry	67	61	58	20	35	27
Indifferent	30	35	37	44	38	63
Very relieved	3	4	5	36	27	10
N	2,189	2,200	1,173	1,471	756	4,559

Source: EB 41.1.

European integration on the other. As the measure of the latter, this analysis uses the dissolution indicator.

Enthusiasm for integration is closely related to views about the scope of EU policy-making: being very sorry if the EU were scrapped ranges from a high of 67 per cent among those who want more EU decision-making and have specific issues in mind to a mere 20 per cent among those who want the EU to have less decision-making power and for whom this is just a general feeling. It is notable that those who say they have specific issues in mind in answering the question are more favourably disposed to integration than those who do not; this is true even among those who favour less EU decision-making than at present. The implication that apathy and lack of involvement are notable sources of low Euro-legitimacy is confirmed by the attitudes of the large segment of the citizenry that has no view on the scope of EU decision-making: Euro-enthusiasm is almost as low in this group as it is among those who favour less EU policy involvement and more than 60 per cent of those with no view on the scope of European policy-making express indifference in the face of a hypothetical dissolution of the Union.

Turning to assessment of the working of democracy, we find that the small minority that sees a *substantial* democratic deficit in the Union shows very little enthusiasm for integration: among this group only 21 per cent would be very sorry if the Union were scrapped; the corresponding figure for the even smaller minority who are very satisfied with the working of democracy in the Union is 72 per cent (see Table 3.5). Thus, at the extremes, attitude to integration is closely

TABLE 3.5. *Attitude towards a hypothetical dissolution of the EU by satisfaction with EU democracy (%)*

Attitude towards EU dissolution	Satisfaction with EU democracy				
	Very satisfied	Fairly satisfied	Not very satisfied	Not at all satisfied	Don't know
Very sorry	72	57	38	21	22
Indifferent	26	39	49	46	66
Very relieved	2	4	13	33	12
N	548	5,099	4,078	1,429	1,326

Source: EB 41.1.

related to judgements about the democratic quality of the Union. For the majority of respondents who take a moderately favourable or moderately unfavourable view of democracy in the Union, attitudes to integration also vary though less dramatically: 57 per cent of the former would be very sorry to see a dissolution of the Union compared to 38 per cent of the latter. Whether negative attitudes to integration lead to negative judgements about democratic quality or whether the influence runs the other way is much more difficult to determine. We cannot, in other words, conclude from the existence of the relationship that a substantial injection of democracy would lead to an immediate and substantial increase in the legitimacy of the Union.

LEGITIMACY AND PARTICIPATION

If the legitimacy of the European Union were more firmly established, turnout at European Parliament elections would presumably be higher. It could also be argued, of course, that more widespread participation would enhance the legitimacy of integration. At the moment, however, we are interested in the possible effect of attitudes to integration on the propensity to turn out to vote. As noted in Chapter 2, some previous research has dismissed this connection. In a preliminary analysis of this issue, this chapter concludes with an examination of the relationship between the various indicators of EU legitimacy and reported turnout at the 1994 European Parliament election.[14]

Of the four standard indicators of attitude to European integration, the benefits indicator shows the weakest relationship with European turnout: there was only a 10 percentage point difference in reported turnout between those who thought their country benefited from membership and those who did not. This weak relationship is not altogether surprising: as shown above, a sceptical view of the benefits of membership *to one's own country* can and often does coexist with positive views regarding *integration as such*. Positive or negative

---

[14] These bivariate analyses are based on the data from non-compulsory voting countries. A multivariate analysis incorporating a wide range of variables, including the effect of compulsory voting, is presented in Chapter 8.

TABLE 3.6. *Type of electoral participation/abstention by attitude to unification of Western Europe (non-compulsory voting countries only) (%)*

Type of electoral participation/abstention	Attitude to unification				
	For—very much	For—to some extent	Against—to some extent	Against—very much	Don't know
Euro-voter	78	71	60	60	56
Circumstantial Euro-specific abstainer	9	10	10	7	9
Circumstantial Euro-and-national abstainer	3	3	3	1	4
Voluntary Euro-specific abstainer	7	11	21	23	16
Voluntary Euro-and-national abstainer	4	6	6	9	15
N	2,007	3,754	1,152	606	643

Source: EB 41.1.

TABLE 3.7. *Type of electoral participation/abstention by attitude to a hypothetical dissolution of the EU (non-compulsory voting countries only) (%)*

Type of electoral participation/abstention	Attitude to dissolution			
	Very sorry	Indifferent	Very relieved	Don't know
Euro-voter	78	61	63	70
Circumstantial Euro-specific abstainer	9	11	8	9
Circumstantial Euro-and-national abstainer	3	3	2	3
Voluntary Euro-specific abstainer	7	17	21	11
Voluntary Euro-and-national abstainer	3	9	7	8
N	3,292	3,106	1,058	697

Source: EB 41.1.

views on membership are more strongly related to participation: 81 per cent of those who say membership is a good thing report having voted, compared to 60 per cent of those who take a negative view. In the case of the unification indicator, outright opposition to European unification is also quite strongly associated with non-participation in European elections: only 60 per cent of those who are very much against efforts to unify Western Europe turned out to vote while 78 per cent of those who were very much in favour did so (see Table 3.6). But it is not just those who are opposed to integration who are less likely to vote; lower turnout is also related to indifference: the gap in the rate of voting between those who indicated that they would be indifferent in the event of a dissolution of the EU and those who would be very sorry to see such an outcome was 17 percentage points (61 per cent compared to 78 per cent—see Table 3.7).

Apart from these contrasts in the rate of turnout between people with different attitudes to European integration, Tables 3.6 and 3.7 bring to light a further important feature of the pattern of turnout and abstention: there is virtually no difference in the rate of *circumstantial* abstention between those with different attitudes to integration. This is as it should be; if circumstantial abstention is really such, that is if it is really due to external constraints, then it should not be related to attitudes to Europe, or to any other attitudes for that matter. The evidence in Tables 3.6 and 3.7 is therefore encouraging confirmation of the validity and importance of the identification of this form of abstention. The corollary of this lack of relationship between circumstantial voting and European attitudes is that almost all of the contrast is concentrated in the categories of voluntary abstention: 23 per cent of those who are strongly opposed to unification were voluntary Euro-specific abstainers compared to 7 per cent of those very much in favour of unification; 17 per cent of those who are indifferent on the dissolution indicator were voluntary Euro-specific abstainers compared to 7 per cent of those who would be very sorry if the EU were dissolved.

Since the other European attitude variables discussed in this chapter tend to show broadly similar relationships to turnout and abstention, there is no need to discuss each in detail; to summarize, turnout is positively related to strength of European identity, to attitudes to the functioning of democracy in the Union, to support for a United States of Europe, and to positive versus negative views about the scope of EU policy-making. Just two qualifications need to be added to this summary. The first is that a very strong sense of European identity does not appear to make any special difference: the rates of participation and of various kinds of abstention are almost identical as between those with a very high and those with a fairly high sense of European identity; the increase in participation and the decrease in voluntary abstention tend to occur as one moves through the lower reaches of the scale of European identity. The second qualification is that views on the functioning of democracy in the Union only make a substantial difference to turnout as between the small groups that take extreme views on this question: 86 per cent of those who are very satisfied with European democracy voted while only 64 per cent of those who are not all satisfied did so; but there was no difference in the rate of participation between the much larger groups who were either 'fairly satisfied' with the working of democracy, on the one hand, or 'not very satisfied' on the other.

On the face of it, therefore, voting and abstention are not just linked to a number of institutional characteristics or to national political attitudes; they are also associated with a variety of views about the European Union. One must pause at this point for the moment and leave for later the question of whether this association holds up under a rigorous multivariate test, however. It is sufficient—but also important—to note already that there is an association between a series of attitudinal variables and the probability of voting and of deliberate abstention. Before examining this matter further, other attributes and attitudes and their possible link to turnout must be examined, beginning with interest in and knowledge of the European Union and the integration process.

4

Interest, Knowledge, and Participation

INTRODUCTION

The evidence considered in Chapter 3 indicated that a substantial segment of the European public is, by and large, indifferent to the European Union and that many Europeans have not got any opinion or formed any attitude on some quite central integration issues. This suggests that any serious assessment of the legitimacy of European integration must go beyond *evaluations* of various aspects of integration such as those covered in Chapter 3 to the matter of how people relate, indeed whether they relate at all, to the process of integration and to the institutions of the Union. Several aspects of this relationship need to be explored. The first is very elementary: to what extent are people aware of the European Union, of its institutions and, in particular, of its Parliament? The fact that the European institutions might cross such a threshold of awareness indicates, however, only the most minimal relationship between the citizens and the process of European integration. As a second measure, therefore, it is essential to assess the degree of interest shown in European politics, an interest which must of course be seen in the context of the extent and limits of people's interest in politics as such. But 'interest' is an elusive notion; this is primarily because it can only be assessed in a subjective way, that is on the basis of respondents' own reports of their degree of interest in European politics or politics in general but also because it is difficult to separate expressions of interest or lack of interest from underlying positive or negative attitudes to Europe or to politics. In order to arrive at an adequate account of how citizens relate or fail to relate to the European Union, it is necessary to assess the cognitive aspect of this relationship: how much do the citizens actually know about the European Union and its institutions? In short, this chapter will examine awareness of, interest in, and knowledge of European politics and European institutions and begin to explore how interest and knowledge in particular might be related to evaluations of European integration and to participation in European Parliament elections.

'AWARENESS' OF EUROPEAN INSTITUTIONS

'Awareness' as measured in the Eurobarometer surveys has a rather special meaning. What is being asked is whether, over a period (three months) respondents 'have heard or read something about' a number of European institutions and policy developments. What is referred to as 'awareness' should therefore probably more accurately be described as 'recall of media coverage' of various institutions or developments. The awareness of respondents in general is not being measured, but rather complex and aggregate combinations of three elements, the extent of media coverage of these institutions or developments, the extent to which interviewees were subjected to this coverage, and the extent to which they were able to remember noticing the coverage. Clearly, we must be careful in drawing inferences from these data; treated with caution, however, they can throw some light on how European citizens relate to the institutions of the Union. As it happens, despite the limitations mentioned, the data are of particular interest in the case of the European Parliament since the question has been asked in relation to the Parliament on a regular basis since 1977; data on the Commission are available since 1987 and on the Council of Ministers and the Court of Justice only since 1994. A number of European policy or general political developments have been included in the question in recent years; two of these—the Single Market and the Maastricht Treaty—are considered here as a means of putting awareness of the European institutions into perspective.

The most striking feature of the data on awareness of the European institutions is the degree to which awareness of the European Parliament was boosted by the occurrence of European elections in 1979, 1984, and 1989 but not in 1994. The heightened awareness at election time is precisely what one would expect; what is surprising is that the 1994 election failed to produce the customary rise. It is also surprising that there is little or no evidence of a cumulative increase in the awareness of media coverage of the Parliament over the last two decades: in 1994 awareness of the European Parliament was only marginally ahead of what it had been in 1977, two years before the first direct elections. In normal circumstances, that is apart from the immediate occasions of the first three European elections, the levels of awareness of media coverage of the European Parliament and of the European Commission tend to be rather similar: both fluctuate around the 45 to 50 per cent mark, awareness of the Parliament tending to be slightly ahead of that of the Commission, and both levels tend to move up or down together; the recent data suggest a slight upward trend that may reflect the role of the Parliament in the process of approving the European Commission in late 1994 and early 1995. The data also indicate that the Council of Ministers and the Court of Justice have a noticeably lower public profile than the Parliament or the Commission. This is understandable in the case of the Court, which, although generally credited with an activist role in integration, is less likely to generate substantial media coverage on a regular basis. In the case of the Council of Ministers, however, the low public profile is more problematic. This is the decisive legislative organ of the Union; in theory it has a significant part to play in ensuring that governance in the Union is at least indirectly representative. Its ranking in the consciousness of the public is clearly out of line with the importance of its actual role.

The level of awareness of media coverage of the four main institutions must also be assessed in the light of the levels of awareness of major policy developments. Figure 4.1 shows that awareness of the Single Market was, for the most part, well ahead of awareness of the Union's institutions; the exception occurred in the run-up to the 1989 European elections. The contrast with the level of awareness of the Maastricht Treaty is even more striking. The Maastricht Treaty burst into the consciousness of the European public in mid-1992: in the autumn Eurobarometer of 1992 some 85 per cent had read or heard something about the Treaty in the previous months, an increase of 30 percentage points on the proportion in spring 1992. This level of media coverage of the Treaty was not of course sustained. The point is not that awareness of European affairs could or should be maintained at this level; the point is that when there was widespread awareness of major issues such as the Single Market or the Maastricht Treaty, there was much less awareness of what the European Parliament was saying or doing about these matters. In short, European issue awareness can by quite high without generating a commensurate awareness of the Parliament as the European institution with the

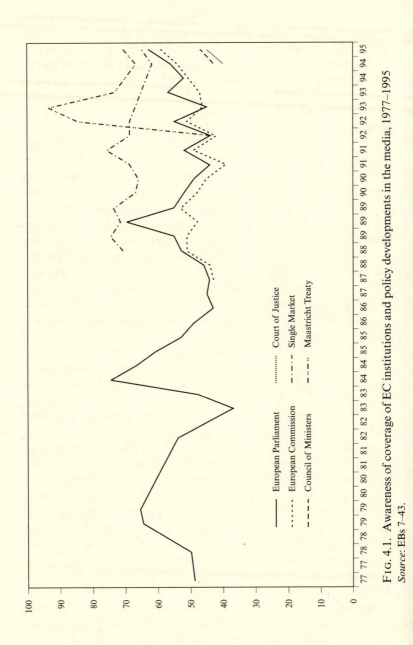

FIG. 4.1. Awareness of coverage of EC institutions and policy developments in the media, 1977–1995
Source: EBs 7–43.

main responsibility for representing the views of the citizens and for acting as a specifically European channel of communication between the policy process and the citizens. As emphasized above, however, awareness in the sense of exposure to media coverage of the Parliament or the other European institutions is only one-half of the equation: no matter what the level of media exposure, citizens respond to media coverage and to European events and European affairs generally with varying degrees of interest.

INTEREST IN EUROPEAN POLITICS

Data on interest in the European Community and its affairs have been collected on a fairly regular basis since the inception of the Eurobarometer surveys in the early 1970s. Unfortunately, the wording of the questions has varied substantially over the period: early versions of the question asked 'are you personally interested' in 'the problems of the European Community' and sometimes prefaced the question by making reference to newspaper, radio, and television coverage of the Community; later versions simply asked 'are you interested' in 'European politics' defined as 'matters related to the European Community' and (rightly) avoided any prior reference to media coverage. Equally if not more seriously from the point of view of obtaining comparable data over time, the response format changed in autumn 1988 from a three-level scale ('very interested', 'a little interested', 'not at all interested') to a four-level scale ('a great deal', 'to some extent', 'not much', or 'not at all').[1] The net result of these variations in wording is that we have comparable data on degrees of interest in European Community affairs only from autumn 1988 on. The compensating factor is that, over the same period, though not with quite the same frequency, we also have comparable data on interest in politics; in fact this question was first asked in a Eurobarometer in 1983. This enables us to analyse interest in European politics (matters related to the European Community/Union) in relation to interest in politics in general.

Interest in politics as such is rather low. The year 1983 can be taken as the benchmark: then, only 42 per cent of the citizens of the Community declared that they had an interest in politics: only 11 per cent

[1] For details of the various questions on interest see Eurobarometer (1994).

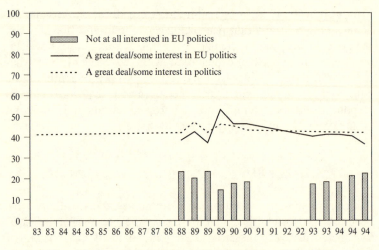

F IG. 4.2. Interest in politics and in EU politics, 1983–1994
Source: EBs 19–42.

said that they had a great deal of interest and 31 per cent indicated
that they were interested in politics to some extent; 34 per cent said
that they were 'not much interested' and 24 per cent not at all
interested. As Figure 4.2 shows, the proportion interested in politics
is remarkably stable: the combination of a great deal of interest and
interested to some extent varies by no more than 5 percentage points
over the nine occasions between 1983 and 1994 on which this question
was asked. This relatively low level of interest may not be regarded as
surprising, though it may be useful for those who are particularly
committed to politics, whether as participants or as observers, to be
reminded that their passion is not shared by the majority of their
fellow citizens.

   In the light of the generally low level of interest in politics as such,
what may be more surprising is that interest in European politics
should be as high as it is: when the comparable question on interest in
European politics was first asked (autumn 1988), 39 per cent
indicated an interest (9 per cent a great deal and 30 per cent to some
extent). This was just four percentage points behind the overall level
of interest in politics as such in the same survey (see Figure 4.1). One
might be tempted to conclude from the similarity of these two proportions that the expression of interest in European politics is here simply
an automatic response following the acknowledgement of interest in

politics as such and that, having indicated some degree of interest in politics, respondents would be reluctant to admit to a lesser degree of interest in European politics or would simply not consider it worth distinguishing between their degree of interest in each.

Certain aspects of the evidence on interest in politics in general and in European politics suggest that this is not the case. For one thing, interest in European politics has, admittedly on only one occasion, well outstripped interest in politics in general: in autumn 1989, in the midst of the dramatic changes in Central and Eastern Europe that were symbolized by the fall of the Berlin Wall, interest in European politics, that is in matters related to the European Community, rose to a record 54 per cent (see Figure 4.2). This sudden rise in interest in European politics, presumably in response to the events of 1989, suggests that what is being measured is not simply a reflection of general political interest. A second point evident from Figure 4.2 gives further confidence that the two measures are reasonably independent and that the level of interest in European politics is not merely a result of the question on interest in European politics being asked immediately after the question on interest in politics in general: on three occasions (twice in 1993 and once in 1994) the European question was asked on its own and the results were not significantly different from those obtained when the European question has been preceded by the general question.

Both questions were asked in the survey on which this study is based, allowing one to examine not just the distribution on each variable but also the relationship between them. The overall levels of interest identified in this study are generally in line with the findings of the other Eurobarometer studies (see the second entry for 1994 in Figure 4.2). The detailed breakdown of interest in European politics is: a great deal of interest 9 per cent, interested to some extent 32 per cent, not much interest 37 per cent, no interest at all 22 per cent. Taking the responses to both questions into account shows that only one-third of people are interested in both politics in general and in European politics but that almost a majority (48 per cent) are interested in neither; those who are interested in politics in general but not in European politics constitute 12 per cent of the sample and those interested in European politics but not in politics in general 9 per cent (see Table 4.1).

All of this indicates that one can have reasonable confidence in the measure of interest in European politics and at least tentatively

TABLE 4.1. *Interest in politics and in European politics (%)*

Interest in politics in general	Interest in European politics	
	A great deal/to some extent interested	Not much/not at all interested/DK
A great deal/to some extent interested	32	12
Not much/not at all interested/DK	9	48

Notes: Entries are percentages of the total sample (N = 12,483).
Source: EB 41.1.

conclude that the majority of European citizens have not got much interest in matters relating to the European Union, but that, on the other hand, they are not much interested in politics as such either. The fact that the level of interest in European politics is not all that much less than the level of interest in national politics does not mean that lack of interest is not a problem for the Union: unlike the component nation states, the Union is still faced with the task of establishing its legitimacy and nurturing commensurate levels of participation; higher than average levels of interest may be necessary to achieve this. Having said all that, however, the fact remains that 'interest' is a somewhat elusive notion that may be highly subjective and may reflect positive or negative views as much as or more than a cognitive orientation. Accordingly, it is essential to examine more direct and objective evidence of how citizens relate to the European Union, specifically, how much do they actually know about it.

KNOWLEDGE OF EUROPEAN AFFAIRS

In 1993, the Eurobarometer moved beyond simply monitoring interest in and exposure to European affairs and began to probe how much citizens know about Europe. In particular, Eurobarometer 39 (spring 1993) asked about the membership of the Community, the location of the Commission, the name of its president, the names of incumbent Commissioners, which is its most powerful institution (in the sense of having the final say on legislation), and who elects the MEPs. Responses to these questions can be scored and combined to form a thirty-point index of knowledge of the European Union, with

0–5 indicating 'no knowledge'; 6–11 'very little knowledge'; 12–17 'some but not much knowledge'; 18–23 'moderately well informed'; and 24–9 'very well informed'.[2] On this interpretation of the scale, 10 per cent of the citizens of the European Union are very well informed and a further 24 per cent are moderately well informed. It appears, however, that two-thirds of European citizens have less than adequate knowledge of the workings of the Community or Union, 26 per cent having 'some but not much knowledge', 24 per cent 'very little knowledge', and 15 per cent 'no knowledge' at all.[3]

Two of the individual items in the foregoing scale that relate directly or indirectly to the European Parliament indicate that the widespread ignorance of the working of European institutions extends to the role and composition of the Parliament. Asked which of the main European institutions is seen to be most powerful 'in terms of having the final say on European Community legislation', a plurality (35 per cent) erroneously attribute decisive power to the European Parliament; 20 per cent, again erroneously, regard the Commission as the most powerful and one-quarter of the citizens simply don't know. Thus 80 per cent of European citizens either don't know who decides or don't realize that the power of decision lies with the representatives of the national governments, i.e. with the Council of Ministers; and, as we have seen, over one-third mistakenly attribute decisive power to the European Parliament. The inadequacy of public knowledge of European institutions becomes even more glaring when the spotlight is placed directly on the Parliament. Asked the apparently simple question 'who elects the members of the European Parliament?' and presented with a card showing two incorrect and one correct response, only two out of five respondents chose the correct response (Sinnott 1997: 8–10).

Widespread ignorance also appears to prevail in relation to the

---

[2] The questions, the response categories, and the scores assigned to them are given in Sinnott 1997. Dividing such a scale up into discrete levels is difficult and inevitably somewhat arbitrary. In assessing the interpretation put forward here, it should be borne in mind that most of the questions are very simple and that, with several of the questions offering only two alternatives, guessing is easy and relatively rewarding. This results in an inflation of the scores relative to the real level of knowledge.

[3] Although direct comparison with levels of knowledge of national political systems is impossible, it is worth noting that a four-item scale measuring knowledge of the national political system that was used in the same Eurobarometer survey showed 78 per cent having a high to very high level of national political knowledge (Eurobarometer 1993: 55–9).

scope of EU decision-making. In autumn 1995, Eurobarometer respondents were asked about the actual allocation of decision-making power between national governments and 'the European Union level' over a wide range of policy areas. The wording of the question was: 'In fact the (nationality) government together with those of the other countries in the European Union have agreed that a number of policy areas will be decided jointly within the European Union, and not by each country separately. Can you tell me which areas of policy are already, at least to some extent, decided at the European Union level?' Among the issues listed in the question were three which provide a particularly telling test of public knowledge of this aspect of integration: 'agriculture', 'foreign policy towards countries outside the EU', and 'defence'. Since it became fully established in the late 1960s, the Common Agricultural Policy has been the pre-eminent common policy of the Union and one of the clearest examples of the transfer of decision-making to the European level. One would presume that after some twenty-five years of the CAP, much of it marked by controversy and frequently punctuated by all-night negotiating sessions in Brussels, the reality of Brussels involvement in agricultural policy would be widely recognized by the vast majority of the mass public. Not so: only 40 per cent of European citizens believe that agricultural policy is 'at least to some extent decided jointly within the European Union/decided at the European Union level'. Likewise, given the development of European Political Cooperation since the early 1970s and the prominence of the issue of a common foreign policy and security policy in recent debate, one would expect a reasonably widespread public realization of the actual decision-making process in regard to foreign and defence policy, i.e. that the former is decided 'at least to some extent' at EU level and the latter is not.[4] The reality is that identical proportions (38 per cent) see foreign and defence policy being decided at EU level; in other words there is a gross underestimation of the extent of European involvement in foreign policy and a gross overestimation of its involvement in defence policy. These findings are entirely consistent with the evidence reported in Chapter 3 that more than one-third of the public does not have any attitude on this central aspect of European integration and

[4] As tortuously specified in Article J4 of the Maastricht Treaty, joint decision-making on defence is a matter for the future: 'The common foreign and security policy shall include all questions related to the security of the Union, including the eventual framing of a common defence policy, which might in time lead to a common defence'.

that the bulk of those who do have a preference tend to think of the matter only in rather general terms.

The preceding paragraphs have summarized a wide array of evidence on knowledge of European affairs taken from several different Eurobarometers. In designing the questions for our study, we were keenly aware that it was essential to include some measures of knowledge but, in the limited space available to us, it was not possible to replicate all of the previous questions or to have a scale that was as broadly based as that summarized above. It was possible, however, to take account of the previous research in designing a more limited set of questions, thereby strengthening confidence in the validity and reliability of the measure of EU knowledge. Among the range of questions which form the scale presented above, the question on the personnel of the EU Commission (President and Commissioners) and the question on which countries were members of the Union suggested themselves as ones which, in a modified format, could be used as economical measures of knowledge of European affairs. The correlations between the individual items dealing with these issues and the knowledge scale described above were 0.70 for the name of the President of the Commission, 0.63 for the names of the individual Commissioners, and 0.66 for the identification of which countries were members of the Community. This provides reassuring evidence that items dealing with the personnel of the Commission and with the membership of the Union are valid measures of a wider array of knowledge of the Union. On this basis, two sets of informational questions were used in Eurobarometer 41.1: first, interviewees were provided with a list of names and asked to identify the names of the President of the Commission and of one of the Commissioners from their own country (or the one Commissioner in the case of the smaller member states); secondly, interviewees were asked to identify the countries belonging to the European Union in 1994 from a list of twelve countries, half of which were not members of the Union.

The results derived from the individual questions show that, despite ten years of considerable exposure, Jacques Delors was not part of the panorama of politicians for half the citizens of the Union in mid-1994: only 48 per cent succeeded in picking out his name from the list as that of the President of the Commission. Moreover, it is perhaps surprising that the proportion of those who could mention the name of the President of the Commission was only somewhat larger than was the proportion (34 per cent) of those who could identify one of the Commissioners or the Commissioner from their own country. If account is taken of the answers given both to the question on the President of the Commission and to the question on the national Commissioners, slightly over a quarter of the respondents (27 per cent) gave two correct answers, and about the same proportion (28 per cent) gave one correct answer, while 45 per cent gave no answer or no correct answer. This is in sharp contrast to the markedly better information which respondents display about senior political figures in their own country:[5] 56 per cent knew the names of both the minister of foreign affairs and the minister for finance of their country and another 19 per cent knew the name of one of them, while only 26 per cent did not know either name or gave incorrect answers (see Figure 4.3). Thus national political figures are not only appreciably better known to respondents than European Union Commissioners of the countries of these respondents; they are appreciably better known than Jacques Delors at the apex of his European career. This confirms that there is indeed an 'information gap' about who is involved in European affairs among European citizens. Levels of declared interest in national and European politics may be rather similar; levels of knowledge of national and European politics are certainly not.

The findings relating to knowledge of the membership of the Union are not particularly encouraging either. If virtually all respondents could identify five countries from the list as either members or non-members, less than half could identify ten countries or more and little over a third (35 per cent) could point correctly to eleven or twelve countries. The countries for which there were the fewest incorrect answers were France (90 per cent), Germany (89 per cent), Spain (86 per cent), and, among the non-members Poland (92 per cent), Hungary (91 per cent), and Turkey (83 per cent). There was apparently greater confusion about Norway, Switzerland, and Austria: in the Austrian case, there could indeed have been some doubt, since the referendum on membership took place in that country a week before the European Parliament elections were held in 1994; thus it may not be altogether surprising that 30 per cent of the respondents should have said that Austria was a member. There was, however, also a

---

[5] Following immediately on the question regarding the members of the Commission, respondents had also been asked to identify the names of the ministers of finance and of foreign affairs of their country, again from a list provided.

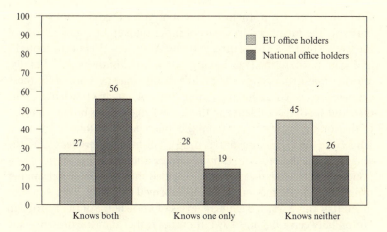

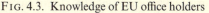

FIG. 4.3. Knowledge of EU office holders
(Commission President and national Commissioner), and of national
office holders (Minister of Finance and Minister of Foreign Affairs), 1994
Source: EB 41.1.

sizeable percentage of incorrect responses with respect to a number of
well-established member states, specifically Portugal, Ireland, and
Denmark: a third or more of the respondents stated that these three
countries were not members. The Danish case is particularly surprising given the fact that Danish voters had, within the previous two
years, initially rejected the Maastricht Treaty and delayed the whole
process of ratification by having to have a second referendum to get
it passed.

An overall index of European knowledge can be constructed from
these questions by combining the answers provided about Commission personnel (0, 1, or 2 points being allocated respectively for no
correct answer, one correct answer, or two correct answers) and the
answers provided about the countries belonging to the Union (0, 1, or
2 points being allocated respectively for giving correct answers about
8 countries or less, 9 or 10 countries, or 11 or 12 countries): respondents could therefore obtain a maximum of 4 points (and a minimum
of zero). Overall, 14 per cent were very well informed (a score of 4)
and 16 per cent moderately well informed (a score of 3). At the other
hand of the scale, 28 per cent had virtually no knowledge (score of
0): they did not know the name of Jacques Delors or of a (the)

Commissioner from their own country and could not identify correctly the membership status of more than eight countries out of the twelve that were presented to them. A further 21 per cent scored 1 and can be described as having 'very little knowledge'. Finally, another one-fifth occupy the middle of the scale (a score of 2); these are here regarded as having 'some but not much knowledge'. The distribution of respondents on this knowledge scale is broadly similar to that on the scale derived from the much larger number of items in EB 39 (see the discussion above, p. 93). The main difference is that the scale used in the present study identifies a larger proportion of respondents as having 'no knowledge'; it also shows a somewhat smaller proportion in the moderately well-informed category. This does not mean that there was a decline in levels of knowledge of the European Union between 1993 and 1994; it means rather that the present scale is a somewhat more demanding one. This is not surprising as it will be recalled that the 1993 scale included some extremely simple items, including one which asked 'Is [name of country] a member of the European Community or not?' The scale used here is a somewhat more rigorous test of knowledge but, we would argue, also a better one. One can conclude therefore that half the sample had no knowledge or very little knowledge of the Union and, as Figure 4.4 indicates, no matter which scale one chooses to use, only a minority of European citizens can be regarded as having an adequate knowledge of European affairs.

The evidence of EU interest and especially of EU knowledge presented so far in this chapter provides indirect support for the conclusion drawn in the previous chapter according to which it is at best a little dangerous to attach too much significance to the ostensibly large majorities who declare themselves satisfied with the process of European integration. Although respondents may be in favour of this process without knowing much about what it entails and how this goal might be implemented, support is unlikely to be truly strong where the substantive content of such 'support' is small and, in some cases, almost non-existent. Low levels of knowledge will also presumably affect the propensity to turn out to vote at European Parliament elections. Before turning to this question, however, it is worth examining the relationship between knowledge of EU affairs and some of the variables already considered, specifically interest in European politics and positive and negative attitudes to aspects of integration.

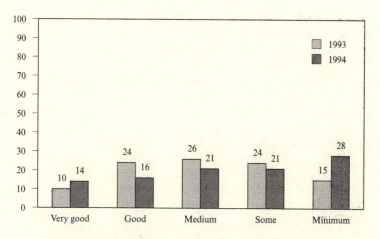

F IG. 4.4. Distribution of respondents on
two indices of European knowledge, 1993 and 1994
Source: EB 39, 41.1.

INTEREST, KNOWLEDGE,
AND ATTITUDES TO INTEGRATION

Is lack of knowledge simply a function of lack of interest? Interest
certainly plays a role but is only part of the story. This can be shown
by comparing the levels of knowledge of those who express different
degrees of interest in European politics (Table 4.2). Thirty-one per
cent of those who express a high degree of interest in European politics are very well informed (obtaining the maximum points (4) on the
scale); a similar level of information is found among only 4 per cent
of those who have no interest. Moreover, the proportions scoring 2
and 3 on the knowledge scale increase with each step up the scale of
interest. On the other hand, it is also clear from Table 4.2 that there
are many who are interested in European matters but who have not
got commensurate knowledge. For example, one-quarter of those
who say that they are very interested in European politics score one
or less on the knowledge scale; similar scores are found among
more than one-third of those who claim to be somewhat interested in
European politics. These discrepancies between interest and knowledge imply a significant failure to translate the public's interest in

TABLE 4.2. *Knowledge of European politics by interest in European politics (%)*

Knowledge of the EU	Interest in EU politics			
	A great deal	To some extent	Not much	Not at all/ DK
No knowledge	10	17	29	48
Very little knowledge	14	19	24	22
Some but not much knowledge	20	24	22	18
Moderately well informed	25	21	15	8
Very well informed	31	19	10	4
N	1,175	4,025	4,313	2,841

Source: EB 41.1.

European affairs into concrete knowledge about Europe's institutions and political processes.

One would also anticipate that support for European integration would be closely related to interest in European politics; indeed, one of the problems with the concept of 'interest' is that there is a high probability that it includes an evaluative component. The empirical evidence confirms that the two are closely related: 78 per cent of those who are very interested in European politics would be very sorry if the EU were dissolved, while only 16 per cent of those who are not at all interested share this sentiment; enthusiastic support for the Union drops by almost 20 percentage points with each step down the scale of interest and indifference grows correspondingly (Table 4.3). It would, however, be a mistake to conclude from this that we have found the key to support for integration, that, as it were, all that needs to be done is to increase the public's interest and the EU's legitimacy would soar. This would be a mistaken inference for two reasons. First the influence is likely to be reciprocal: the reason for the close association between the two variables could be that positive attitudes lead to increased interest rather than or at least as much as that increased interest leads to positive attitudes. The second problem is even more fundamental and has already been adverted to: in measuring *interest* one may, to a considerable extent, also be measuring *affect*. While the first of these two problems also applies to the relationship between evaluation and knowledge (i.e. the influence may be reciprocal), the second does not: measures of affective or evaluative orientation are clearly distinct from measures of knowledge or cognitive orientation.

TABLE 4.3. *Attitude to a hypothetical dissolution of the EU by interest in EU politics (%)*

Attitude to hypothetical EU dissolution	Interest in EU politics			
	A great deal	To some extent	Not much	Not at all
Very sorry	78	61	35	16
Indifferent/DK	13	31	53	68
Very relieved	9	8	12	16
N	1,177	4,030	4,321	2,841

Source: EB 41.1.

The remainder of this section, therefore, will concentrate on the relationship between knowledge of European affairs and the various indicators of favourable and unfavourable attitudes to integration.

Of course, it could be argued that increased knowledge of the workings of the European Union would not necessarily lead to increased legitimacy. Euro-sceptics would no doubt argue that the contrary outcome is the more likely and there are undoubtedly some very well-informed opponents of European integration. However, an examination of the relationship between the level of knowledge of the EU and attitudes to European integration indicates that variations in levels of knowledge may have substantial consequences for support for the Union. Attitude to integration, as measured by the dissolution indicator (reaction if the Union were to be scrapped), is closely related to knowledge. Enthusiastic support for the Union (very sorry if the Union were to be scrapped) goes from 29 per cent among the least informed to 59 per cent among the best informed, an increase of 30 percentage points (see Table 4.4). Note that increased knowledge does not convert those who are implacably opposed: 12 per cent of those with no knowledge would be very relieved if the EU were to be scrapped but so would 11 per cent of those with very good knowledge; this confirms the point that there is a small group of very well-informed opponents of integration. Thus, the effect of increases in knowledge, assuming for the moment that the effect runs in this direction, is to reduce the level of indifference: this declines from 59 per cent among those with no knowledge and 48 per cent among those categorized as having very little knowledge to 30 per cent among those with the highest knowledge score.

TABLE 4.4. *Attitude to a hypothetical dissolution of the EU by knowledge of the EU (%)*

Attitude to hypothetical EU dissolution	Knowledge of the EU				
	Very well informed	Moderately well informed	Some but not much knowledge	Very little knowledge	No knowledge
Very sorry	59	55	44	40	29
Indifferent/DK	30	35	44	48	59
Very relieved	11	10	12	12	12
N	2,486	2,008	2,597	2,293	3,082

Source: EB 41.1.

The evidence on the relationship between knowledge and preferences regarding the scope of EU policy confirms that one of the main effects of increased levels of knowledge is an increase in the likelihood of forming an opinion on EU issues. Whereas 55 per cent of those with the lowest level of knowledge responded that they had not really thought about the matter or that they did not know, this was the case for only 14 per cent of those with the highest level of knowledge. The relationship is so marked that there seems little doubt that knowledge of European politics does enable respondents (or at least a majority of them) to give a substantive answer to the question being asked. Yet the association remains a trend only, as, on the other hand, half the respondents who had little or no knowledge of European matters felt able to have a view about the policy scope of the European Union. Unlike in the case of attitudes to dissolution, however, increases in knowledge are associated in this instance with an increase in opposition to integration as well as with an increase in support for integration: the most knowledgeable are more likely to say that more issues should be decided by the EU and to say that the scope of EU decision-making is about right; but they are also more likely to take the view that 'two many issues are decided on by the EU'. It should be emphasized that the relationship between knowledge and attitudes to integration is almost certainly reciprocal: more knowledge leads to more support and a more supportive attitude leads to the desire for more knowledge and understanding. Even allowing for greater complexity in the underlying causal processes, however, it is clear that knowledge is closely associated with support for European integra-

TABLE 4.5. *Attitude to scope of EU decision-making by knowledge of the EU (%)*

Attitude to scope of EU decision-making	Knowledge of the EU				
	Very well informed	Moderately well informed	Some but not much knowledge	Very little knowledge	No knowledge
More issues should be decided on by the EU	25	21	18	16	12
The number of issues is about right	23	20	17	17	12
On some issues there should be more EU decision-making, on other issues, less	13	17	12	11	8
Too many issues are decided on by the EU	25	20	19	16	12
DK/haven't thought about it	14	22	34	39	55
N	2,487	2,009	2,597	2,295	3,083

Source: EB 41.1.

tion; in this sense knowledge can matter in a very practical and very political way. Our main concern, however, is in what effect it and the related variable of interest in European politics have on participation in European Parliament elections.

INTEREST, KNOWLEDGE, AND PARTICIPATION

Both interest in and a knowledge of European politics are strongly associated with levels of turnout at European elections, the association between interest and turnout being ostensibly stronger than that between knowledge and turnout. The rate of participation rises to 86 per cent among those most interested in European politics and drops to 49 per cent among the least interested; in the case of knowledge, turnout rises to 79 per cent among the most knowledgeable, falling to 59 per cent among the least knowledgeable. By and large, there is relatively little difference in circumstantial abstention between the different levels of interest and knowledge; in contrast, not only does the proportion of voluntary abstainers vary markedly as interest or knowledge varies; but these variations are not identical across the two types of voluntary abstention. As interest and knowledge increase, the proportion of double abstainers, i.e. those who abstain at *both* Euro and national elections decreases: from 14 to 2 per cent across the

TABLE 4.6. *Type of electoral participation/abstention by interest in EU politics (non-compulsory voting countries only) (%)*

Type of electoral participation/abstention	Interest in EU politics			
	A great deal	To some extent	Not much	Not at all/ DK
Euro-voter	86	78	67	49
Circumstantial Euro-specific abstainer	5	10	10	9
Circumstantial Euro-and-national abstainer	2	2	3	4
Voluntary Euro-specific abstainer	5	7	15	23
Voluntary Euro-and-national abstainer	2	3	5	14
N	799	2,732	2,794	1,835

Source: EB 41.1.

TABLE 4.7. *Type of electoral participation/abstention by knowledge of the EU (non-compulsory voting countries only) (%)*

Type of electoral participation/abstention	Knowledge of the EU				
	Very well informed	Moderately well informed	Some but not much knowledge	Very little knowledge	No knowledge
Euro-voter	79	74	69	65	59
Circumstantial Euro-specific abstainer	8	9	10	10	9
Circumstantial Euro-and-national abstainer	2	2	3	3	4
Voluntary Euro-specific abstainer	10	11	12	15	16
Voluntary Euro-and-national abstainer	2	3	5	8	11
N	1,723	1,322	1,752	1,444	1,903

Source: EB 41.1.

spectrum of interest and from 11 to 2 per cent across the spectrum of knowledge. In contrast, voluntary abstention that is specific to the European election varies substantially with interest *but only very slightly with knowledge.* As interest increases, the fall in voluntary Euro-specific abstention is from a high of 23 per cent to a low of 5 per cent; but as knowledge increases, there is only a 6 percentage point drop in voluntary Euro-specific abstention: from a high of 16 to a low of 10 per cent (see Tables 4.6 and 4.7). The fact that the relationship between knowledge about European politics and voluntary Euro-specific abstention is not very close suggests that some of the most knowledgeable adopt anti-integration attitudes; this is much less likely among those who express an interest in European politics. Thus, the group of deliberate abstainers at European elections who normally vote in national elections is likely to include a substantial proportion of very knowledgeable respondents who *abstain* because of opposition to the EU and who are fully aware of what they are doing and why they are doing it.

In summary, there is a marked association between knowledge of European politics and patterns of voting and non-voting; there is also, as noted in the last chapter, an association between attitudes and patterns of voting and non-voting. The question that needs therefore to be examined is whether knowledge, interest, and attitudes independently influence voting and abstention, whether only some of these variables play an independent part, or whether they are all so interlinked that it is not possible to discover the extent to which each of them influences the result. What has therefore to be done is to examine the combined relationship between turnout patterns, on the one hand, and, on the other, knowledge, interest, and views about the European Union: this will be attempted in Chapter 8. But first it is necessary to examine attitudes to the European Parliament and how they may be related to voting and non-voting at European elections.

5

The European Parliament: Power, Responsiveness, Image, and Participation

INTRODUCTION

So far we have been dealing with attitudes to the European Union in general. But the election is about the European Parliament. Does the public see this parliament as the toothless tiger of the critics or as an alert and powerful watchdog on which they can rely to ensure that EU decisions will be in their interests? The question of the perceived power of the European Parliament is crucial. As noted in Chapter 1, the defining characteristic of second-order elections is that there is 'less at stake'. But the reason there is less at stake is said to be because there is less power involved. Commenting on the second-order characteristics that are specific to the European Parliament, Reif and Schmitt point to 'the fact that the representative body which is elected has very little real power, even compared to other second-order elected bodies. Thus even less is at stake' (Reif and Schmitt 1980: 12). This chapter focuses on how the power of the European Parliament is seen by the voters. This will prepare the ground for the analysis of what is at stake in these elections, an analysis that will be presented in Chapter 6. As well as analysing the perceived power of the European Parliament, the present chapter examines the perceived reliability of the Parliament and the affective images it evokes in the minds of the European public. To what extent does it evoke any image at all? If it is admired, what is it admired for? If disliked, why? The chapter will conclude with the now standard question: what is the relationship, if any, between the variables discussed in the chapter and turnout in the election?

PREVIOUS RESEARCH ON PERCEPTIONS OF
THE EUROPEAN PARLIAMENT

Attitudes to the role of the European Parliament have been extensively explored in the Eurobarometer surveys in research sponsored mainly by the European Parliament itself. This research has been reviewed elsewhere (Niedermayer and Sinnott 1995) and the results can be summarized briefly. Its main focus has been on three variables: awareness of coverage of the European Parliament in the media, knowledge of the European Parliament, and perceptions of its importance. The data on awareness of the European Parliament has already been examined in Chapter 4. In regard to knowledge of the Parliament, Niedermayer and Sinnott concluded 'it is apparent that only something between one quarter and one third of the citizens of Europe have even the most minimal grasp of the role of the European Parliament. This is the case whether we look at their knowledge of its composition or of its legislative and other powers. Above all, it emerges that a major source of error is the tendency to exaggerate the power of the Parliament, presumably by projecting on to it a role similar to that played by national parliaments' (ibid. 291).

The third main topic in previous research on attitudes to the Parliament has been the perceived importance of the role played by the Parliament. This has been measured by means of two questions, 'How important would you say is the European Parliament in the life of the European Community nowadays?' and 'Would you, personally, prefer that the European Parliament played a more or less important part than it does now?' Between 1977 and 1983, the proportion saying that the European Parliament played an important role increased from 37 to 51 per cent. Over the following decade this proportion fluctuated between 50 per cent and 60 per cent but seemed quite unresponsive to the very significant changes in the power of the Parliament that occurred over that period. Likewise, responses to the second question (preference regarding the role of the Parliament) hovered between 50 and 60 per cent in the period since 1983 when this question was first introduced. It seems remarkable that, despite its increased powers after the adoption of the Single European Act in 1986, the European Parliament has not come to be seen as more important, and that its repeated attempts to take on a more important role in European politics have not been recognized by the European public.

It may be, however, that the standard questions on the present and future role of the Parliament are not altogether satisfactory measures and do not really get at what the public thinks about the European Parliament. Because of the potential ambiguity of the word 'importance', this question could be understood either as probing how much influence the Parliament actually wields or as asking whether it is a good thing that the European Union should have a parliament. In other words, the question is open to either an empirical or a normative interpretation and, as such, it is not a satisfactory basis for analysing citizens' perceptions of the actual role of the Parliament. As this topic is of central concern in the present context, a more satisfactory measure is required. In an attempt to devise such a measure, respondents in the present study were asked: 'As it stands now, how much power do you think the European Parliament has?' They were asked to give their opinion using the same kind of ten-point scale as that used in Chapters 3 and 4 with, in this instance, the ends of the scale being defined as 'no power at all' (1) and 'a great deal of power' (10). Immediately following this question, respondents were asked to rate their own national parliament on the same scale. Finally, they were asked to judge the likely future impact of both institutions.

THE PERCEIVED POWER AND IMPACT OF
THE EUROPEAN PARLIAMENT

A majority of Europeans place the European Parliament below the midpoint on the power scale. Only 9 per cent, however, go along with the radical criticism of the European Parliament as completely powerless and ineffectual (points 1 or 2 on the scale). The plurality of citizens (42 per cent) give the European Parliament a fairly low but not absolutely negligible power-rating (point 3 to 5). A further substantial group (34 per cent) sees it as having a fairly high degree of power and a tiny minority (7 per cent) attribute a great deal of power to it (see Figure 5.1). The inferences to be drawn from these data depend very much on perceptions of the power of national parliaments; the fact is that that only 19 per cent see their national parliament as being very powerful (compared to 7 per cent for the European Parliament) and almost one-in-three (29 per cent) place their national parliament on the lower half of the scale (compared to 51 per cent for the European Parliament). The differences in the perceptions of the

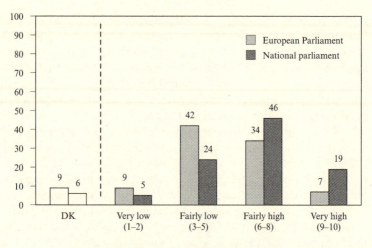

F IG. 5.1. Perceptions of the power of the
European Parliament and national parliaments
Source: EB 41.1.

two parliaments are substantial but it is also clear that voters do not
draw an absolute contrast between a powerless European Parliament
and an all-powerful national parliament. The European Parliament is
regarded as less powerful, but the situation is not seen to be one in
which the national parliaments deal in the coinage of power while the
European Parliament does not.

Consideration of the role of the European Parliament also needs
to take change over time into account. Objectively, the role of the
European Parliament has been significantly enhanced over the last
number of years; it is probable, moreover, that the expansion of its
role will continue whether by the formal grant of new powers or by
the Parliament learning to further maximize the leverage inherent in
the current institutional balance. Does the public have a sense of an
emerging parliamentary power centre in the European Union? In
order to examine this matter, respondents were asked, 'Thinking
about the future, how much effect do you think what the Parliament
does will have on people like yourself?' Responses were again recorded on a ten-point scale and, to have a yardstick by which to assess
these perceptions, respondents were asked the same question regarding the likely future effect of the national parliament.

In this future perspective, the European Parliament does somewhat

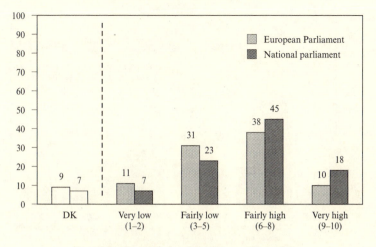

F IG. 5.2. Perceptions of the future effect of the
European Parliament and national parliaments
Source: EB 41.1.

better. Whereas 42 per cent see the European Parliament as currently
having a fairly low degree of power, only 31 per cent see it as having
a fairly low impact on themselves in the future (see Figure 5.2). In-
terestingly, it is only the European Parliament that is seen as being on
a growth curve in this regard: there is no change in the distribution of
perceptions of the national parliaments as between their present
power and their future effect. Consequently, there is a discernible
closing of the gap between the two institutions: as a comparison of
Figures 5.1 and 5.2 shows, the profile of the European Parliament on
this future effect variable is a good deal more similar to the profile of
the national parliaments.

Because the relative powerlessness of the European Parliament is a
central feature to the second-order election model, it is essential to be
as precise as possible with respect to how voters see the relative clout
(present power or future effect) of the European Parliament. Ideally,
one needs to know, for each respondent, whether he or she sees the
European Parliament as having less power than the national parliament and if so, how much less. This can in fact be measured by
subtracting the rating given to the national parliament from the
rating given to the European Parliament. If the result is negative, the
European Parliament is seen by that individual to be less powerful

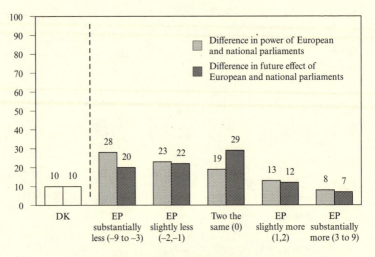

F IG. 5.3. Difference in perceived power and perceived
future effect of European Parliament and national parliaments
Source: EB 41.1.

and the number resulting from the subtraction gives a measure of just
how much less powerful.

The results suggest that the power perceptions that are attributed
to the voter by the second-order election model are far from being
universal. Forty per cent see the European Parliament as being either
just as powerful as or more powerful than their national parliament
and only 28 per cent see it as substantially less powerful (a difference
of 3 scale points or more). In a future perspective, 48 per cent regard
the likely impact of the European Parliament as equal to or greater
than that of the national parliament and only 20 per cent rate that future impact as substantially less than that of the national parliament.
The view that the European Parliament has much less power than
national parliaments, a view that is at the base of the second-order
election model, may be an accurate and objective account of the
Parliament's powers and functions; it is not a view that is shared by a
majority of European citizens.

National parliaments in the member states of the European Union
vary considerably in the role they play in the political system.
Obviously, if one country has, or, more importantly in this context, is
seen as having a very strong parliament and another country a very
weak one, the *relative* ratings of the power of the European Parliament

that emerge from both systems will be very different. Given that one is analysing *perceptions* of both the European and national parliaments and relating one to the other, it is essential to examine these relative power judgements on a country-by-country basis. In the European Union as a whole, national parliaments are judged to be somewhat more powerful than the European Parliament. This is reflected in the position of the point for the EU in the plot in Figure 5.4. Germany, the Netherlands, and Luxembourg, however, tend to regard their own parliaments as quite powerful and the European Parliament as relatively powerless. Denmark would belong to this group were is not for its high rating of the power of the European

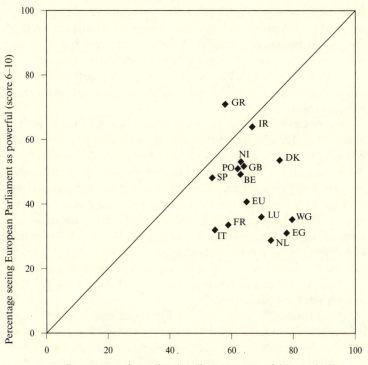

F IG. 5.4. Perception of power of the European Parliament and perception of power of national parliaments by country
Source: EB 41.1.

Parliament, a rating that may have as much to do with Danish concerns about sovereignty as with an objective appreciation of the modalities of power in Strasbourg and Brussels. At the other end of the scale of perceived national parliamentary power, one finds Spain, Italy, Greece, and France. These countries differ radically, however, in their assessment of the power of the European Parliament: Italy and France regard it as very low; Spain as about average, and Greece produces the highest European Parliament power rating of all. The other outlier is Ireland, where the rating of the power of the national parliament is about average but where the European Parliament is given its second highest power rating. Ireland, however, remains just below the diagonal which divides the countries in which the national parliament is seen as more powerful than the European Parliament from the one country (Greece) in which the reverse perception obtains. Even leaving aside the stark exception of Greece, however, this simple graphical portrayal of the perceptions of parliamentary power, national and European, in the different member states suggests that, at least at the level of the electorate, the degree to which this initial assumption of the second-order election model is realized varies considerably.[1]

Perceptions of the relative power of the European Parliament are likely to be affected not only by the baseline of national parliamentary power from which the comparison is being made, but also by the extent to which the voters have accurate knowledge of the political systems both of their own country and of the European Union. Chapter 4 presented evidence of people's knowledge of the European Union. This scale can be combined with one which measures knowledge of the national political system to give an overall index of levels of information about the European and national political systems. The expectation is that those who are better informed will be more likely to see the actual power discrepancies between the European and the national parliaments.

Not surprisingly, knowledge of European and national politics affects the respondents' ability to say anything at all about the power of either the European or national parliament: the proportion giving a don't know response on either the question regarding the power of

---

[1] A more important test of the model will of course be whether perceptions of the power of the European Parliament (absolute or relative) affect electoral participation. This issue is taken up at the end of this chapter and again in Chapter 8.

TABLE 5.1. *Perceived difference in the power of the European Parliament and national parliaments by index of knowledge of the European and national political systems (%)*

Perceived difference in power of EP and national parliaments	Index of European and national political knowledge				
	No knowledge	Very little knowledge	Some but not much knowledge	Moderately well informed	Very well informed
Euro substantially less	18	24	33	39	44
Euro slightly less	23	25	26	28	23
Two the same	32	24	18	15	15
Euro slightly more	18	18	14	11	10
Euro substantially more	10	9	9	7	7
N	1,126	2,589	3,456	1,578	2,226

Source: EB 41.1.

the European Parliament or on that regarding the power of the national parliament or on both goes from 26 per cent among those who score zero on the knowledge scale to 2 per cent among those who score 6 (these don't knows are omitted in the analysis that follows). As Table 5.1 shows, there is also quite a strong relationship between knowledge of European and national politics and how the power of the parliaments is perceived. The European Parliament is considered to be *substantially* less powerful than the national parliaments by 44 per cent of those with a full score on the combined European and national knowledge scale. The same judgement is made by only 18 per cent of those who score zero on the scale; in between these two extremes, the proportion seeing the European Parliament as substantially less powerful drops regularly with each step down the knowledge scale.[2] This finding suggests that the effects of relative power perceptions on the likelihood that someone will turn out to vote may be complex: those who realize that there is a power discrepancy between the two institutions are also much better informed about both European and national politics and therefore more likely

[2] For ease of interpretation, the seven-point scale arrived at by combining the European and national knowledge scales is reduced to five levels using the same labels as used in the European knowledge scale: 'no knowledge', 'very little knowledge' 'some but not much knowledge'; 'moderately well informed' and 'very well informed'.

to be involved and to turn out to vote. This issue will be taken up again at the end of this chapter and in Chapter 8.

THE EUROPEAN PARLIAMENT AND THE RESPONSIVENESS OF EU DECISION-MAKING

The European Union is remote from its citizens. It has recognized its problems in this regard and has repeatedly charged the European Parliament with bringing the Union 'closer to the citizens'. But remoteness and closeness are rather vague notions; what is really at stake here is the responsiveness of EU decision-making: do the citizens believe that the European Parliament can be relied on to ensure such responsiveness? To examine this, the following question was used: 'Many important decisions are made by the European Union (European Community). They might be in the interest of people like yourself, or they might not. To what extent do you feel that you can rely on each of the following to make sure that these decisions are in the interest of people like yourself?' Respondents were asked to evaluate the European Commission, the national government, the European Court of Justice, the Council of Ministers of the European Union, the national parliament, and the European Parliament in these terms. Again, a ten-point scale was used, with 1 indicating 'not reliable at all' and 10 'completely reliable'.

The reliability ratings of all six institutions are presented in Figure 5.5. Only two in five European citizens give the European Parliament a favourable rating (point six or above on the ten-point scale). A mere 5 per cent see the Parliament as being very reliable; 34 per cent think it is fairly reliable; and a majority place it below the midpoint on the scale (37 per cent between points three and five and 14 per cent put it at the lowest two points (one and two) on the scale (see the third column of Figure 5.5). Of course, trust in or reliance on the European Parliament is one thing, trust in or reliance on the entire complex process of European decision-making and on its other individual components may be quite different. The institutional framework of the European Union is complex and its responsiveness could be regarded as being not just a function of the directly elected European Parliament but a function of the entire range of European institutions. The Commission is the guardian of the Treaties and is charged with ensuring that European Union decisions are actually implemented in the member states. The Council of Ministers is effectively the main branch of the legislature of the Union and it can claim to have both a political orientation and a representative basis. The European Court of Justice adjudicates issues in the light of the Treaties. The responsiveness of European decision-making is also affected by the actions taken by national governments in pursuit of national policy objectives. Finally, national parliaments have extensive procedures for monitoring and vetting the legislative decisions and the administrative actions taken at the European level.

In order to locate the contribution of the European Parliament to the perceived responsiveness of European decision-making within this complex institutional context, the ratings of all six institutions in Figure 5.5 are arranged from left to right in terms of the public's increasing sense of their overall reliability (i.e. very high plus fairly high reliability). In terms of ensuring that *European* decision-making is responsive, European citizens, in so far as they believe in such responsiveness at all, look to *national* institutions: their national government (46 per cent at least fairly reliable) and their national parliament (49 per cent). This encapsulates the dilemma of democratic responsiveness in the Union: the institutions to which the citizens look to ensure that decisions are in their interests (i.e. their own national governments and parliaments) are not always the best equipped to achieve this; the institutions which, in theory, ought to be better equipped (the legislative institutions of the Union—the Council and the European Parliament) are less trusted in regard to this vital democratic function.

Among the European institutions, the Commission and the Council of Ministers are felt to be the least reliable, each being rated as at least fairly reliable (a score of 6 or more) by only one-third of respondents.[3] In assessing this, one might argue that the Commission, despite its de facto representative composition and despite its role as guardian of the treaties, is a bureaucratic and quasi-executive body and, therefore, unlikely to be regarded as a prime source of responsiveness. An extenuating argument is harder to make in the case of the Council of Ministers. As noted above, it is the main branch of the legislature of the Union and it is composed of members of elected governments;

---

[3] Respondents appear to have somewhat greater difficulty in answering the question of reliability with respect to European institutions than with respect to national institutions: the proportion of 'don't knows' drops from between 10 and 17 per cent in the case of European institutions to between 3 and 4 per cent in the case of national institutions.

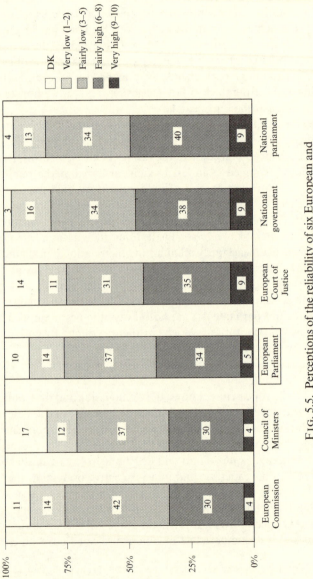

FIG. 5.5. Perceptions of the reliability of six European and national governmental institutions in ensuring the responsiveness of European decision-making

Source: EB 41.1.

furthermore, those who seek to defend the Union against the charge of a 'democratic deficit' frequently point to the representativeness and power of the Council. The evidence in Figure 5.5 shows that this argument does not persuade the citizens; they are no more likely to look to the Council to protect their interests than they are to look to the overtly bureaucratic Commission.

The problem for the Parliament, which ought to be the agent of European responsiveness *par excellence*, is that it is only marginally ahead of these two clearly unresponsive institutions: as noted above, only 39 per cent of European citizens see the European Parliament as even a fairly reliable means of ensuring responsive decision-making. While it is regarded as being slightly more reliable than the Commission or the Council, it is less reliable than the remote and unrepresentative Court of Justice in Luxembourg. At the European level, the most trusted institution is in fact the Court: 44 per cent give it a rating above the midpoint of the scale. Finally, it should be emphasized that no institution, European or national, is even fairly highly regarded as an instrument of responsive European governance by more than 50 per cent of the citizens.

IMAGES OF THE EUROPEAN PARLIAMENT: POSITIVE, NEGATIVE, AND NONE

One of the difficulties that arises in survey research is that the very process of gathering the data may impose concepts and assumptions on the respondent that are really those of the researcher. At the extreme, this can amount to generating an attitude where none previously existed and where the respondent knows nothing whatsoever about the attitude object. For example, this could arise in the present context if a respondent who knew nothing about the European Parliament, on being asked the question about its power, were to respond by calculating that, if it is a parliament and if it is European, it must have some reasonable degree of power, and, on this basis, were to give it a rating of, say, six on the ten-point scale. This would be a classic example of what has been called the problem of non-attitudes. As Converse put it many years ago, the problem arises because 'Whatever our intentions, the attitude questionnaire is approached as though it were an intelligence test, with the "don't know" and the "can't decide" confessions of mental incapacity' (Converse 1970: 177).

This risk can be minimized by various research strategies. One such strategy is to facilitate the expression of 'no opinion' where this seems particularly likely; an example of this can be seen in the discussion of the evidence of preferences regarding the scope of EU decision-making in Chapter 3. Another strategy is to ask some open-ended questions, allowing the respondents to formulate their thoughts and feelings in their own terms (or not to express any thoughts or feelings if they have none). This latter strategy was an important part of this study's attempt to get at the images that people have of the European Parliament. In pursuit of these images, respondents were asked two direct and very straightforward open-ended questions: 'We are interested in the good points and bad points about the European Parliament. First, is there anything in particular that you LIKE about the European Parliament?' Having answered this, the respondent was then asked 'Is there anything in particular that you DISLIKE about the European Parliament?' Each question was followed by a prompt ('What else?') to encourage a full response. The entire response was written down by the interviewer and these verbatim responses were then content analysed or coded to provide evidence of the images ordinary European citizens have of the European Parliament. It will be clear from what has been said that one is just as interested in the 'no opinion' or 'nothing' responses to these questions as in the positive and negative images that are expressed.

Thirty-nine per cent of respondents answered 'no' or 'nothing' to both these questions; in other words, a very substantial proportion of European citizens has *no affective image of the European Parliament* (see Table 5.2). A further one in five say there is nothing they like about the Parliament but go on to identify things they do not like about it; thus the proportion who have either no image or a purely negative image of the Parliament amounts to a substantial majority (62 per cent). The remaining 38 per cent is made up mostly of critical admirers, who harbour both likes and dislikes (27 per cent of all respondents); unalloyed positive views of the Parliament are found among only one in ten. But, perhaps the most important finding resulting from this use of open-ended questions to probe more deeply into attitudes to the European Parliament is that two in five European citizens have no such attitude!

Among those who have an affective image of the European Parlia-

TABLE 5.2. *Affective images of the European Parliament*

	%
No image (no likes/no dislikes)	39
Negative image (dislikes) only	23
Mixed positive/negative image	27
Positive image (likes) only	11
N	12,499

Source: EB 41.1.

ment, likes and dislikes range across a very broad spectrum. Apart from uncovering the extent of 'non-attitudes' to the Parliament, revealing this variety is another major advantage of the use of open-ended questions in this context. Such variety, however, poses major problems for the investigator—the problems of how to summarize, codify, quantify, or otherwise reduce this variety to manageable proportions. As indicated in Chapter 1, the analysis of this kind of data requires a laborious process of coding or content analysis. The major task is to devise a workable coding frame that reveals the underlying themes and variables in the data while respecting their variety. Presentation of the data poses the same problem of summarizing the overall features without sacrificing the richness that lies in the detail. The solution in this case is to report the quantified results of the content analysis and, at the same time, to quote liberally from the verbatim responses in order to illustrate both the general themes and the complexity and particularity of individual attitudes.

Positive images of the European Parliament are dominated by two main types of response: on the one hand, references to building consensus, encouraging cooperation, and overcoming national differences and antagonisms, and on the other, references to specific policy issues. Each of these two types of response occurred among approximately half of those saying there was something they liked about the European Parliament[4] (see Table 5.3).

The first theme—the consensus and cooperation responses—consisted of variations on the idea that the European Parliament

---

[4] Note that, because respondents could mention several things they liked or disliked about the Parliament and because each mention was coded and recorded, the percentages in these tables add to more than 100.

TABLE 5.3. *Positive images of the European Parliament*

	%
Proportion of all respondents having a partially or fully positive image of the EP	38
Of which	
Consensus building	58
Policy issues	52
Representative/democratic	19
General/miscellaneous references	9
Good for own country	6
Institutional	6
Positive references to MEPs	2
N cases	4,720

Note: Due to multiple responses, percentages add to more than 100.

Source: EB 41.1.

provides a vital forum for discussion of differences and for the resolution of conflict. At one end of the spectrum, the responses made general references to the value of discussion based on diverse points of view, as for example, in the case of the Frenchman who said 'The fact that politicians from different countries can discuss jointly all the European problems'[5] or the German version of the same notion: 'The basic idea: various opinions can be better discussed by many peoples. Harmony.'[6] An Italian respondent was more specific about overcoming 'national egoism' and extended the significance of this to the global scale: 'The ability to overcome national selfish attitudes; can give an example of unity to the entire world.'[7] Developing this idea, some respondents came close to the concept known in international relations theory as that of 'a security community', that is an area characterized by long-term dependable expectations that all disputes can and will be settled by peaceful means. In the words of one Danish respondent: 'It is a forum where opinions from the European community can meet, develop, and compete. It symbolizes the fact that a traditionally warlike part of the world can now get together

[5] 'Le fait que les hommes politiques de pays différents puissent se concerter pour tous les problèmes européens.'

[6] 'Grundidee: viele Meinungen können durch viele Völker besser diskutiert werden. Gleichklang.'

[7] 'Il fatto di poter superare gli egoismi nazionali, poter essere un esempio di unità per il mondo intero.'

peacefully. After so much war in Europe, that is the most important.'[8] A German respondent concurred: 'That this entity even exists. Blah-blah is better than boom-boom!'[9]

The theme of the value of unity was sometimes expressed not so much as overcoming conflicting differences but rather as transcending specific national problems or limitations. Three quite different examples illustrate the point. For an Italian respondent, the value of the European Parliament lies in providing an escape from what he sees as the limitations of Italian politics: 'It is the first move towards the Union, it deprovincializes our political life.'[10] For a Spanish respondent, the entire value attached to the Parliament, a value really stemming from European integration itself, consists in leaving behind the isolation of the past: 'That Spain is more linked to Europe than before, it is not isolated as it was under Franco. Never again.'[11] Finally, a British respondent saw the advantages of the unifying role of the Parliament as a means of overcoming British insularity: 'It would prevent this insular feeling which Britain has. It might also curb this horrible thing about being British. I think that is a bad thing. The idea that everything must be British is destructive as opposed to constructive and I hope the EP would redress the balance.'

The other main category of positive responses to the question of likes regarding the European Parliament were references to policies and issues that the respondents associated with the Parliament. Policies of one sort or another were mentioned by 52 per cent of those giving a positive response to the question. Half the references were to economic policies, the other half ranged over a wide gamut of issues from drugs, crime, and terrorism to international relations issues, environmental issues, social policy, consumer protection, and so on.

Since the reputation of the British public in regard to European policy issues is that it focuses obsessively on real or imagined problems of standardization of the minutiae of British life, it is perhaps worth drawing the illustrations of positive policy images attributed to the European Parliament from the British data. In the economic area

---

[8] 'Det er et forum, hvor meninger fra det europæiske fællesskab kan samles, udvikles og brydes. Det er et symbol på, at en pr. tradition ellers krigerisk del af verden nu kan mødes fredeligt. Efter krigstidende i Europa, det er det vigtigste.'

[9] 'Dass es diese Einrichtung ueberhaupt gibt. Lieber Bla-bla als Bum-bum!'

[10] '. . . è il primo passaggio verso l'unione, sprovincializza la nostra vita politica.'

[11] 'Que España está más unida a Europa que antes, no está aislada como con Franco. Nada más.'

many of the references were to policies that are at the heart of the process of economic integration. In some cases, the economic benefits were described almost in technical terms such as mobility of labour and freedom of movement. But there were also more colloquial and down-to-earth expressions of the basic idea such as: 'It's a leveller between countries if tariffs are the same everywhere within the community'; or the response that put a basic proposition of international trade theory in a nutshell: 'We can get more things cheaply from other people and they can get more things cheaply from us.' But the most succinct expression of this aspect of the policy references was undoubtedly the response that said simply: 'Trading is easier, travelling is easier.' The latter also illustrates very well the general nature of many of the responses, even though the question was specifically related to the European Parliament. Some policy responses, indeed, were even more general, in that they referred to very large problems that, on the face of it, the respondent seemed to anticipate the European Parliament could solve, as in: 'It might be able to solve problems that just our country won't be able to do on its own—unemployment, crime, all sorts of things like that' or the respondent who simply said he liked it because 'It could create more jobs for us all.'

Not all of the policy content of the positive images of the Parliament is as general as the foregoing. In the more detailed responses, there was considerable focus on the welfare of workers as in: 'I like the fact that they are aware of welfare issues relating to maternity benefits, leave, part-time workers, issues like that and job protection, more than our government.' Another, longish response also raised issues of this sort and went into even more detailed matters: 'Raising standards on retirement ages, the working week, the Social Chapter. I like the degree of openness in the issues they raise, they make things known like beef, and salmonella in eggs. Also car safety, we can't get the information. Europe or some [European] countries are more open than we are.'

Three policy areas with which the Parliament has been particularly associated—regional policy, environmental policy, and human rights —also struck a chord: 'I think its policies about helping the under-developed parts of the European Union are good—a very positive side of the European Union' and 'Yes—over pollution they seem to be more concerned, over green issues and seem to be able to get the British Government to do something.' Finally, the Parliament's concern with human rights and issues affecting minorities did not go unnoticed: one respondent simply said she liked the European Parliament because 'They are concerned about human rights around the world' and another felt likewise because 'They are more interested to discuss issues which are related to people who are thought of as traditional minorities—refugees and immigrants.'

Apart from these two dominant kinds of response (consensus building and policies), the only other positive response category that emerged with notable frequency consisted of references to the representative or democratic basis of the European Parliament (20 per cent). These included favourable references to its gender balance, or its partisan composition, or simply to the basic fact that it is democratically elected.[12] The latter was succinctly put by a French respondent who said: 'The fact that members of the European Parliament are elected by us, by popular vote, which is fairly representative of ideas prevailing in each country. Nothing else',[13] and by the British respondent who got a decided sense of satisfaction from voting in a European Parliament election: 'It's an elected assembly—it's not nominated by government—I get to vote for my MEP.'

We have quoted extensively from these positive responses for two purposes: to give a balanced picture (we shall illustrate the negatives presently) and, secondly, to bring out the point, noted in passing above, that many of the responses referred to issues and policies actually attributable to the Union as such rather than directly attributable to the Parliament. The Parliament may have contributed to bringing them about but many of them pertain as much to the general process of integration as to its representative or democratic dimension. This could be interpreted to mean that the image of the Parliament is enhanced by the success of general Community or Union policies. On the other hand, it could signify that many people do not differentiate between the Union as such and the Parliament. In other words, the lack of image of the Parliament may be more widespread than indicated by the level of non-response and don't know responses to the likes/dislikes question.

The negative images of the European Parliament tend to be more specific. This is clear from the fact that 63 per cent of those who identified something they dislike about the European Parliament

[12] Gender balance was a minority concern; reaction to it among that minority was more likely to be favourable (37 cases) than unfavourable (13 cases).

[13] 'Le fait que les représentants du parlement européens soient élus par nous, par vote, assez représentatif des idées de chaque pays; rien d'autre.'

TABLE 5.4. *Negative images of the European Parliament*

	%
Proportion of all respondents having a partially or fully negative image of the EP	48
Of which	
Institutional aspects	63
Policy issues	32
Dominance of other countries/bad for own country	27
Negative references to MEPs	18
General/miscellaneous references	7
Unrepresentative/undemocratic	6
N	6,059

Note: Due to multiple responses, percentages add to more than 100.

Source: EB 41.1.

referred to institutional aspects (see Table 5.4); the next most frequent category of complaint (policy- or issue-related negative references) came a substantial way behind (at 32 per cent of those with dislikes). One quarter of the dislikes mentioned reflected a belief that other countries' interests predominated and the respondent's own country's interests were not being catered for or that its sovereignty was being infringed. Finally, almost one in five of those who had negative things to say about the Parliament specifically criticized the MEPs.

In thinking about the predominance of institutional complaints about the Parliament, one must first note an important qualification: a substantial proportion (32 per cent) of those who criticized the European Parliament as an institution did so more in sorrow than in anger, in the sense that they complained that the Parliament is not powerful enough. Such respondents may have a jaundiced view of the Parliament but they are, at the same time, among its well-wishers. A British respondent expressed this kind of complaint in a nice mixed metaphor: 'I believe, from what I know about it, that it doesn't actually have any teeth—I dislike its lip service without any bite.' A German respondent went further in looking for the ultimate degree of parliamentary power: 'The European Parliament can't put a government out of power.'[14] Others, however, were more qualified in their analyses and prescriptions regarding the power of the Parliament.

---

14 'Das Europa Parlament kann eine Regierung nicht ausser Kraft setzen.'

TABLE 5.5. *Negative institutional images of the European Parliament*

	%
Proportion of all respondents having a negative institutional image of the EP	21
Of which	
Not enough power	32
Inefficient	22
Not transparent	19
Too costly	18
Bureaucracy	14
Too many specific issues	8
Indecisive	7
Too powerful	3
N	2,657

Note: Due to multiple responses, percentages add to more than 100.

Source: EB 41.1.

Thus a Dutch respondent argued that that it was partly the Parliament's fault that it was not more powerful: 'Too little power or too little capacity to use power; the Parliament must control better, above all control over the subsidies.'[15] A Danish respondent criticized the Parliament because it lacked influence but the criticism was more than tinged with ambivalence: 'The Parliament has no influence, but I don't know whether they should have more influence, as they are like a coffee club.'[16]

In addition to such more or less friendly criticisms, however, it is clear that real and specific negative comments on the institution occur with considerable frequency: it is seen as inefficient (22 per cent of institutional complaints), not transparent (19 per cent), too costly (18 per cent), and too bureaucratic (14 per cent) (see Table 5.5). Complaints of inefficiency and bureaucracy were often combined as in: 'Too much bureaucracy, too much indecisiveness, loss of time, few concrete and speedy decisions.'[17] Likewise, complaints about cost

[15] 'Te weinig macht, of te weinig gebruik van de macht maken; het parlement moet beter controleren, vooral de controles op de subsidies.'
[16] 'Parlamentet har ingen indflydelse, men jeg ved ikke, om de skal have mere indflydelse, da det minder om en kaffeklub.'
[17] 'Trop de bureaucratie, trop d'indécision, perte de temps, peu décisions concrètes et rapides.'

are often linked to low output and ineffectiveness, as for the Italian respondent who stated that the Parliament was 'Too spendthrift. Having three meeting places is absurd; it is absurd to translate everything into nine languages; overstaffed; unable to take rapid and difficult decisions when there are conflicts among Europeans,'[18] or, as a Danish respondent summed it up: 'It is inefficient in proportion to the sums put aside for it.'[19] To some extent, these perceived weaknesses in the Parliament are the other side of the coin of what other respondents see as the advantage of an international debating forum or talking shop. The German respondent quoted above may see virtue in 'blah-blah', but a Belgian focused on the downside of this: 'too low, too slow, too much palaver'.[20]

Another fairly prominent feature of the institutional complaints is lack of transparency (one in five of all institutional-type criticisms). Somewhat like the criticisms of the Parliament for its lack of power, these negative views are often related to an underlying positive attitude and a degree of interest in the Parliament and its activities; at the very least, these citizens indicate an openness to persuasion. A Danish respondent expressed her frustrations in this regard as follows: 'It is so distant. It is too far away. One is not sufficiently informed and many times it is not expressed clearly enough so that one can understand it.'[21] The demand for more effort in this regard by the Parliament is illustrated by portions of two Dutch responses: 'too little clarification and information', 'too little publicity';[22] and by the Italian respondent who argued: 'I am pro-Europe but I don't see what I could like about the European Parliament given the absence of any information campaign; people know little about it, it seems to work in the dark . . . .'[23] The notion that it operates in the shadows is also expressed by the French respondent who said: 'Elle reste mysterieuse pour nous.'

Whereas positive images of the Parliament were dominated by two

---

[18] 'Troppo dispendioso. Tre sedi sono assurde; assurdo tradurre tutto in nove lingue; troppo personale; incapacità di prendere decisioni drastiche e scomode in occasione di contese europee.'

[19] 'Det er ineffektivt i forhold til de store summer, vi sætter af til det.'

[20] 'Te lag, te traag, te viel palaver.'

[21] 'Det er så fjernt. Det er for langt væk. Man bliver ikke nok oplyst, og mange gange bliver det heller ikke udtrykt tydeligt nok, så man forstår det.'

[22] '. . . te weinig voorlichting en informatie' and 'te weinig promotie'.

[23] 'Io sono europeista ma non vedo cosa mi possa piacere nel parlamento europeo con l'inesistente campagna d'informazione infatti le persone ne sanno poco, sembra che lavori nell'ombra . . .'

features (consensus role and policies), the negative images tend to be dominated by the institutional category just considered. However, other negative features also occur with some frequency: negative policy references, references to the dominance of other countries or to the Parliament (or Union) being bad for the respondent's country, and negative references to MEPs (see Table 5.4). Given that so much media attention is devoted to the latter type of complaint, the matter is worth investigating in some detail. Before doing so, however, it is worth noting that the negative reactions to the Parliament on the basis of its being inimical to one's country's interests are not confined to the British or the Danes. Certainly they occur in these cases—an example in the British case being: 'I do not agree with it making decisions which affect us. They do not understand the minds of the British people'; likewise a Danish respondent saw things very much from a national point of view when he argued that 'Our sixteen have no possibility of being heard. They drown in folly and nonsense.'[24] But, it is not just the British and the Danes: a Portuguese respondent put the matter quite forthrightly: 'In the Parliament the Portuguese members don't succeed in defending our interests; the country managed to lose out on the agricultural front'[25] and a French respondent expressed his dislike of the Parliament on the basis that: 'it affects what belongs to France and French social provisions.'[26]

Turning to complaints about the MEPs, a matter that receives much media attention, the first point to note is that they are not very frequent. Although they are made by 18 per cent of those who have a negative image of the European Parliament, this amounts to only 9 per cent of all respondents. In some cases these negative references amount to no more than the harmless comment that there are too many of them; in even rarer cases, they consisted of robust general condemnation that probably no parliament can avoid or effectively counter, as in 'The stupidity of politicians. I can't be more precise. That is all I can say.'[27] In other cases, however, the negative reaction is more pointed: 38 per cent of those who criticize the MEPs directly refer to their motivation or behaviour, for example, to alleged low

[24] 'Vores 16 har ingen mulighed for at blive hørt. De drukner i ævl og kævl.'
[25] 'No parlamento os deputados portugueses nao conseguem defender os nossos interesses; o pais ficou a perder no caso agricola.'
[26] 'Qu'il touche au patrimoine et aux acquis sociaux Français.'
[27] 'La connerie des politicards, non je n'ai pas a préciser, c'est tout ce que je peux dire.'

rates of attendance and an implied goal of a cushy life: 'Absenteeism at sittings. MEPs tend to regard being elected as a means to the good life.'[28]

Perhaps reflecting a prominent feature of negative press coverage of the Parliament, concern with allegedly excessive salaries and expenses made up one-quarter of the complaints directed at MEPs. An Irish respondent linked this issue to that of responsiveness: 'Their incomes are not justified. I know they are busy people but they become too well-off and forget the people left behind at home'; a British respondent linked it directly to his decision not to vote: 'I think the European parliamentarians, for the work they do, are grossly overpaid and the money would be put into better use elsewhere. . . . too many people in high positions all receiving a high salary. One of the reasons why I wouldn't vote.' Again, however, given the publicity the issue of MEP salaries and expenses gets, it must be emphasized that the issue is raised by only 3 per cent of respondents.

In summary, the exploration of the image of the Parliament among European citizens using an open-ended question technique has revealed, first, that almost 40 per cent of the citizens have no such image; beyond that plurality, 23 per cent have a purely negative image, 27 per cent a mixed positive and negative image, and 11 per cent a purely positive image. Secondly, the evidence indicates that the dominant positive images relate, on the one hand, to the Parliament as a means or symbol of overcoming conflict and, on the other, to its association with a very varied set of positive policy measures. The evidence also suggests, however, that some of these positive images are related to general features of European integration rather than to matters directly attributable to the Parliament. Thirdly, the evidence from the open-ended questions shows that the negative images of the Parliament tend to be more specific and that they focus mainly on aspects of the institution and how it functions. However negative policy associations also occur, as do images of the Parliament as being inimical to the national interest and national sovereignty and negative images relating to the behaviour or remuneration of MEPs. In regard to the latter, given the extent to which such matters have been highlighted by the media, it must be emphasized that such images are found among only small minorities of the citizens. A far,

---

28 'Le manque d'assiduité aux séances des députés européens. Ces députés ont tendance a considerer leur élection comme un moyen de bien gagner sa vie à l'aise.'

TABLE 5.6. *Negative MEP-related images of the European Parliament*

	%
Proportion of all respondents having a negative	
MEP-related image of the EP	8
Of which	
Motivation/behaviour	38
Too distant	35
Salaries too high	23
Too many MEPs	13
Expenses excessive	9
N cases	1,002

Note: Due to multiple responses, percentages add to more than 100.

Source: EB 41.1.

far greater problem than any images of less-than-perfect MEPs, is the fact that the Parliament has no image at all among two-fifths of the citizens. This indeed is a conservative estimate of the extent of the lack of a distinct image of the Parliament because a proportion of the images that have been uncovered here are very undifferentiated and unspecific: they seem to relate as much or more to the Union as such as to the Parliament.

POWER, RESPONSIVENESS, IMAGE, AND PARTICIPATION

What effect, if any, do these perceptions, reliability ratings, and positive or negative images have on participation in European Parliament elections? A key assumption of the second-order election model is that turnout is lower because there is less at stake. In turn, it is argued that there is less at stake because second-order assemblies wield less power. Applying this explanation to the voters, and, if the explanation is to be comprehensive, it must surely apply at this level, the prediction becomes: those who attribute substantial power to the European Parliament will be more likely to vote than those who see it as having little or no power. As Table 5.7 shows, the data provide no support for this hypothesis: turnout is precisely the same whether the

TABLE 5.7. *Type of electoral participation/abstention by perception of the power of the European Parliament (non-compulsory voting countries only) (%)*

Type of electoral participation/abstention	Perceived power of the European Parliament				
	Don't know	Very low (1, 2)	Fairly low (3–5)	Fairly high (6–8)	Very high (9, 10)
Euro-voter	55	70	72	69	71
Circumstantial Euro-specific abstainer	10	5	8	12	7
Circumstantial Euro-and-national abstainer	4	1	3	3	2
Voluntary Euro-specific abstainer	19	18	12	12	13
Voluntary Euro-and-national abstainer	13	6	6	5	7
N	789	674	3,045	2,863	783

Source: EB 41.1.

elector attributes a very low or a very high degree of power to the Parliament or any degree of power in between. The hypothesis suffers an even worse fate if the more precise and comprehensive measure of the perceived difference between the power of the European Parliament and that of the national parliament is used. In this case, such relationship as exists is in the opposite direction to that hypothesized: 75 per cent of those who see the power of the European Parliament as substantially less than that of the national parliament report that they voted in the European Parliament election compared to 64 per cent of those who attribute substantially greater power to the European Parliament.[29] There are several possible reasons for the failure of absolute or relative perceptions of the power of the European Parliament to predict turnout. For one thing, perceptions of the power of the European Parliament are related to knowledge of politics: those who attribute less power are more knowledgeable and therefore, on the basis of the latter characteristic, more likely to vote. Second, the attribution of greater power to the European Parliament does not necessarily lead to positive judgements about its reliability in ensuring the responsiveness of EU decision-making. For some, indeed, the perception of a powerful European Parliament may be the perception of a threat rather than a promise; this is not a factor that is conducive to turning out to vote.[30] Be that as it may, the evidence presented here does not strengthen one's confidence in the second-order election explanation of low turnout. It should be emphasized, however, that this test of the model is not comprehensive; the key element in the interpretation is the notion of there being less at stake in a European Parliament election. One would expect that perceptions of power would be related to this key element but a fair assessment of the explanation requires direct measurement of the less-at-stake dimension. A task that will be taken up in Chapter 6.

In contrast to power perceptions, two of the other variables discussed in this chapter—images of the Parliament and ratings of its reliability—do have a significant effect on turnout. Among those with no affective image of the European Parliament, turnout is 62 per cent; it rises to 75 per cent among those who have a purely positive image

[29] Inability to make any judgement, absolute or relative, regarding degrees of parliamentary power does have quite a significant effect on turnout (see Tables 5.7 and 5.8). This, however, has nothing to do with the second-order election model.

[30] Unless there is an opportunity to vote for a candidate committed to curtailing the power of the European Parliament, but such opportunities are rare.

TABLE 5.8. *Type of electoral participation/abstention by perception of difference in the power of European and national parliaments (non-compulsory voting countries only) (%)*

Type of electoral participation/abstention	Perceived difference in the power of the EP and national parliaments					
	Don't know	EP substantially less (−9 to −3)	EP slightly less (−2, −1)	Two the same (0)	EP slightly more (1,2)	EP substantially more (3 to 9)
Euro-voter	55	75	72	69	65	64
Circumstantial Euro-specific abstainer	10	7	10	10	11	11
Circumstantial Euro-and-national abstainer	4	2	3	3	3	3
Voluntary Euro-specific abstainer	19	13	11	12	13	16
Voluntary Euro-and-national abstainer	13	4	5	6	7	7
N	830	2,255	1,833	1,484	1,058	686

Source: EB 41.1.

TABLE 5.9. *Type of electoral participation/abstention by affective image of the European Parliament (non-compulsory voting countries only) (%)*

Type of electoral participation/abstention	Affective image of the EP			
	No affective image	Negative image only	Positive and negat-ive images	Positive image only
Euro-voter	62	66	78	75
Circumstantial Euro-specific abstainer	11	8	8	10
Circumstantial Euro-and-national abstainer	4	2	2	3
Voluntary Euro-specific abstainer	15	17	9	7
Voluntary Euro-and-national abstainer	9	7	3	4
N	3,012	1,850	2,394	906

Source: EB 41.1.

and to 78 per cent among those who have a mixed (positive and negative) image. This suggests that negative reactions to the Parliament do not lead to lower turnout if they are softened by the attribution of some positive qualities to the Parliament; furthermore, turnout is just as low when the potential voter simply does not relate, favourably or unfavourably, to the Parliament as it is when the image of the Parliament is entirely negative (see Table 5.9). It is also worth noting that all of the variation in abstention in this regard is concentrated in the two categories of voluntary abstention: the image of the Parliament has no effect on the extent of circumstantial abstention, a finding that confirms the importance of distinguishing between these two kinds of non-participation.

A similar pattern obtains in the case of variations in the perceived reliability of the European Parliament in terms of ensuring the responsiveness of EU decision-making (Table 5.10): turnout runs from 61 per cent among those who judge the reliability of the Parliament to be very low to 79 per cent among those who judge it to be very high. Conversely, those who give it a very low reliability rating are four times more likely than those who give it a very high rating to be voluntary Euro-specific abstainers. Given that ensuring the responsiveness of European decision-making is a fundamental function of the Parliament and given that, as shown in Figure 5.5 above, only 39 per

TABLE 5.10. *Type of electoral participation/abstention by perception of reliability of the European Parliament (non-compulsory voting countries only) (%)*

Type of electoral participation/abstention	Perceived reliability of the European Parliament				
	Don't know	Very low (1, 2)	Fairly low (3–5)	Fairly high (6–8)	Very high (9, 10)
Euro-voter	60	61	67	75	79
Circumstantial Euro-specific abstainer	9	7	10	10	8
Circumstantial Euro-and-national abstainer	4	2	3	3	4
Voluntary Euro-specific abstainer	17	20	15	9	5
Voluntary Euro-and-national abstainer	11	11	6	4	4
N	884	1,037	3,002	2,766	465

Source: EB 41.1.

cent give the Parliament a fairly or very high rating on this function, there would seem to be some scope for improving turnout in the European Parliament elections by persuading the voters that the Parliament is capable of defending their interests. Whether attempts at such persuasion are likely to succeed or not depends in large measure on how the electorate responds to the parties, the candidates, and the European election campaign. These matters are examined in Chapter 6.

6

Parties, Candidates, and Campaigns

INTRODUCTION

In reviewing existing research on turnout in general Chapter 1 provided a brief summary of the rational choice approach to the matter. This chapter analyses one of the key concepts of that approach, namely that of 'party differential'. Elections are, by definition, processes of choice. Parties are the main objects of that choice. The voter has, however, to make two decisions: which party to choose and, prior to that, whether or not to vote. In the rational choice approach, parties and the perceived differences between them figure prominently in both decisions. According to the classic formulation of the approach, 'Each citizen in our model . . . compares the utility income[1] he believes he would receive were each party in office. In a two-party system . . . [t]he difference between these two expected utility incomes is the citizen's *expected party differential*. If it is positive, he votes for the incumbents; if it is negative, he votes for the opposition; if it is zero, he abstains' (Downs 1957: 38–9). One should add that, depending on the electoral system, citizens may have varying opportunities to choose between candidates. Accordingly, they may also have a candidate differential and this too may play a role in their decisions on whether and how to vote.

In short, party and candidate differentials can be expected to play a crucial role in the explanation of turnout. Applied to the problem of turnout in European Parliament elections, this approach enables one to restate the second-order election explanation in more general (and

[1] For Downs, utility income is a broad concept, broad enough indeed to encompass altruism: 'It is possible for a citizen to receive utility from events that are only remotely connected to his own material income. For example, some citizens would regard their utility incomes as raised if the government raised taxes upon them in order to distribute free food to starving Chinese. There can be no simple identification of "acting for one's own greatest benefit" with selfishness in the narrow sense because self-denying charity is often a great source of benefit to oneself. Thus our model leaves room for altruism in spite of its basic reliance upon the self-interest axiom' (Downs 1957: 37).

more testable) terms. The central concept of the second-order election model is that, in such an election, there is less at stake. Translated into Downsian terms, this means that party and candidate differentials would be lower and such lower differentials would appear to provide a ready-made explanation of low turnout in European Parliament elections. As Reif and Schmitt put it, 'since less is at stake in second-order elections, fewer voters may consider them sufficiently important to cast ballots' (Reif and Schmitt 1980: 9). The hypothesized 'less at stake' feature of second-order elections can be operationalized by the *difference* between party and candidate differentials in European and national elections. This provides at least a partial measure of the extent to which the European electorates see these elections as second order and makes it possible to test the explanation of low turnout put forward by the model.

PARTY AND CANDIDATE DIFFERENTIALS AND THE SECOND-ORDER ELECTION MODEL

A majority of potential voters approach European Parliament elections with a discernible party differential, i.e. they attach a significant degree of importance to the outcome of the election in party terms; as Figure 6.1 shows, two-thirds of them have either a fairly high (6 to 8) or a very high (9 to 10) score on a ten-point scale which measures how much the voters think it matters which parties win more or fewer seats in such an election. Conversely, only 27 per cent fall below the midpoint on the scale (a further 7 per cent say they do not know). To a greater or lesser degree, depending on the electoral system, elections, including European ones, are also about electing candidates to seats in a parliament. The present study includes a measure of 'candidate differential', i.e. how much it matters to the voter which candidates win or lose seats as a result of the election. Despite the fact that, as we shall see in Chapter 7, candidates receive very little or no emphasis in some of the electoral systems used in European Parliament elections, the candidate dimension is just as important as the party dimension from the voters' point of view: as Figure 6.1 shows, the distribution of responses is almost identical on both scales. Apart from what it shows about how voters regard the candidate issue in European Parliament elections, this finding has

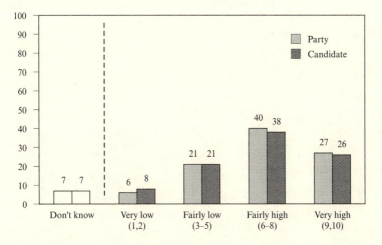

F IG. 6.1. Party and candidate differentials at European Parliament elections
Source: EB 41.1.

important implications for how one interprets the data on European party differentials. It could perhaps have been argued that, when respondents indicate that it matters which party wins more or fewer seats in European Parliament elections, they are simply seeing the European outcome in terms of the national balance of power between the parties. This would mean that their European party differential is really a national party differential. The fact that they are equally concerned about the outcome of the election in candidate terms, despite the fact that this has little or no national repercussions, suggests that differentials at European elections may not be reducible to a concern about the implications for the outcome of the domestic political struggle.[2]

While these party and candidate differentials in European Parliament elections look impressive enough, the key point of the second-order election model is a relative one: second-order status requires that there be *less* at stake than in a first-order (national) election. As noted above, when considered at the level of the voters, this becomes a requirement that there be a widespread *perception* that less is at

---

[2] The possibility that European party differentials are merely a surrogate for party preferences in the national arena will be examined later in this chapter.

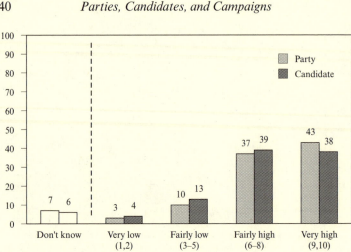

FIG. 6.2. Party and candidate differentials at national elections
Source: EB 41.1.

stake. A first impression of whether this requirement is met can be obtained by comparing the distribution of party and candidate differentials at European and national elections. It is true that very high party differentials are more widespread at national elections: 43 per cent of the electorate attach a high degree of importance to the party outcome in national elections, compared to 27 per cent who do so in the case of European elections (Figures 6.1 and 6.2). However, this 16 percentage point gap is the only real difference between the two; apart from this, the distributions of European and national party differentials are not strikingly different. And, because candidate differentials are slightly less important than party differentials in national elections, the gap between the proportions with very high candidate differentials at European and national elections is only 12 percentage points.

By focusing on the relationship between European and national party differentials for each individual voter (i.e. by subtracting the respondent's score on the national party differential scale from his or her score on the European party differential scale), one can test the central assumption of the second-order model more directly. This shows that more than half of the European electorate regards the matter of which party wins or loses seats as being of equal importance whether the election be a national or a European one. A further 21 per

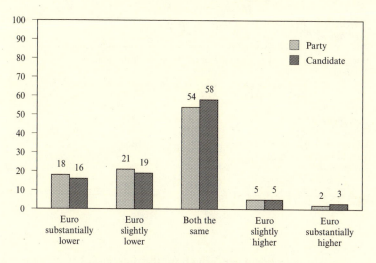

F IG. 6.3. Difference between European
and national party and candidate differentials
Source: EB 41.1.

cent see the party outcome as being marginally less important (a
difference of one or two points on a ten-point scale) at European
elections. The perception that there is *substantially* less at stake in
European Parliament elections (a difference of three points or more)
is found among only 18 per cent of potential voters; it seems un-
warranted to conclude from this that European elections are seen by
the electorate as second-order. As Figure 6.3 also shows, identical
European and national candidate differentials actually occur with
marginally greater frequency: 58 per cent regard the candidate
outcome of the two kinds of elections as being of the same degree of
importance, while only 16 per cent see the candidate outcome of
European Parliament elections as being substantially less important.

The implications of these findings for the application of the second-
order election model to European Parliament elections can be briefly
summarized. First, the great majority of voters do not have either the
absolute or relative power perceptions required by the second-order
election model (see Chapter 5). Secondly, party differentials in European Parliament elections are more widespread and, more importantly, their distribution is more akin to that of party differentials in
national elections than the model suggests. Thirdly, electors also

TABLE 6.1. *European party differential by perceived power of the European Parliament (%)*

European party differential	Perceived power of European Parliament				
	Very high (9, 10)	Fairly high (6–8)	Fairly low (3–5)	Very low (1, 2)	Don't know
Very high (9, 10)	52	28	24	27	19
Fairly high (6–8)	24	49	41	26	23
Fairly low (3–5)	13	17	25	24	14
Very low (1, 2)	7	2	6	18	5
Don't know	5	4	4	4	39
N	1,334	4,356	4,566	991	1,238

Source: EB 41.1.

show fairly widespread concern about the outcome of the election in candidate terms. Fourthly, and perhaps most damagingly, the connection between the power of the Parliament and what is at stake in the election, a connection that is fundamental to the model, is not, by and large, made by the electorate: a majority of those who see the Parliament as having little or no power do not draw what might be described as the 'second-order conclusion' that there is little or nothing at stake. While the above evidence casts considerable doubt on the applicability of the second-order election model to European Parliament elections, the ultimate test of the model as an explanation of turnout in these elections is whether those who believe that there is less at stake in European as compared with national elections are more likely to abstain. This question will be taken up in the final section of this chapter and again in Chapter 8.

In the meantime the role of the election campaign as one possible source of European party and candidate differentials must be considered. Given the low regard in which the campaigns for European Parliament elections are usually held, this seems unlikely; nonetheless, the issue is worth exploring, particularly as it both provides an opportunity to determine what else, if anything, is affected by the campaign and is a necessary preliminary to examining the effect of the campaign and of party and candidate differentials on turnout. In order to pursue these questions, it is first necessary to identify the extent to which the campaign was experienced by the electorate as a whole and by the electorates in each of the member states.

CAMPAIGN EXPOSURE

To assess how the campaign was experienced by European electorates, the following question was asked: 'At the European election we have just had, the parties and candidates campaigned for votes. Did the campaigns come to your attention in any of the following ways?' The interviewer then read out a list of six campaign channels, obtaining the voter's response to each. This provides a measure of the success of the campaigns in getting across to potential voters and an indication of the means by which this was accomplished. The channel most frequently identified as the one through which the campaign came to people's attention was 'coverage of the campaign on TV and radio' (61 per cent). Newspaper coverage comes substantially behind (at 36 per cent) and was closely matched by some mechanisms more directly related to the efforts of the parties and the candidates, such as election leaflets (identified by 39 per cent) and advertising (36 per cent). The process of a two-step flow of communication, which is often mentioned in the context of political campaigning, is indeed found to be valid for a sizeable minority: 24 per cent say that the campaign had come to their attention through 'family, friends or acquaintances discussing the European election'. The sixth mechanism for communicating with voters or mobilizing the vote ('party workers called to your home to ask for votes') was at the very bottom of the list (5 per cent). Across the Union as a whole, one elector in six had no exposure to the campaign, or at least no exposure through any of the channels identified in Table 6.2.

Considerable variations in this general picture appear when campaign exposure is examined at national level, however. The outer limits of campaign penetration can be assessed by examining the inverse of the proportion of respondents who stated that the campaign did not come to their attention in any of the ways mentioned (see Table 6.2). Very high levels of campaign penetration (about 95 per cent) are found in Denmark, Germany, Greece, and Ireland; at the bottom of the range are Belgium (77 per cent), France (69 per cent), and Spain (64 per cent). Exposure to the most pervasive mechanism (TV/radio coverage) varied from upwards of three-quarters of voters (Denmark, Greece, Germany, and Portugal) to less than half (France, Belgium, and Spain). The penetration of newspaper coverage varied even more, ranging from high levels of penetration of 72 per cent in

TABLE 6.2. Channels of campaign exposure by country (countries ranked from left to right in descending order of maximum extent of campaign penetration) (%)

	DK	GE (W)	GE (E)	IR	NI	GR	GB	EC12	PO	LU	IT	NL	BE	FR	SP
Party workers called	0	3	1	44	15	3	12	**5**	5	6	5	1	2	2	9
Election leaflets received	41	38	39	85	89	16	75	**39**	20	45	39	23	44	23	16
Advertising for candidates or parties	57	68	68	61	36	29	33	**36**	23	36	26	31	33	15	17
Newspaper coverage	72	57	66	61	51	43	42	**36**	21	52	27	47	32	17	12
TV/Radio coverage	87	75	79	68	57	85	68	**61**	73	53	59	53	43	47	34
Family/friends, etc., discuss	43	29	29	33	23	48	22	**24**	16	26	23	20	20	19	15
None of the above/DK	3	4	3	3	5	6	9	**17**	13	16	19	18	23	31	36
Maximum extent of campaign penetration	97	96	97	97	96	95	91	**84**	87	84	82	82	77	69	64
N	979	1,052	1,024	930	291	937	1,015	**12,480**	948	483	984	968	946	981	942

Source: EB 41.1.

Denmark, 66 per cent in former East Germany, 61 per cent in Ireland, and 57 per cent in West Germany to lows of 17 per cent in France and 12 per cent in Spain. Political advertising appears to have a substantial reach in only three countries—Germany (68 per cent), Ireland (61 per cent), and Denmark (57 per cent); in the other member states it touches one-third of the population or less, in some cases far less, for example 17 per cent in Spain and 15 per cent in France.

While the ranking of countries on exposure to three of the four main campaign channels (television, newspapers, and advertising) corresponds to the overall ranking, with Denmark, Germany, and Ireland towards the top and Belgium, France, and Spain towards the bottom, there are different styles of campaigning in different countries with respect to the other channels. Thus, the distribution of campaign leaflets reaches almost saturation point in Ireland (85 per cent) and is extremely widespread in Britain (75 per cent), but achieves very low coverage (one-quarter to one-sixth) in France, the Netherlands, Portugal, Greece, and Spain, and moderate levels of coverage (about 40 per cent) elsewhere, including Denmark and Germany. Canvassing in European Parliament elections—party workers calling to people's homes to ask for votes—is the most distinctive channel, being almost unique to Ireland, where it reaches 44 per cent of voters; it plays some small part in Northern Ireland (15 per cent), Britain (12 per cent), and Spain (9 per cent) but is virtually unknown, in European Parliament elections at any rate, in other countries. Finally, the incidence of discussions of the election with family, friends, and acquaintances, something that would tend to amplify the public debate and the campaign, was most widespread in Greece (48 per cent) and Denmark (43 per cent) but occurred at a notably lower rate in other member states.

Campaign exposure can also be looked at in qualitative terms, by taking account of the level of citizen involvement implied by the various channels. Thus, reading about the election in the newspapers and discussing the election with family and friends can be seen as more active ways of attending to the election than, for example, being contacted by party workers or receiving election leaflets, or even noticing advertisements, hearing about the campaign on the radio, or watching coverage of it on television. On the basis of these distinctions respondents can be divided into four categories of campaign exposure: 'none'—those who did not experience the campaign through any of the channels mentioned; 'passive'—those whose exposure to

TABLE 6.3. *Type of campaign exposure by country, ranked from left to right in*

	DK	GE(E)	GR	IR	GE(W)	LU	NI
Fully active	36 ⌉	23 ⌉	24 ⌉	30 ⌉	22 ⌉	17 ⌉	15 ⌉
	80	**71**	**69**	**66**	**64**	**63**	**58**
Partially active	44 ⌋	48 ⌋	45 ⌋	37 ⌋	41 ⌋	46 ⌋	43 ⌋
Passive	16	24	25	29	31	19	36
None	4	5	6	5	5	18	6
N	979	1,024	937	930	1,052	482	291

Source: EB 41.1.

the campaign was limited to being contacted by party workers, receiving election leaflets, or seeing or listening to advertising or radio or television coverage; 'partially active'—those who experienced the campaign through involvement in one active channel (either reading about it in the newspaper or discussing it with family, friends, and acquaintances); and 'fully active'—those who experienced the campaign in both these ways.

This makes it possible to identify two minority groups of equal size at either end of the spectrum, the one in six who had no exposure at all and the one in six who had fully active exposure (see Table 6.3). The majority of the European electorate lies in the middle, and includes slightly less than a third who are passive recipients of campaign messages and slightly more than a third who are partially active agents in the process. If the countries are ranked on the basis of both the partially and the fully active, the two extremes remain the same, Denmark and Spain, but there are also some changes: Britain moves down the ranking and becomes clearly distinct from the countries which have high campaign exposure as measured in this way; so does Portugal, where a remarkably high level of passive campaign exposure leaves little space for active involvement.

Where there is compulsory voting, the campaign does not matter in so far as turnout is concerned. Belgium was below average on almost all of the channels of communication and one-quarter of its electorate did not experience the campaign in any of the ways mentioned; yet, Belgium had over 90 per cent turnout. As they can rely on the law, parties in such systems do not perhaps try as hard to get the vote out. However, even where voting is not compulsory, campaign penetration is not, on the face of it, markedly correlated with turnout. France *descending order of active exposure (sum of partially and fully active) (%)*

NL	EC12	GB	IT	BE	FR	PO	SP
13	16	13	10	9	5	7	3
55	53	51	42	41	32	31	24
42	37	38	32	32	26	24	21
24	31	38	39	32	36	52	35
21	16	10	19	27	32	18	41
968	12,479	1,015	984	946	981	948	942

and Spain have very low levels of campaign penetration and moderate levels of turnout by European Parliament election standards. Ireland has a high and varied campaign penetration and, except when there are concomitant national or local elections, is found among the countries with low turnout. Denmark has the highest level of campaign exposure on any measure and has below average European Parliament election turnout and one of the largest gaps between European Parliament election and national election turnout. Thus, at the aggregate level, the relationship between campaign exposure and turnout appears far from direct. Before examining the relationship at the level of the individual, however, it is worth looking at the effects of campaigning on attitudes to integration, on perceptions of and attitudes to the Parliament, and on party differentials.

CAMPAIGN EXPOSURE AND ATTITUDES TO THE EUROPEAN UNION

In theory, a Euro-campaign should increase the level of awareness and knowledge of the European Union; it might also generate support and enthusiasm for European integration. The Maastricht Treaty specifically assigns such a role to political parties at the European level: 'Political parties at European level are important as a factor for integration within the Union. They contribute to forming a European awareness and to expressing the political will of the citizens of the Union' (*Treaty on European Union*, Article 138a). The campaign naturally should have an effect on how people view the power and the role of the Parliament; it should help to create an image of the Parliament in the minds of the public; it should convey to the public that, in the wake of the Single European Act and of the Maastricht Treaty, the Parliament now exercises substantial power and that, with its co-decision powers, its petition procedure, and its ombudsman, it provides an effective means of ensuring that the decisions made by the EU are in the interests of ordinary people; above all it should convey to the electors a reason or set of reasons why they should vote for one party rather than another or for one candidate or slate of candidates rather than another; it should, in other words, generate party and candidate differentials.

Only a panel survey could measure precisely such presumed campaign effects. Without such a panel study, the best one can do is to compare those with and without any exposure to the campaign and those with varying degrees and kinds of exposure. If one were to find no differences at all, one would be reasonably safe in concluding that the campaign had no effect; if there are differences, it is not possible to conclude that these are *due* to the campaign; the relationship could be the reverse: it may simply be that those who are more pro-integration or are more knowledgeable are more likely to pay more attention to the campaign. Probably the influence runs in both directions. Consequently, if the evidence is negative, one may conclude that campaign exposure has no effect and, if it is positive, that it *may* have had an effect.

At least one clear first conclusion does emerge: *passive* campaign exposure has no effect on attitudes to integration; the support for EU membership is 51 per cent among those with no campaign exposure and 53 per cent among those with passive exposure (see Table 6.4). Thus, being exposed to coverage of the campaign on television and radio or to advertising on behalf of candidates or parties, or being canvassed by party workers makes no discernible difference to people's attitudes to membership of the EU. Second, and on the other hand, *active* campaign exposure is somewhat related to more positive attitudes to membership: among those exposed to one of the two active channels (namely those who either read about the campaign in the newspapers or discussed the election with family, friends, or acquaintances), support for membership rises to 62 per cent and, among those exposed to the campaign through both channels, to 68 per cent. Yet, even if it were assumed that all of these contrasts were due to campaign effects, in other words, that the influence was wholly in one direction, the effects of campaigning on the generation of support for integration would still be limited. While passive exposure has no effect, active exposure has, at most, fairly minor effects on support for the EU; moreover, any effect which may exist arises from some of the uncommitted becoming supportive, not from converting those who are opposed. This picture is confirmed by looking at the relationship between campaign exposure and attitude if the EU were to be dissolved: passive exposure still has no effect. On the other hand, the (maximum) effect of active campaign exposure is slightly greater: support for the EU on this measure rises from 38 per cent among those with passive exposure to 46 per cent among those with partially active exposure, and to 56 per cent among those with fully active exposure; but all the movement also occurs here as a result of a reduction in the proportion of indifference.

As active campaign exposure is associated with lower levels of indifference vis-à-vis the process of integration, one would also expect an association between active campaign exposure and knowledge of the EU. In Table 6.4, the index of knowledge is divided into three levels: low to none, medium, and high to very high. In this case, too, passive exposure has no effect on knowledge of the EU: neither leaflets, nor advertising, nor television coverage, nor radio coverage seems to contribute anything to enhancing the voters' knowledge and understanding of the European Union: while 57 per cent of those with no campaign exposure have a level of knowledge that can only be categorized as 'low to none', the same is true for 53 per cent of those who only experienced the campaign through one or more of the passive channels. Active campaign exposure, on the other hand, is related to level of knowledge: high to very high levels of knowledge are found among 24 per cent of those with no exposure or with passive exposure, among 33 per cent of those with single channel active exposure, and among 44 per cent of those with double channel active exposure. In the case of the knowledge variable in particular, however, the point that the causation could run in both directions must be underlined; it is just as plausible that those with greater levels of knowledge pay more active attention to the campaign, as that active exposure to the campaign in and of itself increases the level of knowledge.

The relationship between campaign exposure and knowledge may even be spurious, with the apparent connection between them being due to the fact that each of these factors is influenced by the level of interest in politics. Those with a high degree of interest in politics as such might pay more attention to the European Parliament campaign and also be more knowledgeable about European affairs (and vice versa for those with little interest in politics). Thus, those respondents

TABLE 6.4. *Attitudes to European integration (membership and hypothetical dissolution) and index of EU knowledge by type of campaign exposure (%)*

	Type of campaign exposure			
	None	Passive	Partially active	Fully active
Attitude towards EU membership				
Good	51	53	62	68
Neither/DK	35	35	28	24
Bad	14	13	10	9
Attitude if EU were dissolved				
Very sorry	38	38	46	56
Indifferent/DK	51	50	43	34
Very relieved	12	12	11	10
EU knowledge index				
High to very high	24	24	33	44
Medium	19	23	21	21
Low to none	57	53	45	36
N	1,970	3,914	4,568	2,022

Source: EB 41.1.

with active campaign exposure might be more knowledgeable without there being a connection between this exposure and an increase in knowledge. This point can be assessed, however, as one can control for the effect of interest in politics by examining separately the relationship between campaign exposure and knowledge for those with high and low interest in politics. If no difference appears between those with different degrees of exposure to the campaign but with the same degree of interest in politics, one could then conclude that the relationship between these two factors is spurious. In fact, a relationship between campaign exposure and knowledge does remain even after controlling for interest in politics, but the relationship is somewhat weaker. High levels of knowledge range from 14 to 25 per cent as campaign exposure increases from none to fully active among those with little or no interest in politics and low to zero knowledge drops from 68 to 56 per cent. In the other group—those with a moderate or high degree of interest in politics—knowledge of the EU is substantially higher but here too it is related to campaign exposure: low to zero knowledge drops from 37 to 24 per cent and high to very high knowledge increases from 42 to 55 per cent as campaign exposure increases from none to fully active exposure. In short, even taking

TABLE 6.5. *EU knowledge by type of campaign exposure by interest in politics* (%)

Level of EU knowledge	Not much interest in politics, or none				At least some interest in politics			
	Type of campaign exposure				Type of campaign exposure			
	Fully active	Partially active	Passive	None	Fully active	Partially active	Passive	None
High to very high	25	20	16	14	55	48	38	42
Medium	20	21	22	18	21	22	25	21
Low to none	56	59	63	68	24	30	37	37
N	687	2,389	2,511	1,330	1,327	2,172	1,387	638

Source: EB 41.1.

into account the fact that interest in politics leads to increases in both EU knowledge and campaign exposure, a relationship does exist between being actively exposed to the campaign and having an increased level of knowledge of the EU.

CAMPAIGN EXPOSURE AND
THE POWER AND ROLE OF THE PARLIAMENT

If the campaign appears to have, at best, only a modest impact on attitudes to and knowledge of the European Union, it may have a greater impact on attitudes to the Parliament, which is, after all, the focus of the process. Does the campaign contribute to strengthening the image of the Parliament in the minds of the electorate? Does it affect perceptions of its power and its reliability in ensuring the responsiveness of EU decision-making? There is a clear relationship between having an image of the Parliament and campaign exposure: half of those with no campaign exposure have no image of the Parliament; this is true of 43 per cent of those with passive exposure, of 34 per cent of those with one level of active exposure, and of 23 per cent of those with full active exposure to the campaign (see Table 6.6). Here, too, the influence could take place in both directions, but the evidence does at least indicate that the campaign may well make a contribution to raising the profile of the Parliament.

Yet, as can be seen from Table 6.6, exposure to the campaign does little or nothing to enhance the perception of the power of the Parliament. Those who had a fully active exposure to the campaign are not more likely than those who had no exposure to regard the Parliament as having a substantial amount of power. Traces of an association between campaign exposure and the perception that the Parliament has a fairly high degree of power do exist but the difference is slight (at most 7 percentage points). It could, of course, be argued that the campaign does not increase the citizens' sense that the European Parliament is powerful because the Parliament is, indeed, not very powerful. Yet, through the Single European Act and through the Maastricht Treaty, the Parliament acquired extensive new powers. Ideally, the existence of these powers should have been conveyed to the electorate by the 1994 campaign. The problem may well be that these powers are obscured in a complex web of special provisions and

TABLE 6.6. *Perceptions of the European Parliament by type of campaign exposure (%)*

	Type of campaign exposure			
	None	Passive	Partially active	Fully active
Image of European Parliament				
No image	50	43	34	23
Power of European Parliament				
Fairly high (6–8)	29	34	35	36
Very high (9, 10)	8	8	7	7
Reliability of European Parliament				
Fairly high (6–8)	27	31	37	42
Very high (9, 10)	6	5	6	7
Future effect of European Parliament				
Fairly high (6–8)	27	37	42	49
Very high (9, 10)	8	9	10	14
N	1,971	3,916	4,570	2,022

Source: EB 41.1.

procedures, requiring a campaign of remarkable sophistication and effectiveness to disseminate an accurate impression of the role of the Parliament among the public.

Several new powers of the Parliament, such as the appointment of a Parliamentary ombudsman and the establishment of a 'petitions' procedure, have been specifically designed to bring the Parliament closer to the people and to enhance the responsiveness of EU decision-making. Yet, as we saw in Chapter 5, only 40 per cent of the respondents feel that they can rely on the Parliament to ensure such responsiveness. The campaign appears to have only a very modest impact in this respect. While full confidence in the reliability of the Parliament is not at all affected by the amount or kind of exposure to the campaign, more limited confidence (points 6 to 8 on the scale) increases from 27 per cent among those with no campaign exposure to 42 per cent among those with fully active exposure. The campaign for the 1994 elections thus had at best only a slight effect in conveying to the public the power that the European Parliament now enjoys and the role that it plays. Moreover, whatever small effect it may have had was entirely dependent on active citizen involvement; the effect of passive exposure was, by and large, negligible. There remains, however, one hopeful straw in the wind: the campaign may have had a somewhat greater impact on the perception of the *potential* power of the Parliament. While only 35 per cent of those with no campaign exposure think that the European Parliament will have either a fairly or a very big effect on people like themselves in the future, 63 per cent of those with fully active campaign exposure held this view, as can be seen from Table 6.6.

CAMPAIGN EXPOSURE AND PARTY AND CANDIDATE DIFFERENTIALS

Important as it may be to examine whether the election campaign tended to increase support for European integration and to enhance the image of the European Parliament, the real purpose of the European campaign, as of any other election campaign, is to persuade the voters to support a particular party or candidate. The campaign must convey to the voters the impression that it matters which party or candidate wins. The 1994 campaign had only a limited success in this regard, as can be seen from Table 6.7: fairly high party differentials increase by only 5 percentage points as one moves from zero to fully active campaign exposure; very high party differentials increase by 10 points. Moreover, exposure to the campaign is not associated with the perception of fairly high candidate differentials and only modestly associated with the perception of very high candidate differentials (24 per cent of those with no campaign exposure have a very high

TABLE 6.7. *European party and candidate differentials by type of campaign exposure (%)*

| | Type of campaign exposure | | | |
	None	Passive	Partially active	Fully active
European party differential				
Fairly high (6–8)	37	39	40	42
Very high (9, 10)	26	24	28	36
European candidate differential				
Fairly high (6–8)	36	39	39	38
Very high (9, 10)	24	23	27	36
N	1,971	3,914	4,568	2,020

Source: EB 41.1.

candidate differentials, compared to 36 per cent of those with fully active exposure).

Thus, in relation to the presumed purpose of an election campaign, the 1994 campaign for the European Parliament had only a marginal effect in providing the voters with a choice that they felt mattered. It does not follow that the campaign had an equally marginal effect on turnout, it could lead to a higher turnout by reminding the voters of the existence and importance of the Parliament, by encouraging them to see the election as an opportunity to express their support for European integration as such, or, at a minimum, simply by bringing the election to their attention. Moreover, party and candidate differentials may affect turnout without being a product of the campaign. The electorate may be deaf to the current campaign appeals of the parties and candidates and still think that it matters which party or candidate wins. Furthermore, if the campaign and the existence of party differentials have independent effects on turnout, the effects may be cumulative. If this were so, turnout would be highest among those with high party differentials and active campaign exposure and lowest among those with no party differentials and no campaign exposure or only passive exposure, while those for whom these two variables were mixed (high differentials and low exposure or low differentials and high exposure) would lie in between these extremes. It is essential therefore to look at the relationship between campaign, party, and candidate differentials and turnout. However, as compulsory voting is likely to override the effect that low campaign exposure or low party differentials might have on turnout, the analysis of the relationships between the three variables will be confined to the non-compulsory voting countries only.

PARTY AND CANDIDATE DIFFERENTIALS, THE CAMPAIGN, AND PARTICIPATION

This examination of the relationship between party differentials and turnout focuses first on the merits of the second-order election explanation of turnout. The model states that turnout in second-order elections is lower because less is at stake. What is at stake in a European Parliament election, in the eyes of potential voters, can be assessed in terms of their European party differential. Fairly high party differentials are quite widespread in European Parliament

TABLE 6.8. *Type of electoral participation/abstention by difference between European and national party differentials (non-compulsory voting countries only) (%)*

Type of electoral participation/abstention	Difference between European and national party differentials				
	Euro substantially lower	Euro slightly lower	Both the same	Euro slightly higher	Euro substantially higher
Euro-voter	64	72	70	69	59
Circumstantial Euro-specific abstainer	10	10	9	11	11
Circumstantial Euro-and-national abstainer	2	2	3	3	7
Voluntary Euro-specific abstainer	18	11	12	10	15
Voluntary Euro-and-national abstainer	6	5	7	7	8
N	1,807	1,693	4,050	393	208

Source: EB 41.1.

elections, a finding that suggests that low turnout may not be due to the feeling that there is less at stake. However, the crucial test of the less-at-stake explanation consists in examining whether turnout is lower among respondents who see less at stake in European Parliament elections than they do at national elections, or, in operational terms, among respondents with a *lower* party differential at European Parliament elections *compared* to their party differential at national elections. As discussed above, the latter can be measured by subtracting each respondent's score on the national party differential scale from his or her score on the European scale. When this is done and the resulting measure is related to participation and abstention, it emerges that there is no difference in the rate of turnout between those who have a slightly lower party differential at the European level and those whose party differential is the same at both levels; among those who have a substantially lower party differential at European Parliament elections compared to national elections, turnout is a mere 6 percentage points lower than it is among those who say that what is at stake in party terms in the two elections is identical.[3] If party differentials are viewed as giving an indication of what the voters see to be at stake in an election, these findings provide little or no support for the view that turnout is lower because voters see less at stake in European than in national elections.

It is important to emphasize that although the perception that there is less at stake (a relative judgement) plays little or no role in determining turnout, the perception that the stakes are high or low (an absolute judgement) does appear to have a marked effect. As can be seen from Table 6.9, turnout rises from 48 per cent among those with a very low to zero European party differential to 78 per cent among those with a very high European party differential. Having a sense that something is at stake in the European Parliament election increases the likelihood of voting. It might seem logical to further claim that, 'there is less at stake in European Parliament elections than in national elections, therefore turnout is lower'. There is little or no evidence of this logic operating among the electorate, however. A majority feels that what is at stake in the two kinds of elections is the same and only one in five sees a substantial difference, as noted

---

[3] The results are the same in relation to candidate differentials: there is only a 5-point difference in turnout between those respondents whose European and national candidate differentials are identical and those whose European candidate differential is substantially less than their national one.

TABLE 6.9. *Type of electoral participation/abstention by European party differential (non-compulsory voting countries only) (%)*

Type of electoral participation/abstention	European party differential				
	Very low (1, 2)	Fairly low (3–5)	Fairly high (6–8)	Very high (9, 10)	Don't know
Euro-voter	48	64	73	78	50
Circumstantial Euro-specific abstainer	8	10	10	8	8
Circumstantial Euro-and-national abstainer	2	3	2	2	6
Voluntary Euro-specific abstainer	26	16	10	9	21
Voluntary Euro-and-national abstainer	16	7	4	3	15
N	602	1,726	3,205	2,058	564

Source: EB 41.1.

earlier. Moreover, as has just been shown, even the group that sees a substantial difference in what is at stake is not much less likely to vote. The electorate is influenced by what it sees to be at stake; it does not, however, make the apparently simple, but in reality highly sophist-icated, calculations required by the second-order election model. Whatever the value of the second-order model may be as an account of elite perspectives on European Parliament elections, it does not appear to correspond with the reality of European voters' perceptions and attitudes, at least not in so far as the determinants of participation and abstention are concerned. At this stage, however, this judgement must remain tentative, pending the inclusion of all the relevant variables in the multivariate analysis in Chapter 8.

In order to complete this preliminary analysis of the relationship between European party differentials and turnout, one final issue must be addressed. Could it be that the relationship between turnout and European party differentials is merely a reflection of a basic attachment to parties at the national level? On this interpretation, the real influence at work would run from party attachment to turnout and the 'European party differential' would be merely a surrogate measure of voters' feelings about their national political parties. Although there may be controversy about how it should be measured, about its applicability across systems, and about its consequences for voting choice, party attachment has been an influential concept in the study of voting behaviour and the possibility that it is the real influence at work here must be dealt with. The idea is a simple one: voters do not necessarily make a fresh party choice at each election; rather, they possess what has been variously described as a degree of affective support for, a standing decision in favour of, a sense of loyalty or feeling of closeness to, or an identification with a certain party. This influences not only their propensity to vote for the party in question but also their perceptions of politics and even the positions they adopt on issues. As noted, measurement of the concept has not been uncontroversial. The two main operationalizations of the concept of party attachment have been party identification and party closeness. The following analysis uses the latter measure, as this is the approach that has been taken to party attachment in Eurobarometer surveys since 1978.[4]

Table 6.10 shows the rate of turnout at each level of party differential *and* each of three levels of party attachment. For the interpretation that it all comes down to national party attachment to hold, there should be no differences along the rows of the table; within a given level of party attachment, European party differentials should make no difference. In fact it makes a difference at all levels of party attachment. The effect is most obvious at intermediate levels of attachment where turnout varies from 48 per cent among those with no or almost no European party differential to 79 per cent among those with a very high party differential. The range is from 40 to 62 per cent among those with no party attachment and 65 to 86 per cent among those who are very or fairly close to a party. In short, the effect of

[4] Within the Eurobarometer there are significant differences in the wording of the party-attachment question, mainly between a relative closeness question ('do you feel closer to one party than to the others?') and an absolute closeness question ('do you feel close to any particular party?'). An ordinal form of the question has been asked in Germany and between 1989 and 1994 in Spain and a quite different form of party attachment question has been asked in Denmark. It can be shown that these different wordings affect the levels of party attachment elicited. The present research, taking place as it did within the context of the Eurobarometer, had to adopt the basic Eurobarometer question format, including its cross-country variations. The comparative difficulties have, however, been overcome in this study by the insertion of a supplementary question asking all respondents who gave a negative answer to the initial question whether they 'feel a little closer to one of the parties than to the others'. This supplementary question provides the data required to construct a functionally equivalent measure of the overall levels of party attachment across all twelve member states. For a discussion of the methodological issues involved see Sinnott (1998).

TABLE 6.10. *Type of electoral participation/abstention by European party differential by party attachment (non-compulsory voting countries only) (%)*

Party attachment	European party differential				
	Very low (1, 2)	Fairly low (3–5)	Fairly high (6–8)	Very high (9, 10)	Don't know
Very/fairly close	65	72	82	86	70
Merely a sympathizer/a little closer to one party	48	65	74	79	52
None	40	55	60	62	42

Note: Entries are the percentage voting in the European Parliament election in each category of party attachment.

Source: EB 41.1.

European party differentials on turnout cannot be reduced to increases in turnout arising from the voters' attachment to parties at the national level.

Exposure to the campaign is also associated with higher turnout. The increments in turnout from one level of exposure to the next may not be very large but, overall, there is a 23 percentage point difference in turnout between those with no campaign exposure and those with fully active exposure. This, however, is clearly a case in which the relationship could be spurious, as both turnout and exposure could be a function of interest in politics. This can be readily assessed: if the increase in turnout with increasing campaign exposure is merely due to increased levels of political interest, there should be no relationship between exposure and turnout among those with similar levels of interest in politics. For those with at least some interest in politics, the campaign has indeed very little effect: turnout is 76 per cent among those with no campaign exposure and 85 per cent among those with fully active exposure (see Table 6.12). Among those with 'not much' or no interest in politics, however, the relationship between exposure and turnout is marked: it rises from 49 per cent among those with no campaign exposure to 72 per cent among those with fully active exposure. In short, campaign exposure appears to make a difference to the rate of participation, but only among those with less interest in politics: those who are interested in politics turn out to vote more or less regardless of their exposure to the campaign.

Of course, the impact of the campaign on turnout is related to

TABLE 6.11. *Type of electoral participation/abstention by type of campaign exposure (non-compulsory voting countries only) (%)*

Type of electoral participation/abstention	Type of campaign exposure			
	None	Passive	Partially active	Fully active
Euro-voter	58	64	71	81
Circumstantial Euro-specific abstainer	9	10	10	7
Circumstantial Euro-and-national abstainer	5	3	2	2
Voluntary Euro-specific abstainer	17	15	12	8
Voluntary Euro-and-national abstainer	11	8	5	2
N	1,214	2,541	2,988	1,410

Source: EB 41.1.

a range of other variables as well. For example, we have seen that campaign exposure is related to modest increases in European party differentials. The question then is: do the effects of these variables on turnout simply overlap or are they cumulative? In the latter case, turnout would be lowest among those with no campaign exposure and little or no party differential and highest among those with fully active campaign exposure and a very high party differential. Table 6.13 confirms this expectation: turnout rises from 36 per cent among the former to 91 per cent among the latter. *Within* each level of campaign exposure, turnout increases with increases in perceived party differentials; except in the case of respondents with fully active campaign exposure, increases tend to be largest as one moves through the first grade of party differential, i.e. from very low to fairly low, and to taper off at the top of the scale. *Between* the different levels of exposure, the pattern is more uneven; there is little difference between zero and passive exposure, no matter what the level of party differential, differences are larger as one moves between passive and partially active exposure and are most noticeable between those with partially active and fully active exposure, especially for those with lower levels of party differential.

Party and candidate differentials at European Parliament elections are widespread; their distribution is not markedly different from the distribution of national party and candidate differentials; and

TABLE 6.12. *Type of electoral participation/abstention by type of campaign exposure by interest in politics (non-compulsory voting countries only) (%)*

Type of electoral participation/abstention	Not much interest in politics, or none				At least some interest in politics			
	Type of campaign exposure				Type of campaign exposure			
	None	Passive	Partially active	Fully active	None	Passive	Partially active	Fully active
Euro-voter	49	58	65	72	76	74	78	85
Circumstantial Euro-specific abstainer	9	10	10	9	9	9	10	6
Circumstantial Euro-and-national abstainer	6	4	3	2	3	2	1	1
Voluntary Euro-specific abstainer	21	17	15	12	10	12	9	6
Voluntary Euro-and-national abstainer	15	10	8	5	2	3	3	1
N	801	1,556	1,441	419	413	982	1,542	988

Source: EB 41.1.

TABLE 6.13. *European electoral participation by European party differential and type of campaign exposure (non-compulsory voting countries only) (%)*

Type of campaign exposure	European party differential				
	Very low (1, 2)	Fairly low (3–5)	Fairly high (6–8)	Very high (9, 10)	Don't know
None	36	53	64	69	38
Passive	42	62	70	73	50
Partially active	53	65	76	79	57
Fully active	62	77	80	91	71

Note: Entries are the percentage voting in the European Parliament election in each category of exposure/party differential.

Source: EB 41.1.

relatively few potential voters judge that there is substantially less at stake at European Parliament elections than at national elections. Those who do are not markedly less likely to vote in the European Parliament election. These findings provide little support for attempting to explain abstention in European Parliament elections in terms of the second-order election model. Meanwhile, the campaign for the European Parliament, exposure to which varies widely between the member states, has some effect on the perception that the party outcome of the elections matters, but the effect is limited. Likewise, there is some evidence that the campaign may affect attitudes to integration but the magnitude of this effect falls well short of fulfilling the mission given to the parties by the Maastricht Treaty. Both party differentials and campaign affect turnout; in particular, their combined effect is substantial: at the extremes it more than doubles the rate of turnout (from 36 to 91 per cent). Yet, it must be remembered that the factors influencing turnout examined in this chapter are part of a complex set of factors that together boost or decrease turnout; these multivariate effects will be considered in Chapter 8. Meanwhile, the variations in campaign exposure identified in the present chapter are a timely reminder that one is not dealing with a single homogeneous European electorate but with (in 1994) twelve different electorates operating in twelve different competitive contexts. These national variations are the subject matter of the next chapter.

7

Turnout in Context:
A Comparison of Member States

INTRODUCTION

There are two aspects to the puzzle posed by turnout at European
Parliament elections. One is its low overall level relative to turnout in
national elections—an average difference of 20 percentage points
across the Union as a whole in the four elections between 1979
and 1994. Much of the discussion in the previous chapters has been
devoted to the sources and implications of this discrepancy; this
exploration will be taken up again in the following chapter, as it is
essential to look at the combined effect of the variables that have been
examined separately so far and thus build a composite picture of
the factors affecting participation. Meanwhile, the other aspect of
abstention at European elections must be considered, namely the
enormous variations that exist *between* the member states. While 91
per cent of the electors voted in Belgium in 1994, only 36 per cent did
so in the United Kingdom, the Netherlands, or Portugal. It is to the
examination of these inter-country variations that this chapter is
devoted. In order to highlight the problem, the countries will be
considered in three groups of four as defined by their positions in the
ranking of turnout in the European Parliament elections of 1994. The
three groups are, in descending order of turnout between the groups
and within each group: (1) Belgium, Luxembourg, Italy, and Greece;
(2) Germany, Spain, Denmark, and France; (3) Ireland, the United
Kingdom, the Netherlands, and Portugal. As it happens, this grouping is very close to the one that would be arrived at by categorizing the
countries in terms of presence or absence of compulsory voting and
Sunday voting; the only difference would be that Portugal and
Denmark would be swapped between groups two and three. This

concordance tells us something about the institutional sources of high and low turnout. However, since these and other institutional factors (concurrent national or regional elections and proportionality of the electoral system) have been discussed in Chapter 2 and since the precise weight of their impact will be considered in Chapter 8, there is no need to deal with them again in the present chapter, though the arrangements in this regard in each country are noted in the appropriate place in the tables.

This chapter broadens the scope of institutional comparisons to include other aspects of the electoral system and deals also with aspects of the context of the elections whose potential effect cannot be ruled out. Thus the configuration of the party systems and the significance of parties for the voters may well account for some of the differences in turnout among countries. Moreover, the positions adopted by the parties in relation to European unification and the nature and intensity of the campaigns they conducted seem prima facie likely to have some impact on the public and therefore potentially result in higher or lower rates of abstention. Accordingly, in this consideration of country differences, it will be necessary to look at the presence or absence of Europe-related conflicts in the party system, at the campaigns at national level and at the broad political culture of European integration in each country.

Within each of the three groups of countries, country analyses are articulated in the same four sections. The first section looks at various indicators of turnout and at the way abstention is distributed across countries between its European and national components and between its circumstantial and voluntary components. The second section examines country differences in terms of the institutional context in which the election in each country took place. A third section considers aspects of the political context of the election ranging from structural aspects of the national party systems to the specifics of the campaign for European elections in each of the countries of the Union. The fourth section returns to the attitudes of citizens vis-à-vis the construction of Europe that were analysed in earlier chapters, this time focusing, however, on individual countries, in order to assess how far these attitudes vary from one member state to another. The chapter concludes with some reflections on the implications for our understanding of variations in European Parliament election turnout.

HIGH TURNOUT COUNTRIES:
BELGIUM, LUXEMBOURG, ITALY,
AND GREECE

Turnout and abstention

Despite the fact that all four countries in this first group have or have recently had compulsory voting, turnout varies quite substantially between a pair with very high participation and a pair with rather lower participation (Belgium and Luxembourg having 91 and 89 per cent turnout respectively, on the one hand, compared to Italy and Greece with 75 per cent and 72 per cent respectively, on the other). Although European Parliament election turnout fell in both Italy and Greece in 1994, the contrast between these two pairs of countries is not new but is reflected in the average European turnout between 1979 and 1994 (see Table 7.1). Italy and Greece are also distinctive in this group of four high-turnout countries in regard to the gap between turnout in the most recent European election and in the previous national election: while this gap was 2 per cent in Belgium and zero in Luxembourg,[1] it was 11 per cent in Italy and 10 per cent in Greece.

When it occurs, abstention in all four countries is likely to be circumstantial, overwhelmingly likely to be so in Greece, where voluntary abstention appears, on the basis of these data, to be virtually non-existent. Deliberate abstainers formed slightly over a quarter of all abstainers (or 1 and 1.6 per cent of the respondents respectively) in Luxembourg and Belgium. The Italian findings are appreciably different, both in overall proportions and in the extent to which they affected specifically European elections. Eleven per cent of the Italian sample stated that they abstained—over twice the proportion of reported abstainers in the other three samples; of these, almost three-quarters (nearly 8 per cent of the sample) abstained at Euro-elections only. Moreover, deliberate abstention is noticeably higher than in the other three countries of the group: 26 per cent of the abstentions come from deliberate abstainers at European elections only and a further 16 per cent from deliberate abstainers at European elections who had previously abstained at national elections (see Table 7.1). These deliberate Italian abstainers constituted 5 per cent of the Italian

---

[1] The lack of any difference in the case of Luxembourg is not surprising, since the elections were concurrent.

TABLE 7.1. *Patterns of turnout and abstention by member state (%)*

	BE	LU	IT	GR	GE (W)	GE	GE (E)	SP	DK	FR	IR	GB	NL	PO	EU
Actual turnout															
EP election 1994 (EPE94)	91	89	75	72	60	60	62	59	53	53	44	36	36	36	58
Change since 1989	0	1	-6	-8	-2	n.a.	n.a.	5	7	4	-24	0	-12	-16	-4
EP elections 1979-94	91	88	81	77	61	61	62	61	50	55	56	34	48	53	63
Last national election (NE) (prior to EPE94)	93	89	86	82	79	78	75	77	82	86	69	78	78	68	78
Gap between EPE94 and last NE	-2	0	-11	-10	-19	-18	-12	-18	-29	-33	-25	-41	-43	-33	-20
Reported EP abstention (as proportion of abstainers)															
Circumstantial Euro-specific	50	0	47	35	22	22	21	26	39	24	31	36	29	32	31
Circumstantial Euro-and-national	22	74	12	62	5	4	1	14	2	15	8	9	6	12	10
Voluntary Euro-specific	9	0	26	3	46	49	59	34	50	34	42	38	49	40	40
Voluntary Euro-and-national	20	26	16	0	27	25	19	27	9	27	20	18	17	16	20

sample—not a large proportion by comparison with those found in other member states of the European Union, but yet a significant one. Thus, while the idea that voting was compulsory probably lingered on, it must already have begun to be felt less binding: abstention may well increase somewhat in the future at European elections, as it already did at the national parliamentary election of 1996.

Institutional context

In addition to having compulsory voting and voting on a Sunday, all four high-turnout countries have PR systems for European Parliament elections, but with significant variations. Greece and Luxembourg have national lists; Italy and Belgium have regional lists, in the latter case the regional lists coinciding with linguistic areas. The distance between Euro-parliamentarians and electors is thus greater in Greece (with lists of 25 names) than even in Italy (where the average number of seats per region is 17), let alone in Belgium and Luxembourg. Except in Greece, preferential systems exist, with varying consequences, the effect being small in Belgium. The proportionality attendant on the different (national) electoral systems also varies, being high in Belgium and Luxembourg and lower in Italy and Greece. Finally, in terms of differences in the institutional context of the 1994 European Parliament election, the position of the European election relative to national elections varies very considerably across these four states. Luxembourg is the extreme case where, because of the regular concurrence of national and European Parliament elections, the position of the European Parliament election relative to the national election was exceptional on two counts: it took place a full five years after the 1989 national (and European) election and it coincided with the 1994 national election. In Belgium, the time since the last national election was above the European average (31 months as compared to 24 months); in Greece and Italy it was very much below average (8 months and 3 months respectively) (see Table 7.2).

Political context of the election: national and European aspects

Party systems also differ. Greece and Luxembourg have a small number of large parties: Greece was even close to having a two-party system during most of the 1980s, while Luxembourg remained effectively a two-and-a-half party system. Both party systems had moderate volatility throughout the 1980s. Belgium and Italy, on the other hand, both have a large number of parties, thirteen and sixteen respectively in the Parliament in existence in 1994, although the number of 'effective' parties is only, also respectively, eight and seven. The level of voter volatility is high in Belgium and Italy, at 10.1 and 8.7 respectively. There are substantial differences between the real characteristics of the party systems of these two countries, however: the large number of Belgian parties has more a symbolic than a practical effect; despite their split on linguistic lines, the major parties continue to collaborate in government or in opposition almost as in the past. Thus the traditional Belgian two-and-a-half party system model of the 1950s and 1960s has not entirely ceased to be realistic; in Italy, on the other hand, the fractionalization of the party system grew gradually throughout the post-Second World War period: the events of the early 1990s contributed to increasing rather than decreasing this trend, although this had been expected to be checked by the (partial) introduction of a majority electoral system. The real division among the four countries of the group from the point of view of the structure of the party system is thus between Italy and the others. Party attachment differs appreciably among the four countries: it is very high in Greece (80 per cent), but, somewhat surprisingly, it is lower in Belgium (60 per cent) and Luxembourg (66 per cent) than in Italy, where it is about average (72 per cent), despite the near-collapse of the whole party system that occurred in the early 1990s in that country.

The truly significant parties of the four countries are very favourable to European integration, including in Greece, at least since the mid-1980s. Yet this overt consensus covers some undercurrents of opposition. Whether these differences actually emerged as part of the context of the 1994 European election can only be ascertained by examining the situation country by country.

In Belgium, opposition has occasionally emerged among marginal parties: since the 1990s, this opposition has manifested itself through the Flemish nationalistic Vlaams Blok (van Deelen 1996: 42). However, the 1994 campaign in Belgium has been described as 'low key and almost dull. It was undramatic and at times barely perceptible . . . The campaign was affected, not to say dominated by national issues' (Fitzmaurice 1994: 331); this author continues (332): 'Belgium almost more than any other member-State, has shown a passive, permissive elite-level consensus about European issues in the past. Europe has served Belgium well, economically and politically. It was an article of faith that was never questioned or examined but, equally, never updated.' Van Deelen adds (1996: 42): 'Central in the campaign were concrete policy areas in which the European Union should act, such as the fight against the economic recession and unemployment. . . . It was in the specific discussion of policy areas that differences between parties surfaced.' In summary, Belgium, or more accurately, Flanders does have an anti-EU option in the party system but, in 1994, this could at most be described as a weak feature of the context of the election.

In Luxembourg, the main parties are solidly pro-European Union, though the Communist party has not shared this enthusiasm. When it came to the election itself, however, because elections for the European Parliament are held on the same day as national elections, 'the campaign concentrated as usual almost entirely upon a range of domestic issues' (Hearl 1994: 352). On the other hand, it was noted that 'most parties stressed the necessity of the European Monetary Union, a social Europe, a European army and a political union'; but they stressed 'also stronger links between the national parliament and the European parliament' (van Deelen 1996: 52).

Italy also has residual anti-European options in the party system: at a minimum, the position of the right-wing National Alliance was, in 1994 at least, somewhat ambiguous as was that of the reconstructed Communist party ('Rifondazione'), which inherited some of the uncertain views about European integration that had characterized the Italian CP in earlier years. Meanwhile, however, Italy was regarded as being too occupied with internal politics and the new party system to generate a debate on Europe (Irwin 1995: 187). The campaign has been characterized as 'a low-key affair focused primarily on domestic issues and themes . . . The parties paid lip-service to European issues but only debated those issues such as market deregulation and a social Europe which had a resonance on domestic political divisions' (Daniels 1996: 143).

The Greek Socialist party was somewhat ambivalent towards European integration in 1994, though it did change afterwards under the leadership of Simitis. The largely Communist extreme-left is opposed to it. The 1994 campaign has been described as 'very low-key' and 'dull', a dullness which was interrupted only by two events, an assassination attempt against three Communist candidates and a

Supreme Court ban against a Macedonian minority party (Dimitras 1994: 344). 'On most major issues concerning the European Union's future, [the main parties] were roughly in agreement, although with some differences in emphasis', while the Communists advocated a complete Greek withdrawal (Verney and Featherstone 1996: 113). Overall, 'domestic concerns continued to be central, with much speculation about possible developments within the two big parties' (ibid. 114). Thus of these four countries, at a stretch only Greece and perhaps Belgium could be said to have fallen into an intermediate category in terms of the presence of an anti-EU current in the 1994 election: in the other two, neither the campaign nor the underlying party system had any discernible European content.

Overall campaign penetration was well above average in Greece and lower than average in Belgium; measured in terms of *active* attention to the campaign, however, Italy joins Belgium in the below average category. High European party differentials were substantially more widespread in the two countries with high active campaign attention—Luxembourg and Greece, where two-thirds of the electorate paid active attention to the campaign and where high European party differentials were found among 39 and 46 per cent of the electorate respectively. Greece was distinctive in another respect: the perception of substantial candidate differentials in the European election in Greece was as frequent as the perception of substantial party differentials and was in fact the highest in the Union; this is all the more remarkable given that the Greek electoral system makes no provision for candidate choice (see Table 7.2).

The political culture of European integration

By and large, the citizens of the four countries with high turnout find themselves in a political environment favourable to the European Union. Yet this does not prevent these citizens from displaying substantial differences towards the construction of Europe, not all of them being in expected directions.

Belgium

Belgium provides most surprises among these four countries. The support of its citizens is almost entirely passive, as if Belgians accept the European Union simply because it happens to exist. This

TABLE 7.2. *Context and features of the European Parliament elections 1994, by member state (%)*

	BE	LU	IT	GR	GE (W)	GE (E)	GE	SP	DK	FR	IR	GB	NL	PO	EU
Institutional contextual aspects															
Compulsory voting	Yes	Yes	Yes	Yes			No	No	No	No	No	No	No	No	Var
Weekday/Sunday voting	Sun	Sun	Sun	Sun			Sun	Sun	Wk	Sun	Wk	Wk	Wk	Sun	Var
Electoral system	RL	NL	RL	NL			NL	NL	NL	NL	STV	FPP	NL	NL	Var
Number of constituencies	3	1	5	1			1	1	1	1	4	84	1	1	10.5
Constituency size (seats)	8.3	6	17.4	25			99	64	16	87	3.8	1	31	25	5.4
Choice of candidate within party	Yes	Yes	Yes	No			No	No	Yes	No	Yes	No	Yes	No	Var
Prominence of candidate on ballot	Lo	Hi	Hi	Lo			Lo	Med	Hi	Lo	Hi	Hi	Lo	Med	Var
Proportionality (national elections)	Ho	Hi	Lo	Lo			Hi	Med	Hi	Lo	Hi	Lo	Hi	Med	Med
National political context															
Number of parties in national parliament	13	5	16	4			5	7	8	5	7	11	9	5	7.7
Effective number of parties	8.4	3.9	7.3	2.2			2.6	2.7	4.4	3	3.5	2.3	5.4	2.2	4.0
Level of voter volatility (1980s)	10.1	15.9	8.7	6.4	6	—	6	7	9.7	11	8.1	3.4	8.5	6	7.7
Level of party attachment (1994)	60	66	72	80	73	68	73	73	81	67	51	78	89	78	71

High party differential in NE (9–10)	33	53	39	65	53	55	58	46	51	34	38	41	35	26	43
Time since last national election (months)	31	60	3	8		42		12	42	15[a]	19	26	1	32	24
Concurrent election	N	Nat	N	N	N		SR	SR	N	N	SL	N	N	N	Var
European political context															
Presence of anti-EU parties/lists	W	No	No	W	W	W	W	No	S	S	N	W	N	W	Var
No experience of EPE94 campaign	23	16	19	6	4	5	3	36	3	31	3	9	18	13	17
Active experience of EPE94 campaign	41	63	42	69	64	69	71	24	80	32	66	51	55	31	53
High party differential in EPE (9–10)	25	39	29	46	28	31	39	31	22	23	23	24	17	15	27
High candidate differential EPE (9–10)	21	33	30	47	25	27	39	29	37	21	35	23	16	18	29

[a] Taking the 1988 Presidential election, the length of time was 76 months.

EPE = European Parliament election
FPP = First Past the Post
Hi = High
Lo = Low
Med = Medium
N = None

Nat = National
NE = National election
NL = PR national list
RL = PR regional list
S = Strong
SL = Some local

SR = Some regional
STV = PR STV
Var = Varies
W = Weak
Wk = Weekday

lukewarm character of the attitudes of Belgians towards the construction of Europe is remarkable, given that the country is in the centre of Europe and that the capital of Europe is in Belgium. It may be that the presence of the European institutions creates day-to-day difficulties and even excites a degree of jealousy among some citizens, as only a minority benefits from the existence of these institutions. Belgians show average support for membership of the Union. However, most surprisingly at first sight, only a minority—and not even a very large minority—would feel very sorry if the Union were dissolved: indeed, with 33 per cent falling in this category, the proportion of Belgian respondents who would feel sorry is lower than the average for the whole Union (42 per cent). This low proportion of positive answers is due essentially to the fact that the 'indifferents' plus the 'don't knows' form a very substantial majority (61 per cent). While there is above average endorsement of a European identity, widespread Belgian public indifference to integration is confirmed by the well above average figure of 37 per cent expressing no interest at all in European politics, by the higher than average proportion having a very low knowledge of European affairs and by the fact that 52 per cent have no image, positive or negative, of the European Parliament. Lack of a sense of involvement in the affairs of the Union is also evident in the attitude of Belgians towards EU accountability. Belgians are a shade above average in their assessment of the overall responsiveness of EU decision-making and slightly more favourably disposed than average to the role of the European institutions in ensuring such responsiveness but they are not particularly prone, as the citizens of several other member states are, to feel that their national institutions (government and parliament) can help very much in relation to European matters. In short, Belgian support for integration is moderate at best and Belgians remain distinctly unexcited by and uninvolved in the whole process.

Luxembourg

Luxembourgers are also very supportive of the Union, but in a highly pragmatic manner. There is almost no opposition at all to membership of the Union (4 per cent) and 39 per cent, which is well above average, are *very much* in favour of unification. Yet this strong support is more directed towards what the Union is currently than towards future developments. For one thing, the majority of Luxembourgers are quite satisfied with the working of democracy in the Union. There is also a small but significant minority—equal to that in the Union as a whole—who strongly believe that a United States of Europe is a bad idea (18 per cent); more ominously, 28 per cent (also close to the European average) believe that their government is more committed to the idea of a United States of Europe than they are themselves. Luxembourgers' support for integration is grounded in widespread interest in EU politics and a high level of information on European affairs—the second highest in the Union; it is also enthusiastic support: only 28 per cent of Luxembourger citizens would be indifferent if the Union were to be dissolved—19 percentage points below the European average. Despite the very favourable attitudes to integration noted above, Luxembourgers' endorsement of a European identity is only average. Also, somewhat surprisingly, a clear majority of Luxembourgers have no image, good or bad, of the European Parliament. Perhaps this reflects the gap between their reliance on national as opposed to European institutions to ensure EU responsiveness. At 66 per cent, their belief in the responsiveness of European decision-making is the highest in the Union; it would appear, however, that this responsiveness is seen as being achieved through national institutions: Luxembourgers' reliance on European institutions is only a shade above average while their reliance on their national government and on their national parliament is very strong (67 and 69 per cent compared to 48 and 51 per cent in the Union as a whole). This gives an added dimension to Luxembourg's resistance to reforms aimed at reweighting EU decision-making procedures in favour of the larger member states. The Luxembourgers are strongly pro-Europe but they do not demand 'more Europe'; they are content with the European status quo.

Italy

Italians are very supportive of the Union, but their support appears affective rather than instrumental or practical. Italians are not as sure as Greeks that their country benefited from the Union; yet they are none the less well above average in their enthusiasm for the Union: 58 per cent would be very sorry if the Union were dissolved, compared to 42 per cent in the Union as a whole. Only 10 per cent think that a United States of Europe would be a very bad idea and despite consistently having one of the most pro-integration governments in

Europe, very few Italians think that their government is too favourable to such a notion. At first sight it would seem that these high levels of support are accompanied by a strong sense of commitment and involvement. For example, the proportion of Italians who have a sense of being European is high—among the highest in the Union. In fact, however, these views are probably based mainly on sentiment, as, although their declared interest in European affairs is relatively high—higher than that of the Belgians, for instance—Italians display a very low level of information about Europe, 59 per cent scoring from 0 to 1 on the knowledge scale. Despite an apparent enthusiasm for Europe, 43 per cent of them have no image, good or bad, of the European Parliament. The gap between theory and practice is also evident in attitudes to EU responsiveness: 55 per cent believe that EU decision-making in general is responsive but only about one-third believe they can rely on any given institution to achieve such responsiveness; this means that, with the exception of the European Court, Italians tend to be about average in their belief in the efficacy of EU institutions and well below average in their believe in the efficacy of their own government and parliament in regard to European matters. Italians appear therefore to like not so much what the Union is, but what it could represent. They are critical about their own institutions as well as about those of the Union: yet they are strongly in favour of the Union and identify strongly with Europe. Their apparently high support is turned towards the future, towards what the Union might be. They are, in short, European idealists with, at best, a moderate level of involvement.

Greece

Greek support for European integration is strong, certainly stronger than that of the Belgians. Greeks are pleased with membership and a clear majority feels that Greece has benefited from it. There is above average support for the idea of the United States of Europe and very limited feeling that their own government is too favourable to such a development. Very few Greeks express no interest whatsoever in European affairs and they are also less likely than average to show no engagement with EU issues. The proportion being indifferent to a possible dissolution of the Union is about average; this distinguishes Greece from Belgium on the indifferent side and from Luxembourg on the highly committed side. A low level of knowledge of EU affairs occurs with about average frequency and Greeks are also about average in the frequency of not having any image of the European Parliament. Limited Greek involvement in the European project is confirmed by a surprisingly low level of European identification. The proportion of Greeks who even lean towards a European identity is appreciably smaller than in the Union as a whole—36 per cent. Despite Greek support for the Union and acknowledgement of the benefits of membership, the European decision-making process is not widely viewed as responsive. Only 30 per cent feel confident that EU decisions will be in the interest of Greece. In terms of confidence in specific institutions, even the Court of Justice is not singled out as being more reliable in the way it is held to be among the citizens of most other member states. Greeks do not show much reliance on their national government or on their national parliament in relation to European affairs either. These are significant qualifications to the initial impression of strong Greek support for integration; given the combination of high approval of membership, high level of perception of benefits, a low level of European identity, it seems that Greek support for integration is of a rather realist and instrumental kind that is accompanied by no more than an average level of involvement.

MEDIUM TURNOUT COUNTRIES: GERMANY, SPAIN, DENMARK, AND FRANCE

Turnout and abstention

The countries with medium turnout also fall into two pairs: Germany and Spain with relatively higher turnout (60 and 59 per cent respectively) and Denmark and France with somewhat lower turnout (53 per cent in each). Although this contrast is more or less reflected also in the average European turnout over the four elections from 1979 to 1994, it has not obtained at each of the European Parliament elections: all four countries have experienced ups and downs in European Parliament turnout and have not shown any consistent trends. It is noticeable indeed that in three of the four countries (Denmark, France, and Spain) turnout was up significantly in 1994 (see Table 7.1). Finally, if we compare turnout in the 1994 European election with turnout in the last national election before 1994, the largest gaps are found in France (33 percentage points) and Denmark (29 percentage points); the gap is 18 percentage points in both Germany and Spain. Overall proportions of circumstantial and voluntary abstention are very similar and very close to the European average in three of the four countries, the division being between two-fifths circumstantial abstention and three-fifths voluntary abstention. Germany differs from this trend in that voluntary abstention constitutes an appreciably larger proportion of the total (about three-quarters). Germany and Denmark differ from the other two in that it was very rare for those who abstained at the European election for circumstantial reasons to have also abstained in the previous national elections (see Table 7.1). Denmark alone is also distinctive, however, in regard to the predominance of Euro-specific abstention among voluntary abstainers.

Institutional context

All four countries have national list systems of proportional representation for the European election: three of the countries (Germany, France, and Spain) have adopted an identical form of PR, based on a single national list with no candidate preferences and with the proviso that lists have to obtain 5 per cent of the votes to share in the seat allocation; Denmark differs from the others in making provision for candidate choice within the list and also, because of its size, in having far fewer names on the lists: there were no less than 99 names on the German lists, 87 on the French lists, 64 on the Spanish lists, but only 16 on the Danish lists.

These arrangements mean that European election laws differ strongly from national election laws in all four countries; but the contrast is particularly marked in France, which has the single-member, two-ballot system at its parliamentary elections, while in the other three countries various forms of proportional representation are in force. The sharpness of the contrast between the two types of electoral systems may account to an extent for the relative lack of enthusiasm shown by the French for the European contest, as was pointed out in Chapter 2. The different French electoral system for national elections also accounts for the poor proportionality of electoral outcomes in French legislative elections; proportionality in national elections is medium in Spain and high in Germany and Denmark. Finally, in terms of the institutional context of the elections, the European Parliament elections occurred relatively soon after national legislative elections in Spain (12 months) and in France (15 months) but well after national elections in Germany and Denmark (42 months in each case). If one considers time since the last national election as an indicator of the place of the European elections in the electoral cycle, the French case is ambiguous; at least, the answer depends on which national electoral cycle one is talking about. In terms of national legislative elections, the European Parliament election occurred early in the cycle; in terms of French presidential elections, however, it occurred very late.

Political context of the election: national and European aspects

The national party systems of the four countries in this group are different in many of their details; they have one fundamental characteristic in common, however, that of being 'adversarial' rather than 'consociational'; the distinction between government and opposition is sharp, although the 'adversarial' character of contests is less marked in Germany and Denmark than in France and Spain. Within this framework, Germany and Spain come close to being two-and-a-half-party systems, while France has tended to have a multi-party system with a dominant party, this dominant party having been successively the Gaullist party and the Socialist party. In all three countries there is a substantial concentration of parties, with their 'effective' number varying only between 2.6 and 3 and even their absolute numbers varying between 5 and 7. Denmark presents substantial contrasts to the other three party systems: it is much more clearly a multi-party system, the total number of parties being 8 and the effective number 4.4.

There are also, however, differences of detail between all four party systems. France has had by far the most complex and also the least stable party structure of the four countries. However, there have been substantial changes within the party systems in the other countries, the main one being the collapse of the UCD in Spain in 1982, admittedly before the country joined the European Union. Party system changes have occurred everywhere in relation to smaller parties, the most important of these changes having been the very marked decline of the Communist party in France; even the German party system has been affected to an extent by the emergence of the Greens, the Republicans, and the PDS (ex-East German Communists). These various developments in party systems are reflected in the fact that voter volatility within this group of countries is highest in France and higher there in particular than in Germany or Spain and that party attachment is somewhat lower in France than in the other three countries (though not lower than in the former East Germany). The most striking contrast, however, is in relation to the occurrence of high national party differentials: these occur among 55 per cent in Germany, 51 per cent in Denmark, but only among 34 per cent in France.

What differentiates above all the party systems of the four countries of this group is the extent of differences in party positions on European integration. In three of the four cases, the main parties are broadly supportive, but there is also opposition and it varies appreciably in importance. In the fourth case there are radical differences both within and between the parties.

In Germany, there were two marginal anti-Union parties, the Republicans and the PDS: they obtained together less than 10 per cent of the votes and did not gain seats in the European Parliament. In the campaign itself there was substantial European content, with the far right stimulating a debate on European issues, although, with so many elections having taken place in 1994, it was difficult for the parties to mobilize their supporters (Klingemann 1994: 338; Paterson et al. 1996: 66). Thus the traditional consensus with regard to European policy was somewhat disturbed. 'For instance, the rise of the Greens in the 1980s broke the broad consensus . . . [The] suspicion of the established political settlement . . . did not gel with what has essentially been an elite-dominated inter-governmental process . . .' (Paterson et al. 1996: 75). Overall, however, the campaign was dominated by domestic issues rather than by transnational or supra-national issues, a tendency which was probably further reinforced by the fact that there had been so many other electoral contests during the year.

In Spain, the only doubts about the Union were to be found among elements of the Isquierda Unita (grouped around the Communists) which did well at the 1994 election, obtaining 13 per cent of the votes. The actual campaign centred on national issues 'with scarcely any reference to European policies' (Vallès 1994: 362). It has been argued that 'the European election was turned into a quasi-plebiscite over the acceptance of the government born from the previous general election of 1993 and over the parliamentary alliance between [Socialists and United Left]' (ibid. 364). All parties stressed, at least to some extent, the need to deepen European integration and to strengthen the role of the European Parliament. However, these issues were largely subsumed under more pressing matters once the campaign was under way.

Even in the light of some expression of opposition to integration in the party systems of Germany, France, and Spain, the Danish case stands out as being quite distinctive in this respect. In Denmark the cleavage between pro- and anti-Union manifests itself in divisions within the major parties, especially within the Social Democrats, in divisions between the main parties, mainly between the Social Democrats and the Liberal party, and in the fact that there are anti-integration 'parties' or lists that confine themselves to the European arena. This situation may in part boost turnout, as those who are against Europe can find an outlet for their views. On the other hand, the campaign in Denmark has been characterized as utterly dull, because issues were played down (Nielsen 1996: 58). Two of the major political parties, the Liberals and the Social Democrats, turned the campaign into a general contest between the party leaders, although neither of them was a candidate at the election. Despite the presence of clear anti-European Union and anti-integration parties and lists, it has been argued that the campaign missed the main point: 'The European parliament has never been taken very seriously by the public or national politicians . . . little was said about what was going on and the European parliament's increased role' (ibid.). Thus substantial European issues did not dominate over domestic issues despite the fact that there were disagreements between parties and lists about European integration. Denmark is, however, still the clearest case of a country where alternative approaches to the issue of European integration are presented to the voters in a European Parliament election and is, accordingly, rated 'strong' on this variable in Table 7.2.

There has always been a substantial undercurrent of opposition to integration also in France, where both the Communists (a major party up to the 1980s) and the Gaullists (at least under De Gaulle and to an extent afterwards) took an anti-supranational stance; as the Gaullist party was becoming more amenable to the Union, a forceful opposition emerged from another quarter of the Right, that of the National Front. There have also been dissenting voices even in the Socialist and Centre parties, although these have traditionally been supportive of the idea of 'Europe'. These divisions are reflected in the fact that the Maastricht Treaty obtained the slimmest of majorities at the 1992 referendum. The diversity of views was accentuated in the 1994 election when two specifically anti-European Union lists, one of the Centre-right and one of the Left, were fielded alongside the National Front and the Communist lists. This does not, however, mean that the campaign was dominated by European issues and it was in fact difficult to distinguish many of the twenty parties and lists from each other. 'The issues which the protagonists debated—unemployment, above all—were cast in domestic terms. Those which had a European dimension but were not of immediate domestic significance—Europe's institutions, above all—were all but ignored by the candidates' (Gaffney 1996: 97). Some references were made to cross-national issues such as immigration and drugs, but other issues of relevance for the European Union such as competition policy, interest groups, regionalism, and foreign policy were hardly mentioned (ibid.). According to some, despite the opportunity that voters had to choose between 'pro-European' and 'Euro-sceptical' parties, the public did not pay much attention to this choice: the voters made up their minds on the basis of general attitudes (Grunberg 1994: 338). One might indeed go further and argue that what the profusion of lists, both pro- and anti-Europe, seems to have achieved is to confuse the voters rather than help them. On the other hand, relative to most other countries, the actual alternatives which were available to the voters in France represented a wide range of alternative approaches to European integration. Indeed, it could be argued that about a third of the electorate voted, ostensibly at least, for anti-Union parties if one adds the 10 per cent of the National Front, the 12 per cent of the Centre-right anti-Union list, the 3 per cent of the anti-Union Socialist list, and the 7 per cent of the Communist list. Accordingly France, like Denmark, is coded 'strong' on the variable 'presence of anti-EU parties or lists' in Table 7.2.

Campaign penetration varied enormously between these four countries: it was virtually total in Germany and Denmark and very partial in France and especially in Spain. This is also reflected in the rate of active attention to the campaign, which varied from 80 per cent in Denmark and 64 per cent in Germany to 32 per cent in France and 24 per cent in Spain.[2] The relationship between the party differ-

---

[2] Spaniards hold the record for lack of experience of the European election campaign as well as the record of the lowest level of active experience of the campaign; the fact that, in these circumstances, the turnout should have been relatively large is worth noting.

ences as outlined above, the rate of campaign attention, and the occurrence of high European party differentials is complex: high European party differentials occur with somewhat greater frequency only in former East Germany and occur least frequently in France and in Denmark. One might explain the low French perception of party differences on Europe either by the relatively low campaign penetration or by the difficulties for some voters arising from a profusion of lists and from the changed electoral system,[3] there is no such ready explanation in the Danish case. One should note, however, that European candidate differentials are quite high in Denmark, a factor that may reflect intra-party differences on Europe and does suggest that Danish campaigning may have had some effect.

The political culture of European integration

The main contrast in the political culture of European integration within this group of medium-turnout countries is, not surprisingly, between Germany, France, and Spain, on the one hand, and Denmark, on the other; yet, there are surprising similarities between Denmark and the other three and not all of the contrasts are in what might be thought of as the predicted direction. For instance, in all four countries, membership of the European Union is seen as good to almost the same extent, at a little below the Union average of 61 per cent. Danes are in fact less likely to feel indifferent about a possible dissolution of the Union and they are only marginally less likely than the Spanish or the French to see themselves as having a European as well as a national identity. Moreover, differences within this group of medium-turnout countries are not confined to contrasts between Denmark and the rest nor to the realm of general attitudes to integration.

Germany

German support for that country's membership of the Union is, at 53 per cent, somewhat below the Union average, having dropped by 20 percentage points since 1989. Some of that decline is due to the evaporation of Europhoria in former East Germany, where support for membership has fallen by 37 percentage points; nonetheless it has also dropped substantially (by 15 points) in West Germany. Germans

---

[3] This point is discussed in some detail in Chapter 2.

are about average on opposition to integration and there is also some degree of opposition to the idea of the United States of Europe; the German attitude with respect to the suggestion of a hypothetical dissolution is not very different from that of the French: on this measure, they are even slightly less enthusiastic vis-à-vis the Union than their neighbours to the West. On the other hand, they are significantly more likely than average to endorse a European identity and less likely to opt for a purely national identity. The proportion of Germans who are not at all interested in the politics of the European Union is slightly less than the Union average; yet this interest does not translate itself into commensurate levels of knowledge: 52 per cent of Germans score 0 to 1 on the knowledge scale, a proportion that is significantly higher than the EU average and higher in particular than the corresponding proportions in Denmark, Luxembourg, the Netherlands, Ireland, and Greece. Not surprisingly, perhaps, low scores are particularly prevalent in former East Germany but the proportion of very poorly informed citizens in West Germany itself is also significantly above the proportions in the five countries mentioned. The belief of Germans in the overall responsiveness of EU decision-making is a shade below average and their sense of the reliability of European Union institutions is not very high, except for the Court of Justice, which is positively singled out. On the other hand, Germans believe that their national political institutions ensure that Union decision-making is responsive: substantial majorities feel they can rely on their national parliament and on their national government to render the Union accountable. In summary, the Germans can be said to show slightly less than average support, average enthusiasm, and above average self-reliance.

Spain

Although they are not as enthusiastic as the French or Germans and although more of them than of the French or the Germans are indifferent to the possibility of secession, the Spanish are similar to the French and the Germans in their overall support for their country's membership of the Union, that is they show a level of support slightly below average. They are also somewhat less interested, less engaged, and less knowledgeable than the European average and less inclined to have an affective image of the European Parliament. Their perception of benefits accruing to Spain from membership is remarkably low and is matched only by the British (both on 39 per cent). They are strikingly low also on confidence in the overall responsiveness of EU decision-making (35 per cent) and, with the exception of the Commission, are below average in their reliance on the ability of European and especially of national institutions in this regard. This lack of belief in the effectiveness of institutions reinforces the sense of disengagement from the European process already hinted at in the somewhat lower levels of knowledge of and interest in EU affairs among Spanish citizens. Given that Spanish support for membership has declined from a high of 75 per cent in 1989/90 to 55 per cent in 1994 one is left with the overall impression that the Spanish approach to the Union is marked by a certain disenchantment.

Denmark

Among the many distinctive features of Danish attitudes to European integration is that a clear majority (58 per cent) regard a United States of Europe as a 'very bad idea'; this is almost 40 percentage points higher than the EU average on this scale. This is not, however, accompanied by any above average rejection of European identity. Apart from their rejection of a United States of Europe, 24 per cent are against Danish membership and 37 per cent to some degree opposed to European unification. At the same time, a clear majority of Danes believe that their country has benefited from membership of the Union and show a confident approach to political responsiveness at European Union level. In terms of overall confidence in the responsiveness of EU decision-making, the Danes rank second highest in the Union. Their approach to this matter is overwhelmingly intergovernmental and national: they rely heavily on their national government and their reliance on their national parliament is the highest in the Union while their reliance on the European Parliament is the lowest (see Table 7.3). Consistent with this discriminating and complex set of attitudes, Danes have by far the highest level of knowledge of European affairs and only tiny proportions indicate that they have no interest in European politics or have no view on the scope of EU decision-making. If one were to attempt to sum up Danish attitudes, one might hazard the description 'critical engagement'. Whatever the complex of causes involved, the result was, as we have seen, a moderate level of turnout in the election and above average levels of Euro-specific abstention, of both kinds.

TABLE 7.3. *The political culture of European integration by member state (%)*

	BE	LU	IT	GR	GE (W)	GE	GE (E)	SP	DK	FR	IR	GB	NL	PO	EU
Attitudes to integration															
Membership good	60	79	71	69	54	53	50	55	54	55	79	47	82	49	61
Membership bad	8	4	6	8	11	10	8	13	24	13	5	21	3	11	11
Membership good—change 1989/90–94	−13	1	−8	−6	−15	−20	−37	−20	−4	−13	3	−7	−2	−22	−8
Country benefited from EU	51	73	53	72	49	47	42	39	62	44	86	39	71	67	57
Dissolution—very sorry	33	67	58	52	43	41	33	42	35	48	57	27	47	26	42
Unification—very much in favour	15	39	36	38	25	23	18	27	23	22	34	20	23	29	26
Unification—against	17	16	6	12	20	22	30	13	37	19	10	29	20	18	19
US of Europe a bad idea (1–2)	14	18	10	18	15	16	19	10	58	20	13	35	17	11	20
Govt. more in favour of US of Europe	23	28	16	14	42	43	45	26	57	29	21	39	39	24	31
Satisfied with EU democracy	51	67	43	41	47	43	29	44	40	47	63	37	41	49	45
EU interest/involvement/ knowledge															
Not at all interested	37	14	20	17	16	16	16	29	8	21	34	24	17	37	23
Dissolution—indifferent/DK	61	28	39	43	45	47	52	52	37	42	40	48	46	67	47
No view on scope of EU decision-making	41	30	35	28	42	42	42	44	14	33	47	27	31	58	37

Tend to endorse European identity (6–10)	56	48	56	36	60	57	52	47	41	49	37	26	46	47	46
Endorse national identity only (1–2)	16	17	12	27	10	12	16	13	23	16	26	41	22	9	20
No image of EP	52	57	43	42	26	28	34	51	24	40	40	37	27	62	40
Very low level of EU knowledge (0–1)	51	21	59	39	47	52	59	52	11	49	36	44	32	49	43
Responsiveness of EU decision-making															
Confidence in responsiveness of EU	53	66	55	30	43	41	38	35	53	55	60	38	50	56	48
Tend to rely on Commission (6–10)	43	43	34	28	37	35	29	35	30	36	44	23	39	33	34
Tend to rely on national government (6–10)	47	67	37	37	60	59	51	32	67	50	49	35	67	45	48
Tend to rely on Court of Justice (6–10)	47	49	37	34	54	50	40	38	54	42	64	44	58	40	46
Tend to rely on Council of Ministers (6–10)	44	44	33	32	42	40	33	33	39	37	45	20	46	33	37
Tend to rely on national parliament (6–10)	49	69	39	43	64	63	53	36	71	48	45	38	69	51	51
Tend to rely on European Parliament (6–10)	47	46	39	38	45	43	36	37	35	44	49	28	44	38	40

France

The overwhelming impression obtained from examining a profile of French attitudes to integration is that it is all very average; with slight variations up or down on particular variables, the French are average on support, average on opposition, average on interest, average on knowledge, and average in their reliance on the capacity of both European and national institutions to ensure EU responsiveness. Two points should be noted in this regard: first, the average European position, and thus the French position, on the reliability of institutions in ensuring the responsiveness of decision-making is not very comforting; secondly, there is no trace of traditional French inter-governmentalism in French public opinion: the French are no more likely than Europeans in general to rely on their national government or their national parliament and are considerably less likely to do so than the Luxembourgers, the Danes, the Dutch, or the Germans. It is perhaps a little odd in the light of this that they are a shade more likely than average to feel confidence that EU decision-making as a whole is in the interest of France. It is then even more odd that the only point on which they are really different from the European average is in having a less widespread perception that France has benefited from membership (only 44 per cent of French people take this view compared to 57 the per cent in the Union as a whole who believe that their country has benefited). In the light of the recurring emphasis in the literature on integration on a Franco-German motor force behind integration, it should be emphasized the French public opinion is not in the vanguard of the drive for integration and, secondly, it is even less so than its putative partner, Germany. If one were to suggest a summary description of French attitudes to integration, it would be that the French are average Europeans.

LOW TURNOUT COUNTRIES: IRELAND, THE NETHERLANDS, BRITAIN, AND PORTUGAL

Turnout and abstention

The four low turnout countries in 1994 can also be subdivided but this time the division is three and one: three with extremely low turnout (The Netherlands, Portugal, and the United Kingdom, all on 36 per cent) and one with, by comparison, moderately low turnout, namely the Republic of Ireland on 44 per cent. This grouping breaks down, however, when one moves to average turnout in European Parliament elections since 1979: the United Kingdom is the only case with consistently low turnout (an average of 34 per cent); the other three have moderately low averages, these being due to declining trends in European turnout in the Netherlands and Portugal and to oscillating turnout caused by concurrent local or national elections in the Irish case.

A further rearrangement of these four countries emerges if one examines turnout in national elections: turnout in the national election prior to the European Parliament election was low in Ireland and Portugal (69 and 68 per cent) and, at 78 per cent, moderately high in Britain and the Netherlands. This means that the current gap between national and European turnout is smallest in Ireland and Portugal (25 per cent and 33 per cent respectively) and largest in the Netherlands and Britain (43 and 41 per cent respectively). In regard to types of abstention, the four countries do not stray far from the European average of two-fifths circumstantial and three-fifths voluntary, with abstention in both categories tending to be Euro-specific rather than European and national (see Table 7.1).

Institutional context

Three of the low European turnout countries vote on a weekday and one, Portugal, on a Sunday. They have markedly different electoral systems. Mainland Britain (but not Northern Ireland) has the first-past-the-post system, the Republic of Ireland and Northern Ireland have PR-STV (Proportional Representation Single Transferable Vote), and Portugal and the Netherlands, the list system. At first sight, the Dutch and Portuguese systems are the most similar: both operate single national constituencies with, respectively 31 and 25 seats, and with a medium to high degree of proportionality, highest in the Netherlands. The two countries differ at least in principle in terms of candidate choice: while this is generally recognized to be ineffective in the Netherlands, it is not available at all in Portugal. Ireland's PR-STV system is intermediate: constituency sizes are relatively small (3 to 5 seats) and PR-STV provides ample scope for candidate choice and results in a high but not extremely high degree of proportionality. Mainland Britain, of course, with the first-past-the-post system single-member constituencies and the complete absence of any proportional element is different in all respects. Yet, if Britain provides evidence for the view that, as has been argued, turnout is affected by the proportionality of the electoral system, the 1994 result in the Netherlands constitutes a counter-example, although it may also be that the absence of candidate choice within parties and the rather large number of seats per constituency, both of which characterize the Netherlands, play a part in decreasing turnout, but the evidence is not overwhelming, to say the least. The length of time since the last national election also spanned a wide range: from two years and eight months in Portugal to one month in the Netherlands.

Political context of the election: national and European aspects

The differences between the party system of these four countries are modest enough—from five to eleven parties, with Britain having most, if the absolute numbers of parties in parliament are counted, as the House of Commons includes a panoply of nationalist parties from its various 'peripheries' and, in terms of the 'effective' number of parties from 2.2 and 2.3 in Portugal and the United Kingdom to 5.4 in the Netherlands, Ireland, at 3.5, being intermediate. This situation reflects the fact that Britain has a stable two-party system, that the Portuguese system comes close to two-and-half-party status and that Ireland has oscillated between a two-and-a-half-party system and a multi-party system with a dominant party. Throughout the 1980s voter volatility was about average in Ireland and the Netherlands, somewhat lower in Portugal and very low in Britain (the Labour landslide of 1997 was still several years away). Party attachment is very high in three of the four countries of the group—78 per cent in Britain and Portugal and 89 per cent in the Netherlands being attached to a political party; in stark contrast, in Ireland only 51 per cent show any degree of attachment to party, a smaller proportion by far than in any other country of the Union. Despite this lower level of attachment, however, party differentials in national elections are as high in Ireland as in the Netherlands or in Britain; Portugal is the exception in this regard, having the lowest level of perception of substantial differences arising from which party wins or loses seats in a national election of any of the twelve countries in question.

In Ireland, inter-party consensus has traditionally prevailed on

European issues. Some disagreement has occasionally surfaced, albeit never to an extent that a large number of voters would be affected; against this background, there were media complaints that the 1994 campaign was the most issue-less so far. The success of the Greens in winning two of Ireland's fifteen seats suggests that this view may be exaggerated and there is probably a European or 'ambassadorial' dimension to the competition between leading political personalities that is a prominent feature of European Parliament elections in Ireland (Sinnott 1995c: 258). Moreover, in 1994 'the substance of the campaign was not completely devoid of European content' (Marsh 1994: 346), although, according to another observer, 'the European Parliament election campaign in Ireland was muted, spasmodic, disjointed and often dominated by issues and events that had little to do with the future evolution of the European Union and the role of the European parliament within it' (Moxon-Browne 1996: 128). It is therefore perhaps exaggerated to locate Ireland in an intermediate category with respect to the Europeanness of the campaign, although this is suggested by Irwin (1995: 187).

As is well known, one of the four countries of the group, Britain, has had sharp intra-party divisions over Europe, first mainly within the Labour party and later mainly within the Conservative party; this particular characteristic may be a disincentive to vote, especially since there is no opportunity for candidate choice: pro-integration voters may abstain if their party's chosen (and only) candidate is from the anti-European Union faction; anti-integration voters may do likewise in the opposite situation. In Britain in 1994, however, there was a substantial basis for a more lively campaign since the prime minister, John Major, had appealed to 'Euro-sceptic' right-wing voters by advocating the possibility of a 'multi-speed' Europe and by emphasizing his commitment to preserving the national veto. Yet the contest was nonetheless described as 'a low-key campaign in which few issues caught the headlines and the underlying current of almost all the media coverage was the question of the leadership of the country's two major parties', since John Smith, the Labour leader, had died a week before the campaign was to begin (Mortimore 1994: 341). European issues thus were second to national issues and, at the level of the parties and their strategies, the election to the European Parliament was almost a textbook second-order election, Labour having made it clear that it regarded the election primarily as a referendum on the Conservative government (ibid. 343). Thus, even in Britain, the amount of European debate in the campaign remained relatively small, although it was clearly among the countries where the debate was largest (Irwin 1995: 187).

There is extensive agreement on European issues between the political parties in the Netherlands, though it must be added that some small parties exist exclusively for the purpose of contesting European elections. Even given this long-standing and widespread consensus, the 1994 European Parliament campaign has been characterized as 'probably the most uneventful election ever held in the Netherlands' (Irwin 1994: 357). The author adds that 'there was far more attention in the newspapers on the question of which parties would combine to form a new cabinet than on substantive issues related to Europe' (ibid. 358), despite the fact that the outgoing prime minister, Ruud Lubbers, had announced his candidacy to the European presidency. In reality 'the Dutch Euro-elections lost much of their relevance for national political life and were generally held in a very serene atmosphere' (van Deelen 1996: 47), this last statement suggesting that there was indeed very little interest on the part of either the elite or of the people.

In Portugal, in contrast, opponents of the European Union of the Right and Left had an opportunity to vote according to their views, since the CDS on the Right and the Communists on the Left were opposed to the Union: these two parties obtained together a little under a quarter of the votes. As regards the 1994 campaign, Portugal can probably be placed in an intermediate category. On the one hand, it has been said that 'the European election has been more about who will govern Portugal than how Europe is to be managed' (Goldey 1994: 361); on the other, it has also been argued that 'most of the parties put forward European issues in the Euro-election campaign. In particular, the future design of the European Union was passionately discussed with reference to Portugal. Two parties [the social democrats and the socialists] remained highly ambivalent on the issues of European Union', while the other two (the right-wing CDS and the Communists), campaigned 'on an anti-Maastricht and anti-loss of national sovereignty platform' (Magone 1996: 152).

Campaign penetration in these countries was also varied and did not necessarily reflect the substance or lack of substance of the particular campaigns as summarized above. Thus, for example, despite the fact that, as we noted, there is broad consensus about the European project among Irish parties, the 1994 European campaign was widely and actively followed by Irish voters; on the other hand, given the consensus between the parties in the Netherlands and given, as we noted, that a national election had occurred one month previously and most minds were fixed on the question of the formation of the government coalition, it is not surprising that Dutch attention to the campaign was no more widespread than average or indeed that the campaign completely escaped the attention of one in five Dutch voters. Overall campaign penetration in Portugal was up to the European average, but, for very many Portuguese, the experience of the campaign was essentially passive: only 31 per cent reported paying any degree of active attention to the campaign, a proportion that put it, together with France and Spain, at the bottom of the ranking of active involvement.

Whether due to limitations of campaign penetration or to inherent limitations in the substance of what the parties were attempting to communicate, European party differentials were below average, indeed were the lowest in the Union, in the Netherlands and Portugal. Despite a lack of party conflict on European issues in Ireland and the mainly intra-party conflicts in Britain, party differentials were close to the European average. The campaign, or perhaps one should say, the campaign in conjunction with the electoral system, may have had a further effect in Ireland: European candidate differentials in Ireland were higher than party differentials. This is a characteristic that Ireland shares with Denmark.

The political culture of European integration

At first sight, the essential difference seems to be between the British and the Portuguese, on the one hand, and the Dutch and Irish, on the other. The Netherlands and Ireland both show widespread positive assessment of membership, an assessment that is way above the European average (82 and 79 per cent respectively compared to the European average of 61 per cent). In contrast, Britain and Portugal show the two lowest rates of approval of membership (47 and 49 per cent respectively) and have almost identically low levels of enthusiasm (27 and 26 per cent respectively). This simple contrast begins to break down, however, when one probes further into the culture of European integration in each country.

Ireland

Ireland leads the field by a generous margin in recognition of the benefits of membership of the Union. Support for EU membership is also high, matching that in the Netherlands and Luxembourg; furthermore, the Irish express above average Euro-enthusiasm: 57 per cent would be very sorry if the European Union were dissolved; very few of them are opposed to a United States of Europe. Disengagement begins to appear, however, in the fact that they do not have a commensurate sense of being European and they are slightly above average in the proportion endorsing an exclusively national identity. Although their level of information is about average, they express above average lack of interest in European politics and show extensive non-engagement with EU issues. Non-engagement and a degree of complacency are also evident in their evaluation of EU decision-making. They have an exceptionally high level of satisfaction with the way democracy works in the European Union, a level (63 per cent) that is exceeded only by that of the Luxembourgers (67 per cent). Furthermore, at a general level, they are quite confident that EU decisions will be in the interest of Ireland. However, with the exception of the role of the European Court of Justice, they have only limited confidence in the reliability of particular institutions to ensure that this will be the case. If the expression 'critical engagement' can be used to characterize Danish attitudes, the Irish might be regarded as uncritical but somewhat disengaged.

The Netherlands

We have seen that the Dutch show a level of support for membership very similar to that of the Irish. Meanwhile, while not approaching Danish levels of engagement, they are more interested in European politics, more concerned with European issues, and somewhat more knowledgeable than the Irish. Should they therefore be characterized as the Irish are but just somewhat more committed? This does not seem to be the case for a number of reasons. First, despite their very high approval of their country's membership of the Union, they are no more enthusiastic about integration than the average European and they are about average in the proportion of people strongly in favour of unification. Secondly, despite their overwhelming support for Dutch membership and despite their historical role as one the prime movers of integration, they are only a shade more likely than the average European to have a sense of European identity. Thirdly, in spite of the strong contrast between Dutch and Danish attitudes to membership, the Dutch approach to the responsiveness of Union decision-making is similar to that of the Danes. They are about average in overall confidence that EU decisions will be in the interest of the Netherlands but they are convinced that the main political mechanisms of accountability are the national government and the national parliament. In sum, the Dutch are positive in their approach to integration but not keenly so and they show a strong streak of self-reliance.

Britain

As was mentioned earlier, Britain and Denmark are often bracketed together as hotbeds of Euro-scepticism; yet the similarity ends more or less with attitudes to integration as such. The British are much less likely to believe that their country has benefited from membership or to have confidence that EU decisions are in the interest of Britain. They are also less interested in European politics than the Danes and much less well informed. Their most distinctive characteristic, and one which marks them off not just vis-à-vis the Danes but vis-à-vis everyone else is the small size of the group that shows any degree of endorsement of a European identity and the correspondingly large proportion who reject almost any trace of such an identity. A further striking contrast lies in attitudes to accountability. Their confidence in the responsiveness of European decision-making as a whole is significantly below average and the lack of confidence is accentuated when it comes to assessing individual institutions: by and large, the British have confidence in neither national nor European institutions, a fact that suggests that they are not just disengaged but alienated. When this finding is linked to the widespread rejection of European identity—at 59 per cent by far the largest in Europe, the British view is perhaps best characterized as disaffected.

Portugal

We have seen that Portugal vies with Britain for the position of being the country that is least supportive of membership of the Union. This is not because the Portuguese are actually opposed to membership or to particular aspects of the integration process: they are exactly average on opposition to membership and on support for unification and show somewhat less than average opposition to the idea of a United States of Europe and less than average exclusively national identification. Moreover, the benefits of membership to Portugal are recognized by two-thirds of the Portuguese people. The reason for the low level of support is that, across all the indicators of attitude to integration, large proportions of the Portuguese are uncommitted: 40 per cent say they don't know or choose the 'neither/nor' category in the question on membership (a figure matched only by the people of former East Germany) and no less than 74 per cent are indifferent in the face of a possible dissolution of the Union. It should be emphasized that all of this seems to be a matter of indifference and lack of interest rather than lack of knowledge—the Portuguese are in fact a shade above average on the knowledge scale—but 37 per cent of them have no interest whatsoever in European politics, 58 per cent have no view on the scope of EU policy-making, and 62 per cent have no image, positive or negative, of the European Parliament. Portuguese citizens are in many ways detached from Europe and the whole European edifice seems remarkably distant from them. The relative separation of Portuguese citizens from the European Union manifests itself also in judgements passed about the responsiveness of EU decision-making. The overall Portuguese assessment in this regard is slightly more positive than the European average but the reliability of particular institutions tends to be average or a little below. In short, the most striking characteristic of Portuguese attitudes to the Union is their detachment from the issues and processes of European integration.

A COMPARISON OF HIGH-, MEDIUM-, AND LOW-TURNOUT COUNTRIES

Let us suppose that there are no differences among the member states of the European Union from the point of view of the legal requirement to vote; let us further suppose that the election takes place on the same day of the week (Sunday or weekday), that the electoral system is one in which the principle of proportionality is accepted everywhere (as the European Parliament has recommended should be the case), and that there is no concomitant election alongside that for the European Parliament. Can one then suggest what the rate of participation in the individual member states might be?

TABLE 7.4. *Categorization of member states in terms of support for European integration and involvement in European affairs*

Support	Involvement		
	High	Medium	Low
High	Luxembourg	Italy	Ireland
		Greece	
Medium	Netherlands	France	Belgium
		Germany	Portugal
			Spain
Low	Denmark	–	United Kingdom

There does seem to be an opportunity to do so, at least in a broad manner, if one considers the patterns of 'political culture' with respect to European integration that have just been outlined. Broadly speaking, countries can be categorized in terms of two dimensions—support for integration and degree of involvement in EU affairs. The first of these dimensions is measured by the various indicators of evaluation of the European Union considered above and the second dimension is measured by the indicators of interest, commitment, knowledge, and relationship to the various institutions. Placement of the countries along these two dimension, which, it must be emphasized is an impressionistic and approximate exercise, results in the arrangement of countries shown in Table 7.4.

If one knew nothing about the countries concerned other than the information conveyed in Table 7.4, one would anticipate that turnout would be highest in countries in or near to the top left-hand corner of the table and lowest in countries in or near the diagonally opposite corner. One would anticipate that it would be moderate in countries in the middle of the table. Because countries in the two cells at opposite ends of the other diagonal are subject to contrary influences (deriving from high support and low engagement in one case and from low support and high engagement in the other), one would anticipate that the turnout would reflect these cross-pressures and, therefore, also be moderate. In summary, the expectation would be: high turnout in Luxembourg, Greece, Italy, and the Netherlands; moderate turnout in Germany, France, Denmark, and Ireland; and low turnout in Belgium, Portugal, Spain, and Britain.

If patterns of turnout expected in this way are compared to the recorded levels of turnout at the 1994 European elections, some similarity can be observed. There are sharp differences with respect to three countries only: the Netherlands, which 'should' have a much higher turnout, and Spain and especially Belgium, which 'should' have a lower turnout. Meanwhile, the rates of turnout in Italy, Greece, Luxembourg, Germany, Denmark, France, Ireland, Portugal, and Britain broadly correspond to expectations.

One could extend this logic to suggest that in countries in which citizens are strongly attached to 'their' parties, in countries in which citizens are strongly disillusioned by the government and have outlets to register their protest, and in those in which those who are opposed to the Union also have outlets to register this opposition turnout is likely to be higher than where none of these characteristics obtains. Likewise electoral systems may exercise some influence over and above the degree to which they are proportional. For instance, while large districts may lead to greater proportionality, they may also result in lower turnout as some electors may not be happy with a system in which constituencies are so populous that they have no means whatsoever of getting to know their representatives. If Britain moves to a list system, this aspect would counter the presumed tendency for a more proportional system to increase turnout. For instance, too, some electors may be reluctant to vote at European elections if the electoral system adopted for these elections is markedly different from that which prevails at national elections, whether that national electoral system is truly proportional or not and whether or not it is less proportional than the European electoral system. Particular aspects of the elections in individual countries may also affect turnout; for example, the very marked fall in turnout in the Netherlands—of nearly 12 per cent—has been attributed to 'electoral fatigue' resulting from the European elections following closely the holding of national elections which in turn had followed closely the holding of local elections.

The above arguments have been made not with a view to 'explaining' turnout by reference to this or that attitude or political factor but with a view to illustrating the fundamental point that institutions, political structures, attitudes, and behaviour operate in symbiosis and interact with each other. It is essential therefore to combine institutional, contextual, and attitudinal approaches to the problem of explanation and thus to bring the analysis closer to the real diversity and complexity of actual political behaviour. This is the task attempted in the next chapter.

8

Sources of Participation
and Abstention

INTRODUCTION

Previous attempts to explain turnout in European Parliament elections have raised as many questions as they have answered; some authors have thrown up their hands in despair while others have reached the puzzling conclusion that attitudes to the European Union have nothing to do with the matter. The sources of low turnout are undoubtedly complex. It is equally certain that the question has large implications for an understanding of the legitimacy of the European Union and, at a practical level, for any steps that might be taken to improve turnout. This chapter tackles the problem of explanation, first, by examining a set of factors that have not been taken into account so far, namely, the various social and demographic characteristics of the electors that might encourage or inhibit participation. Having thus completed the survey of potential independent variables, the chapter organizes them in a rough model and also returns to the typology of participation and abstention to clarify the precise nature of the dependent variable or, as will be seen in a moment, the dependent variables that must be explained. One can then proceed to a multivariate analysis of participation in European Parliament elections. This somewhat more complicated step in the analysis is essential in order to identify the effects of each individual variable while holding the simultaneous effects of all other variables constant. Only in this way can one be sure that any given variable, say, for example, the index of EU knowledge, actually has an independent effect on turnout.

DEMOGRAPHIC CORRELATES OF
PARTICIPATION AND ABSTENTION

Apart from the analysis of the circumstances which inhibit participation, the discussion so far has focused mainly on the attitudes and
perceptions of voters and non-voters. We have seen some substantial
differences between these two groups and between the various sub-
types of abstainers. But we have also seen that some citizens vote
despite being badly informed, not very interested, unaffected by the
campaign, or oblivious of party differentials. And there is the other
side of the coin: some people abstain despite possessing a range of
attitudes, perceptions, and knowledge that would have led one to
expect them to be participants. Some of this may be due to a set of
influences which have not been considered so far, namely, the demographic factors that are regularly cited in research on participation.
These can be thought of as direct (positive or negative) influences in
themselves; for example, old age may be thought to diminish the
propensity to vote by reducing mobility, or interest, or the capacity to
absorb new information and to recall what had once been learned;
likewise, education seems likely to increase the propensity to vote
because it provides the resources which make voting and all that must
precede voting (knowledge of the issues or of the parties or the candidates or of the significance of the elections etc.) easy. Alternatively,
these and other demographic characteristics may be proxies for or
indicators of other factors; for example church attendance may not
lead directly to attendance at the voting booth but it may indicate a
propensity to be involved and active or it may reflect a high sense of
duty, either of which could increase the propensity to vote. The final
preliminary step before undertaking a multivariate analysis of all the
potential determinants of participation and abstention is to examine
the demographic background to turnout using the fivefold typology
of participation and abstention as the dependent variable and a broad
range of independent socio-demographic variables, beginning with
the inevitable trio of age, sex, and status.

The relationship between age and turnout is usually said to be
curvilinear, i.e. voting is lower among the young and the old and
higher in the middle of the age distribution. Table 8.1 suggests that
there is an element of truth in this observation in regard to participation in European Parliament elections but that the fall-off in voting

TABLE 8.1. *Type of electoral participation/abstention by age (non-compulsory voting countries only) (%)*

Type of electoral participation/abstention	Age								
	25 and under	26–35	36–45	46–55	56–65	66–70	71–5	76–80	81 and over
Euro-voter	53	60	71	74	78	78	79	76	70
Circumstantial Euro-specific abstainer	12	12	8	8	7	7	8	9	11
Circumstantial Euro-and-national abstainer	7	3	2	2	1	1	1	1	8
Voluntary Euro-specific abstainer	14	15	14	13	11	11	10	8	8
Voluntary Euro-and-national abstainer	14	9	5	3	4	2	2	5	4
N	1,009	1,733	1,539	1,370	1,165	573	413	208	152

Source: EB 41.1.

that is expected as a consequence of old age occurs only at a very ripe old age and is not dramatic. Initially voting increases with each decade, rising from 53 per cent among those aged 25 and under to 60 per cent among the 26–35-year-olds to 71 per cent among the 36–45-year-olds. Participation reaches and maintains a high plateau in the age groups between 56 and 80: equal proportions (approximately 77 per cent) show up as having voted among those aged 56 to 65, 66 to 70, 71 to 75, and 76 to 80.[1] Only among those 81 and over is there some falling off (to a turnout rate of 70 per cent). It is also important to note that age affects the various kinds of abstention differently. Circumstantial abstention tends to be higher among the young (25 and under) and among the very old (aged 81 and over); presumably the circumstances which increase circumstantial abstention in these two groups are very different: mobility and a wide range of alternative opportunities or competing attractions among the former and im-mobility and a generally diminished range of opportunity and activity among the latter. In contrast to this, voluntary abstention shows no curvilinear relationship to age: it is simply most prevalent among the young and least prevalent among the very old. Furthermore, voluntary abstention in both the European and the previous national election is really found in significant proportions only among the young: 14 per cent of those aged 25 abstained voluntarily in the European election and had also abstained in the previous national election. In summary, participation increases with age, especially in the early decades of the voting lifespan; once acquired, the inclination to vote is not easily lost and it is only with seriously advancing old age that there is a slight tendency for participation to diminish. Circum-stantial abstention is more prominent among both the young and the very elderly whereas voluntary abstention is more prevalent only among the young.

Many studies have shown that, even when one controls for the effects of different levels of education, women are less interested in politics than men. This difference has been shown to extend to interest in European politics and to several aspects of attitudes to European integration (Wessels 1995*a*: 111–24). When it comes to participation in European Parliament elections, however, the data in Table 8.2

[1] As with the analyses of participation and abstention in Chapters 3 to 6, this socio-demographic analysis is confined to the non-compulsory voting countries. The combined effects of compulsory voting, the socio-demographic variables and the other variables considered so far are examined in the second part of this chapter.

TABLE 8.2. *Type of electoral participation/abstention by gender (non-compulsory voting countries only) (%)*

Type of electoral participation/abstention	Gender	
	Male	Female
Euro-voter	71	67
Circumstantial Euro-specific abstainer	9	10
Circumstantial Euro-and-national abstainer	3	3
Voluntary Euro-specific abstainer	13	13
Voluntary Euro-and-national abstainer	5	7
N	4,025	4,137

Source: EB 41.1.

show that there is only a slight difference in participation between men and women: 71 per cent of male respondents reported having voted in the European Parliament election compared with 67 per cent of female respondents. In view of the extensive changes in the status of women over the last thirty years, it is not surprising that gender differences in participation are somewhat sharper among the older age groups: taking 55 as the dividing line for this purpose, there is a 2 percentage point difference in participation between men and women aged up to 55 compared to a difference of 7 percentage points between the sexes in the older generation. Gender also interacts with marital status in a way that partly reflects the age effects just noted and is partly independent of them. Table 8.3 shows that there are no differences between single men and single women or, despite the fact that they are presumably much older on average, between widowed men and widowed women. There is, however, a modest difference between married men and married women and a more substantial difference between men and women who are divorced or separated (divorced or separated women voting less frequently) and between men and women who are cohabiting. The combined impact of these variables is considerable: the rate of participation is highest among married men (75 per cent) and lowest among women who are cohabiting (50 per cent).

The third part of the basic socio-demographic trio is socio-economic status. The problem is that status or social class is capable of almost infinite nuances of meaning and measurement. A first approximation can be attempted by looking at respondents' subjective social class, that is, their response to the question, 'If you were asked

TABLE 8.3. *Type of electoral participation/abstention by gender and marital status (non-compulsory voting countries only) (%)*

Type of electoral participation/ abstention	Male					Female				
	Single	Married	Living as married	Divorced/ Separated	Widowed	Single	Married	Living as married	Divorced/ Separated	Widowed
Euro-voter	62	75	60	68	72	62	70	50	61	71
Circumstantial Euro-specific abstainer	10	8	16	8	9	10	9	13	9	10
Circumstantial Euro-and-national abstainer	4	2	4	3	3	5	2	8	2	3
Voluntary Euro-specific abstainer	14	12	14	17	12	11	14	18	17	11
Voluntary Euro-and-national abstainer	10	4	7	4	4	12	5	11	11	5
N	927	2,563	228	147	160	728	2,339	201	286	583

Source: EB 41.1.

TABLE 8.4. *Type of electoral participation/abstention by subjective social class of the EU (non-compulsory voting countries only) (%)*

Type of electoral participation/abstention	Subjective social class					
	Upper class	Upper middle	Middle class	Lower middle	Working class	Refused/ DK
Euro-voter	72	76	72	70	64	67
Circumstantial Euro-specific abstainer	11	10	9	9	9	11
Circumstantial Euro-and-national abstainer	3	1	3	2	3	3
Voluntary Euro-specific abstainer	8	10	11	14	16	10
Voluntary Euro-and-national abstainer	6	3	5	5	8	9
N	112	557	3,205	1,103	2,646	495

Source: EB 41.1.

one of these five names for your social class, which would you say you belong to: middle class / lower middle class / working class / upper class / upper middle class?' If respondents refused to classify themselves or mentioned another social class designation or replied don't know, these responses were also noted. The majority of respondents chose one of the first three standard class categories mentioned in the list (middle class / lower middle class / working class). A very small proportion opted for an upper-class self-assignment and a somewhat larger proportion for the designation of upper middle class. Participation in European Parliament elections is highest (76 per cent) among those seeing themselves as upper middle class and lowest (64 per cent) among the self-identified working class (Table 8.4).

While subjective social class tells one something about the respondent, its weakness is precisely that it is subjective; one does not know what meaning different respondents attach to the terms. Accordingly, it is necessary to tackle the complex and difficult problem of measuring social class by reference to respondents' occupations. The occupational question in the 1994 post-European Parliament election Eurobarometer asked respondents for their current occupation and, if the respondent was not doing any paid work at the time, asked whether they had done paid work in the past and if so what was the occupation. If the respondent was not the person contributing most of the household income, this question was followed with another on the current or former occupation of the main income-earner. Responses to these questions were coded into the major categories of non-active, self-employed, and employed. A detailed breakdown was then made within each of these: for example, among the self-employed, between farmer, fisherman, professional, owner of a shop, business proprietor, etc. and, among the employed, between employed professionals, general management, middle management, skilled manual worker, and unskilled manual worker. Regrettably, the survey did not use the full panoply of Eurobarometer occupational questions and it is, therefore, not possible to further refine the measurement of occupation by looking, for example, at the number of employees in the case of managers or business proprietors. In the absence of such concrete data, and because of the importance of distinguishing in particular between the upper and lower levels of the self-employed, a proxy measure based on overall household income and number of consumer durable goods possessed by the household has been used to distinguish within the self-employed between the bourgeoisie and petty bourgeoisie and analogously between large farmers and small farmers. Use was made of the consumer durable variable because substantial proportions of the sample refuse to divulge information on household income.

The foregoing data provide two measures of occupational class. The first of these applies to the bulk of the population and is arrived at by attributing the occupational class of the head of household or main income earner to those who fall into the category of non-active. This will be referred to as 'socio-professional status'. The second variable is labelled 'occupation'; it includes all of the categories of occupation recorded plus the various categories of non-activity (household duties, student, unemployed, or retired). Table 8.5 presents the breakdown of participation and abstention by the first of these measures, socio-professional status. The main contrast is between the professional and managerial class (78 per cent turnout) and manual workers (64 per cent) with the bourgeoisie and petty bourgeoisie and other white collar workers lying in between; farmers and their dependants are also found to be more frequent participants. The abstainers in these various status groups are scattered over the four types of abstention though there is evidence of a slight concentration of voluntary Euro-only abstention in the manual working class.

This measure of socio-professional status has the advantage of

TABLE 8.5. *Type of electoral participation/abstention by socio-professional status (non-compulsory voting countries only) (%)*

Type of electoral participation/abstention	Socio-professional status						
	Professional managerial	Bourgeoisie	Petty bourgeoisie	Other white collar	Manual worker	Large farmer	Small farmer
Euro-voter	78	70	69	69	64	74	76
Circumstantial Euro-specific abstainer	8	11	11	9	10	8	6
Circumstantial Euro-and-national abstainer	2	1	3	3	3	5	4
Voluntary Euro-specific abstainer	10	13	10	12	16	9	10
Voluntary Euro-and-national abstainer	3	5	6	7	8	3	4
N	1,657	456	412	1,108	3,730	96	286

Source: EB 41.1.

TABLE 8.6. *Type of electoral participation/abstention by occupation (non-compulsory voting countries only) (%)*

Type of electoral participation/ abstention	Occupation										
	Professional managerial	Bourgeoisie	Petty bourgeoisie	Other white collar	Manual worker	Large farmer	Small farmer	House-persons	Student	Un-employed	Retired
Euro-voter	78	72	67	67	62	83	75	65	66	61	78
Circumstantial Euro-specific abstainer	8	11	12	10	11	6	8	10	10	8	8
Circumstantial Euro-and-national abstainer	2	2	3	3	3	0	3	3	7	3	2
Voluntary Euro-specific abstainer	11	12	11	13	16	9	10	15	10	18	10
Voluntary Euro-and-national abstainer	2	4	7	8	9	2	4	7	8	10	3
N	838	316	246	793	1,804	47	107	1,185	403	585	1,820

Source: EB 41.1.

including as many respondents as possible in its purview. This, however, is achieved by *attributing* a particular status to a relatively large number of respondents on the basis of the occupation of the head of household or main income earner. It is essential, therefore, to also look directly at the occupational class of individuals themselves, accepting the fact that a substantial number of people will fall into the non-active categories. Concentration on the actual occupation of respondents is particularly important in the analysis of participation and abstention because these may be affected not so much by socio-economic status as by the constraints and opportunities that accompany different occupations. Table 8.6 shows the range of participation and abstention among respondents by occupation. The occupational categories with the highest level of voting are large farmers (83 per cent—though here it should be noted that the number of cases is rather small), those with a professional managerial occupation (78 per cent), and those who are retired (78 per cent). Considerably lower rates of participation are found among manual workers (62 per cent) and the unemployed (61 per cent).

If one thinks of different occupations as providing different opportunities or as imposing different constraints on participation, it may be that Sunday versus weekday voting interacts with occupation to produce different levels of turnout in different occupational classes. Table 8.7 provides some support for this interpretation: it appears that Sunday versus weekday voting makes relatively less difference for the bourgeoisie and other white collar workers, while making a more substantial difference among the professional managerial class, manual workers, and the petty bourgeoisie. Within the professional managerial class there is a 15 percentage point difference between rates of participation among those who vote on a Sunday and those who vote on a weekday. A difference of a similar scale is found among manual workers, and a difference of 13 points among the petty bourgeoisie. Among the bourgeoisie, on the other hand, the difference between Sunday and weekday voting is only 5 percentage points. The view that this is in part due to greater constraints arising from weekday voting receives some support from the greater prevalence of *circumstantial* abstention in weekday voting countries among the professional managerial class and among manual workers. Both groups are presumably affected by different but equally compelling time constraints. Apart from such circumstantial considerations, the main differences between occupational groups can, however, be

TABLE 8.7. *Type of electoral participation/abstention by occupation (urban), by day of voting in EP election (Sunday/weekday) (non-compulsory voting countries only) (%)*

Type of electoral participation/abstention	Professional managerial		Bourgeoisie		Petty bourgeoisie		Other white collar		Manual worker	
	Sunday voting	Weekday voting	Sunday voting	Weekday voting	Sunday voting	Weekday voting	Sunday voting	Weekday voting	Sunday voting	Weekday voting
Euro-voter	85	70	74	69	71	58	70	62	69	54
Circumstantial abstainer	6	13	11	15	13	18	10	16	10	18
Voluntary abstainer	9	17	15	16	16	24	20	22	22	29
N	431	407	179	137	175	71	439	354	987	817

Source: EB 41.1.

thought of as arising from two major sources. A social class interpretation would emphasize the view that people in different occupations and of different socio-economic status have a different stake in the society and, accordingly, different incentives to participate in the political process. An alternative interpretation could be that the different occupational levels are important not in themselves but because they indicate different levels of resources that are relevant to voting. This raises the question of impact of education as one of the main factors that may equip the individual with the knowledge and the skills necessary to function effectively in the political world.

Because of differences in educational systems across the European Union, measuring educational attainment in terms of the distinction between primary, secondary, and tertiary levels and the various types and gradations within each of these is a complex task. Many surveys, including, the Eurobarometer, rely on a simple expedient: they ask respondents the question: 'How old were you when you stopped full-time education?' This provides a rough but useful quantitative measure of educational attainment and is the basis on which the impact of level of education will be examined here. The range of age of completion of full-time education is defined as 14 or less, 15 to 16, and then by year up to 24.

Participation does increase with education: from 63 per cent among those who completed their education at age 15–16 to 82 per cent among those who completed their education aged 24 or over (see Table 8.8). There is also, however, a hint of a curvilinear effect at the bottom end of the scale which is puzzling: turnout is significantly higher among those who completed their full-time education at age 14 and under compared with those who completed their education aged 15 or 16. This anomaly disappears, however, when one controls for the effect of age: the *increased* rate of participation among those with *least* education is found only among the over-35s whereas in the younger generation turnout is equally low in both the lowest educational categories. Thus, the reason for the somewhat higher turnout among those with the lowest level of education shown in Table 8.8 is that the vast majority of those who completed their education aged 14 or under are older people and, irrespective of level of education, older people have a greater propensity to vote. This may be simply because they have acquired the habit of voting or developed a sense of obligation to vote as they have grown older; alternatively it may be because, through experience, they have acquired the knowledge and skills to

TABLE 8.8. *Type of electoral participation/abstention by age respondent finished education (non-compulsory voting countries only) (%)*

Type of electoral participation/abstention	Age finished education									
	14 years and under	15/16 years	17 years	18 years	19 years	20 years	21 years	22 years	23 years	24 years and over
Euro-voter	70	63	66	68	69	70	70	73	76	82
Circumstantial Euro-specific abstainer	9	10	10	10	10	10	11	10	11	6
Circumstantial Euro-and-national abstainer	2	3	2	4	3	3	2	2	2	2
Voluntary Euro-specific abstainer	14	16	15	12	12	12	13	12	7	8
Voluntary Euro-and-national abstainer	6	9	7	7	6	5	4	4	4	2
N	1,934	1,874	738	854	437	421	306	287	195	712

Source: EB 41.1.

enable them to cope with the political world that their limited education may not have imparted to them.

One way of simplifying and making sense of the political world is to have an ideology, the most common ideological framework being based on a broad distinction between left and right. While being at the lower end of the occupational scale or having lower levels of education may reduce either the incentive or the resources that are necessary for voting, ideological alignment may compensate for both these negative factors. This interpretation receives some support from the fact that there is quite a strong contrast between those who have no degree of left–right identification, on the one hand, and those with a strong ideological identity, on the other: the rate of participation among those who were unable or unwilling to place themselves on a left–right scale was 55 per cent; this increases to 67 per cent among those who placed themselves on the centre of the scale and to 74 to 75 per cent among those opting for a strong ideological position, be it left or right (see Table 8.9). Note that non-alignment on the left–right scale is associated with overall political disengagement: 17 per cent of this group were double abstainers (voluntary abstainers in the European Parliament election *and* abstainers also in the previous national election); this was the case of only 3 per cent of those with right-wing self-placement and 5 to 6 per cent of those with a left-wing or centrist ideological position.

Returning to the question of possible socio-demographic factors that may affect turnout, it has been suggested that frequency of religious practice may encourage habits of participation and link individuals to a mainstream social network or it may inculcate norms of civic responsibility that are conducive to electoral participation. The Eurobarometer provides data on frequency of religious practice for those acknowledging an affiliation with one of the main Judaeo-Christian religions. This can be used to produce a Judaeo-Christian religious practice scale ranging from 'none' (respondent explicitly denies having a religious affiliation, has a non-Judaeo-Christian religious affiliation, or acknowledges an affiliation but never practices) through various degrees of practice up to attendance at religious services more than once a week. Participation really only varies at the extremes of this scale: between the 64 per cent rate of participation among the non-affiliated/non-practising/other religion, on the one hand, to the 83 per cent among the small minority who attend religious services several times a week (see Table 8.10). Note that electoral

TABLE 8.9. *Type of electoral participation/abstention by strength of ideological attachment (non-compulsory voting countries only) (%)*

Type of electoral participation/abstention	Strength of ideological attachment					
	Strong left	Moderate left	Centre	Moderate right	Strong right	Refused/DK
Euro-voter	75	72	67	73	74	55
Circumstantial Euro-specific abstainer	5	10	10	11	8	8
Circumstantial Euro-and-national abstainer	2	3	3	2	2	4
Voluntary Euro-specific abstainer	12	11	14	11	13	17
Voluntary Euro-and-national abstainer	6	5	6	3	3	17
N	630	1,713	2,968	1,448	481	922

Source: EB 41.1.

TABLE 8.10. *Type of electoral participation/abstention by religious practice (non-compulsory voting countries only) (%)*

Type of electoral participation/abstention	Judaeo-Christian religious practice				
	Non-affiliated/ non-practising/ other	Once a year or less	A few times a year	Once a week	Several times a week
Euro-voter	64	68	72	74	83
Circumstantial Euro-specific abstainer	10	10	9	9	5
Circumstantial Euro-and-national abstainer	3	2	2	3	3
Voluntary Euro-specific abstainer	15	14	12	11	6
Voluntary Euro-and-national abstainer	9	6	5	3	3
N	3,213	1,242	1,921	1,451	287

Source: EB 41.1.

participation does not increase significantly as one moves through the apparently important barrier between 'a few times a year' and weekly practice. There may be a variety of reasons for this: weekly church attenders are more likely to be Catholics and Catholics have a marginally lower rate of turnout than those of other denominations; secondly, weekly religious practice is officially required of Catholics and so may not be as closely related to participation in other activities as much as it would if it were entirely voluntary.

In concluding the socio-demographic analysis at this point, however, one must emphasize the limited nature of the inferences one can make on the basis of examining bivariate relationships of this kind: in order to trace the sources of participation and abstention it is essential to undertake a multivariate analysis.

THE INDEPENDENT AND DEPENDENT VARIABLES: AN OVERVIEW

The first task is to decide which of the very large range of possible influences on turnout in European Parliament elections to include in the analysis. The potential independent variables can be considered under six headings: (1) institutional and political context, (2) personal characteristics of the voter, (3) general political attitudes and attitudes related to the second-order election model, (4) attitudes to the European Union, the European Parliament, and the election itself, (5) exposure to the campaign, and (6) country-specific effects. These six sets of variables are laid out in Table 8.11 as a basic reference point for the analysis that follows and as a means of attaching short labels to the variables that can then be used to identify them in the subsequent presentation of the statistical results.

Contextual variables comprise compulsory voting, the day of voting, the proportionality of the electoral system, the coincidence of national elections, the coincidence of regional or local elections, and the timing of the election relative to the last national election. These are all what are called systemic effects: they differ only as between member states or between regional or local political units and all the individuals within the state or other political unit are subject to the same context for the election in question. The first three in this subset of the variables in Table 8.11 are part of the *institutional* context of the election; these have been discussed at some length in Chapter 2 and elsewhere in this book. The other three variables in the set are aspects of the *political* context or environment in which a European election takes place. Clearly, that environment is radically different if the European election coincides with a national election. It is different again if there are concurrent regional elections. The last variable—the time that has elapsed since the last election—is more difficult to pin down and, though it has been mentioned earlier, requires some further discussion.

Distance in time since the last national election is thought to affect turnout in a European Parliament election because of a presumed electoral cycle: if national elections have just recently occurred, neither voters nor parties will be interested in the European election; the further back in time the last national election, the greater the involvement, by way of anticipation or preparation, of both voters and parties in the electoral process and, it is argued, the greater the turnout in the European election. A hypothesis of 'electoral fatigue' has also been advanced: if a European election occurs very soon after a national election, it is assumed that voters find it difficult to muster up the energy to do it again. It is, however, difficult to operationalize this notion and also to separate it from the presumed electoral cycle effects. In their work on turnout in European Parliament elections, Franklin, van der Eijk, and Oppenhuis reverse the time since the last

TABLE 8.11. *Independent variables used in multivariate analysis of types of abstention*

Variable categories and labels	Variable definitions
Institutional and political context	
Compulsory	Compulsory voting
Weekday	Weekday voting
Proportional	Proportionality of the electoral system
National E	Concurrent national election
Regional E	Concurrent regional election
Time elapsed	Number of months since last national election
Personal characteristics	
Age 25<	Aged 25 and under
Age 26–35	Aged 26–35
Age 81>	Aged 81 and over
Manual	Occupational status: manual worker
Education	Age completed education
Religious pract	Frequency of religious practice
Other address	Registered to vote at another address
General political attitudes and SOEM attitudes	
Party attach	Degree of party attachment
Interest-P	Interest in politics
Info-national	Knowledge of national politics
Left–right	Degree of ideological alignment
Dissat natnl democ	Not at all satisfied with national democracy
Natnl pty-diff	National party differential
Power of EP	Perceived power of European Parliament[a]
Diff power EP–NP	Difference in power of EP and national parliament
Less at stake	European party differential minus national party differential
Attitudes to the European Union and European Parliament	
Pro-EU as it is	Support for the European Union as it is
Pro rapid intg	Support for rapid European integration
EU-involvement	Level of involvement in the integration process
EU-knowledge	Knowledge of the European Union
EP reliability	Perceived reliability of European Parliament[a]
Euro pty-diff	European party differential[a]
Euro cand-diff	European candidate differential[a]
Campaign exposure	
Campaign	Exposure to the EP election campaign[a]
Particular systemic effects	
DK or FR and anti-rapid intg	Danish or French and opposed to rapid integration
GB and right-wing	British and right-wing

[a] For the purpose of this analysis, these variables are treated as categorical variables, the categories being those used in Chapters 5 and 6. Logistic regression treats one category as a base line against which to assess the effect of each of the other categories.

election measure, treating it as time until the next election (Franklin et al. 1996: 317–20); however, how voters, or indeed commentators, estimate time to the next election in systems that do not have fixed parliamentary terms is not clear. In this prospective approach, the time-to-next-election variable and the concurrent national election variable become conflated: time to next election is coded zero in the case of a concurrent national election. In developing a theory of the sources of turnout as such, Franklin accords a considerable role to this combined variable as an indicator of 'electoral salience' (Franklin 1996: 228–30).

The *personal characteristics* variables comprise the main variables that have been discussed in the first part of this chapter: age (being either young or very old), occupational status (being a manual worker or being unemployed), education, and religious practice. In preliminary multivariate analyses, gender proved not to have any significant effect and was not included in the final analysis. The last variable in this set is whether or not the individual elector is registered to vote at his or her present address or at another address. It might seem that this belongs with the institutional variables that govern the conduct of the election. However, it differs radically from the institutional variables mentioned above in that, while they are systemic characteristics, it is an individual-level characteristic. Though it does not fit entirely comfortably in what is mainly a set of socio-demographic characteristics, the least inappropriate course is to include it in this category of potential independent variables.

The third set of possible influences on turnout includes party attachment, interest in politics in general, level of political knowledge (of national politics), strength of left–right attachment, and evaluation of the working of democracy at national level. Some interpretations of the sources of turnout emphasize that, after contextual factors have been taken into account, turnout in European Parliament elections is largely a function of general political preferences and orientations. In the analysis that follows, therefore, one point to note will be whether participation in European Parliament elections is affected by general political attitudes *and also* by European attitudes, as one would intuitively expect, or whether, as some have strongly argued, European attitudes play no significant role. In addition to these general political variables, several additional variables are included in order to make the test of prevailing interpretations of turnout and abstention as comprehensive as possible; these are:

perceptions of the power of the Parliament, differences in the perception of the power of the European Parliament and of national parliaments, the perception of party differentials in national elections, and, finally, the indicator of there being less at stake in a European Parliament election, i.e. the difference between European party differentials and national party differentials (see Table 8.11). These variables all figure in one way or another in the second-order election explanation of turnout. Although the bivariate analysis threw considerable doubt on the efficacy of the variables derived from that model, it is essential to include them in the multivariate analysis as a check on the negative conclusions about the second-order election explanation of turnout that were tentatively drawn in Chapters 5 and 6.

In the case of attitudes to the European Union and the European Parliament, one faces the difficulty of having a very large number of potential independent variables with a correspondingly more acute problem in choosing which to include in the analysis. In dealing with this problem, factor analysis has been used in an attempt to identify the key dimensions underlying attitudes to European integration. A factor analysis of seventeen[2] indicators of attitudes to the European Union identified three underlying attitudinal dimensions. The first is *support for the European Union as it is*, a dimension that is defined in terms of three of the four standard Eurobarometer indicators (i.e. unification, membership, and benefits) and by general confidence in EU decision-making and positive assessment of the working of EU democracy (see Table 8.12). The second dimension is *support for rapid and far-reaching integration*. This is defined by the questions measuring preference regarding the pace of integration, support for the formation of a European government responsible to the European Parliament, support for a United States of Europe, and by the difference between the respondent's position on the latter issue and his or her perception of the national government's position. The third and final factor is *degree of involvement in the integration process*. This is defined by indifference towards a hypothetical dissolution of the EU, by declared interest in European politics, by whether the respondent has thought about the question of the scope of EU decision-making, by having or not having an affective image of the European

---

[2] Most of the items used in the factor analysis have already been discussed in earlier chapters. In addition to these, however, we have included some standard Eurobarometer items that we have not previously considered. The wording of all the questions is presented in the Appendix.

Parliament, and, finally, by the rate of don't know responses to the questions on the European Union and European integration. In short, in place of the large number of individual items, one can use these three factors or dimensions as three summary variables that tap clearly distinct aspects of attitudes to the Union (see Table 8.11). The other variables that go to make up the set of EU and EP attitudes and orientations are: the index of knowledge of the EU described in Chapter 4, the question on the reliability of the European Parliament, and the perception of European party and candidate differentials.

The next variable could be seen as belonging to either the national or the European category. In principle, exposure to the campaign could be either a national or a European influence on turnout because the campaign could be experienced by the voters in either national or European terms. For this reason and because it does not obviously belong either with the contextual variables, or with socio-demographic or attitudinal factors, the campaign is placed in a category of its own in Table 8.11. Whichever way it is experienced by the voters, and much more research is needed to discover this, the campaign is the element in this whole process that is most directly under the control of the Parliament, the parties, the MEPs, and the aspirants to that position. It is therefore essential to ascertain what effect, if any, it has on turnout, in particular whether it has an effect that is additional to the effects of the other variables considered.

In addition to these general effects, particular influences may affect turnout in particular countries; though this is not the place to embark on a comprehensive analysis of these effects, two stand out and are worth exploring briefly. The first relates to Denmark and France. In the European Union as a whole, we expect that opposition to European integration will tend to lead to abstention in the European Parliament election. In Denmark, however, opponents of integration have a well-established alternative for which they can vote in European Parliament elections. In France in 1994, on paper, the opportunity to express an anti-integration view also existed, though the anti-EU option was much less well established.[3] In both countries, therefore, one should find that, contrary to the general trend, opponents of integration are less rather than more likely to abstain. In order to test this hypothesis, an interaction effect—being Danish or French and being opposed to European integration—is included in our set of

---

[3] On both these points see the discussion in Chapter 7.

TABLE 8.12. *Factor analysis of attitudes to the European Union and to European integration*

	Factor 1	Factor 2	Factor 3
Support for Western European unification	**0.58**	**0.46**	0.16
Support for country's membership of EU	**0.71**	0.32	0.13
Benefited from membership of EU	**0.74**	0.10	0.09
Confidence in EU decision-making	**0.69**	0.24	0.10
Satisfaction with EU democracy	**0.63**	0.09	−0.03
Preference for pace of European unification	0.27	**0.55**	0.01
European/national identity	0.32	0.39	0.25
Support for formation of a European government	0.26	**0.62**	0.02
Support for United States of Europe	0.13	**0.83**	0.06
Difference between respondent's support for United States of Europe, and respondent's perception of national government's support for same	0.05	**0.78**	−0.02
Indifference towards dissolution of EU	−0.22	−0.02	**−0.56**
Interest in European politics	0.22	0.08	**0.67**
Don't know/haven't thought about level of EU decision-making	0.04	0.01	**0.70**
No affective image of European Parliament	0.14	−0.03	**−0.62**
Don't Know response rate[a]	−0.04	−0.03	**−0.75**
% of total variance	28.4	13.8	7.8
Eigenvalue	4.27	2.08	1.17

[a] Total no. of Don't Knows on all EU-related questions, excluding those testing knowledge of the EU.

Interpretation of factors
Factor 1: Support for the European Union.
Factor 2: Support for rapid and far-reaching European integration.
Factor 3: Involvement in the European integration process.

Source: EB 41.1.

variables. The measure of opposition to integration used is the support for rapid and far-reaching integration factor identified in Table 8.12. The second potential particular effect arises in Britain. In general, one would expect individuals who profess an ideological orientation, whether left or right, to be more likely to vote in a European Parliament election. At the time of the 1994 European Parliament election, however, the Conservative government in Britain was suffering an unprecedented level of unpopularity. In such circumstances one would expect higher rates of abstention among Conservative voters. In testing this hypothesis right-wing self-identification has been used as the measure of potential support for the Conservatives. No doubt, there are many other effects that would be worth exploring; the two chosen here, however, are of particular interest because they enable us to test effects that may run counter to general trends.

In addition to selecting the appropriate independent variables, it is also vital to consider how best to define the dependent variable itself. Fortunately, this can be done more briefly. The dependent variable is usually simply assumed to be: *voted in the European Parliament election versus did not vote*. The typology of participation and abstention outlined in Chapter 2 suggests that this is a serious oversimplification. There are four kinds of abstention arising from whether the failure to vote is specific to the European election or occurs in conjunction with abstention in the last national election and whether the basis of non-participation is circumstantial or voluntary. In attempting to explain abstention in European Parliament elections, it is essential to distinguish these four types; in order of importance, they are: voluntary Euro-specific abstention, circumstantial Euro-specific abstention, voluntary Euro-and-national abstention, and circumstantial Euro-and-national abstention.

THE SOURCES OF ABSTENTION IN EUROPEAN PARLIAMENT ELECTIONS

Given a dichotomous dependent variable (in the case of the first type mentioned in the previous paragraph, for example, Euro-voters versus voluntary Euro-specific abstainers), the appropriate multivariate statistical technique is logistic regression. This is particularly so when the distribution of the variable is skewed. Logistic regression estimates the odds of being in one response category rather than another on the basis of a series of independent variables, measuring the effect of each individual variable while holding all the other variables constant (Aldrich and Nelson 1984). The effect of a variable is indicated by the size of the logistic coefficient for that variable (the columns headed B in Table 8.13) and by its associated standard error (the SE columns). Based on the ratio of these two, one can calculate a test of the significance of the effect of each variable (the Wald statistic); significant effects are indicated by the asterisks in the third column of each section of Table 8.13. Finally, some intuitive sense of the size of the effect of each independent variable can be gleaned from the fourth column in each section of the table; this gives the factor by which the odds of the event occurring[4] change when the independent variable in question changes by one unit. If this factor is one, the variable has no effect. If it is very close to one, the variable, while it may have a statistically significant effect, does little to change the odds of the outcome one is interested in. The more the factor either exceeds one or is less than one, the greater the effect of the variable (positive in the case of the factor exceeding one and negative in the case of the factor being less than one). Given this amount of statistical information and given the need to compare the effects of a large number of independent variables on four distinct dependent variables (the four types of abstention), presentation of the results is inevitably fairly complex. To ease this problem somewhat, the presentation has been subdivided into two tables: Table 8.13 deals with Euro-specific abstention, leaving circumstantial Euro-and-national abstention to be dealt with in the following table.

Two of the three institutional variables included in the analysis make a substantial contribution to predicting the variable of greatest interest: voluntary Euro-specific abstention. They are compulsory voting and weekday voting. The effect of compulsory voting is very strong, reducing the odds of being a voluntary Euro-specific abstainer by a factor of 0.08 (see Table 8.13). This is not surprising—if voting is compulsory or quasi-compulsory, people will tend to vote irrespective of their degree of interest and irrespective of their views about Europe. Looking across at the second section of Table 8.13, one can see that compulsory voting also reduces the odds of being a circumstantial abstainer but not by nearly as much; again, this is perfectly understandable: there are some circumstances that inhibit participation that simply cannot be overcome. However, because compulsory voting is not, realistically speaking, available as a means of dealing with the problem of low turnout in European Parliament elections,[5] these findings are not as interesting as the sheer size of the statistical effect would, at first sight, imply. The advantage of including the variable in the analysis it that doing so allows us to consider the effects of other variables while taking into account the compulsory voting factor. Thus, even allowing for the fact that compulsory voting has a very substantial effect and that all the compulsory voting

---

4 The odds of an event occurring are defined as 'the ratio of the probability that it will occur to the probability that it will not' (Norusis 1994: 6).

5 See the discussion in Chapters 2 and 9.

TABLE 8.13. *Logistic regressions of voluntary and circumstantial Euro-specific abstention*

	Voluntary Euro-specific abstention				Circumstantial Euro-specific abstention		
Variable	B	S.E.	Exp(B)	Variable	B	S.E.	Exp(B)
Institutional and political context							
Compulsory	−2.576	0.236**	0.076	Compulsory	−1.087	0.150**	0.337
Weekday	0.911	0.107**	2.486	Weekday	0.965	0.106**	2.625
Proportional	0.015	0.007*	1.015	Proportional	−0.020	0.007**	0.981
National E	−4.201	4.821**	0.015	National E	−4.469	3.069**	0.012
Regional E	−1.305	0.409**	0.271	Regional E	−0.873	0.426*	0.418
Time elapsed	−0.188	0.176	0.829	Time elapsed	−0.085	0.172	0.918
Personal characteristics							
Age 25<	0.458	0.148**	1.581	Age 25<	0.545	0.143**	1.725
Age 26–35	0.383	0.102**	1.466	Age 26–35	0.461	0.102**	1.586
Manual	0.210	0.097*	1.233				
Education	−0.074	0.044	0.929	Education	−0.066	0.043	0.936
Relig pract	−0.231	0.036**	0.794	Relig pract	−0.123	0.036**	0.885
Other address	0.691	0.194**	1.995	Other address	0.886	0.161**	2.425
General political attitudes and SOEM attitudes							
Party attach	−0.221	0.036**	0.802	Party attach	−0.126	0.036**	0.882
Interest-P	−0.131	0.061*	0.877	Interest-P	−0.131	0.061*	0.878
Info-national	−0.183	0.060**	0.832	Info-national	−0.197	0.061**	0.821
Natnl pty-diff		*		Power of EP		**	
Fairly low	0.457	0.273	1.580	Fairly low	0.198	0.189	1.219
				Don't know	0.376	0.253	1.456
Fairly high	0.681	0.255**	1.976	Fairly high	0.437	0.188*	1.548
Very high	0.629	0.256*	1.876	Very high	−0.202	0.234	0.817

	B	SE	Exp(B)	B	SE	Exp(B)
Attitudes to the EU and EP						
Pro-EU as it is	-0.341	0.049**	0.711			
Pro rapid intg	-0.172	0.047**	0.842	0.092	0.045*	1.096
EU-involvement	-0.279	0.065**	0.756	-0.130	0.063*	0.878
EP reliability		**				
Fairly low	0.054	0.128	1.055			
Don't know	-0.393	0.198*	0.675			
Fairly high	-0.183	0.153	0.833			
Very high	-0.656	0.295*	0.519			
Euro pty-diff		**				
Fairly low	-0.575	0.164***	0.563			
Fairly high	-0.956	0.165***	0.384			
Very high	-0.918	0.182***	0.399			
Euro cand-diff		**				
Fairly low	-0.348	0.158*	0.706			
Fairly high	-0.504	0.152***	0.604			
Very high	-0.608	0.160***	0.545			
Campaign exposure						
Campaign		**			*	
Passive	-0.167	0.126	0.846	-0.019	0.140	0.981
Active1	-0.541	0.131**	0.582	0.014	0.138	1.014
Active2	-0.683	0.167**	0.505	-0.407	0.172*	0.666
Particular systemic effects						
DK or FR and anti-rapid intg	-0.331	0.095**	0.718			
GB and right-wing	0.778	0.292**	2.178			
Constant	-1.173	0.674		0.157	0.635	
Initial log likelihood function	5164.02			4557.61		
Improvement in fit	1229.58			558.17		
Degrees of freedom	46			46		

* = 0.05; ** = 0.01; *** = 0.001.   *Source*: EB 41.1.

countries vote on a Sunday, the day of voting has an independent effect on abstention: weekday voting increases the odds of being a voluntary Euro-specific abstainer by a factor of 2.49 and has a similar effect on circumstantial Euro-specific abstention. Why weekday voting might increase the likelihood of circumstantial abstention is clear: for some citizens, weekday voting simply imposes a direct obstacle to participation; as a consequence, they abstain, citing circumstances as their reason. But why should weekday voting be associated with increased voluntary abstention? The reason has to do, presumably, with the balance of costs and benefits. Weekday voting attaches a relatively high cost to voting; for some of those who explain their abstention in voluntary terms, the day of voting appears to be the factor that tilted the balance in the negative direction. The analysis suggests that, had these voluntary abstainers had the opportunity to vote on a Sunday, some of them would have taken part. The fact that weekday voting is conducive to voluntary and not just to circumstantial abstention increases its importance as an impediment to participation. Anticipating somewhat, one should also note that weekday voting has a somewhat weaker but still quite substantial effect on voluntary Euro-and-national abstention (see Table 8.14 below).

The institutional-context variable that does not contribute to predicting either of the types of abstention considered in Table 8.13 is the proportionality of the electoral system (the effect of this variable is statistically significant for both forms of Euro-specific abstention but is in the wrong direction in one case and is trivial in size in both). These findings are contrary to the results of previous research on turnout in European Parliament elections. There are two possible reasons for this discrepancy. The first is that we have included attitudinal variables that were not included in previous research and that capture more direct influences on turnout. Secondly, the proportionality hypothesis as applied to European Parliament elections may be somewhat fanciful: it may be expecting an unrealistically high degree of sophistication of the electors to imagine that the degree of proportionality that characterizes their national election outcomes actually influences their behaviour in European Parliament elections.[6]

Turning to the political contextual variables, again two out of the

---

[6] In order to maximize the comparability of the findings with those of previous research, the measure of the proportionality of electoral systems used here is that reported in van der Eijk and Oppenhuis 1996: 425.

three variables have a significant impact. Both concurrent national and regional elections substantially reduce the odds of being either a voluntary or a circumstantial Euro-specific abstainer, the effect of concurrent national elections being particularly pronounced.[7] This is as one would expect; in fact these results merely confirm the observations made in Chapter 2 on the basis of the data in Table 2.1 in the case of the concurrent national election effect and on the basis of the map in Figure 2.1 in the case of the regional election effect. It is useful, however, to have the effects confirmed by the statistical analysis and to be able to measure the effects of the other variables while taking them into account. Note that the tendency for concurrent elections to reduce abstention applies only to the two forms of Euro-specific abstention. Concurrent regional elections do nothing to reduce the odds of Euro-and-national abstention (see Table 8.14), presumably because most of those who abstained in the last national election are as likely to abstain in a regional election as in a European Parliament election. In the case of a concurrent national election, abstention in one election is almost automatically associated with abstention in the other; in this sense, a concurrent national election is associated with double abstention, a situation reflected in the positive B coefficient for this variable in the first section of Table 8.14.

The political contextual variable that does not appear to have a significant effect on participation or abstention is time since the last national election. We have used several operationalizations of the variable (the number of months since the last lower house election, the same measure but using the presidential election instead of the National Assembly elections in the case of France, both of these as a proportion of the maximum term of the assembly or office in question and, finally, the time until the next election, which is the measure used by Franklin et al. (1996). None of these variables has any effect on any of the forms of abstention.[8] This remains the case even if the

---

[7] The concurrent national election variable does not meet the criterion of significance in either the analysis of voluntary or of circumstantial Euro-specific abstention on the basis of the usual Wald test. However, Norusis points out that, when the B coefficient is particularly large, the Wald test is unsatisfactory, producing a statistic that is too small and leading one to fail to reject the null hypothesis when in fact one should do so. The alternative test is to build the model, first without and then with the variable in question, and to base the decision on the change in the log likelihood (Norusis 1994: 5). When this is done, the concurrent national election effect turns out to be significant in both analyses.

[8] The results reported in Tables 8.13 and 8.14 for this variable are based on the

concurrent national election variable is not included in the model, a situation that ought to give the maximum opportunity to the 'time' variable to play a role, since, to varying degrees depending on how it is operationalized, the time variable incorporates the concurrent election phenomenon. If we concentrate purely on the time elapsed or time to next election part of the variable, which we can do by omitting Luxembourg from the analysis, the result is the same.[9] While it is clear from the results reported in the previous paragraph that a concurrent national election makes a substantial contribution to increasing the level of turnout, these findings regarding the time variable cast doubt on the proposition that time since the last national election and the concurrence of a national and European election can be combined to form a single measure of electoral salience. In terms of our under-standing of turnout in European Parliament elections, the results tend to undermine the second-order election view that such turnout is a function of the role of European Parliament elections in the national political arena.

Research on turnout as such has identified a number of socio-demographic variables that affect people's propensity to vote and it would be surprising if these did not also affect turnout in European Parliament elections. As indicated in Table 8.12, the analysis ex-amined the possible impact of three categories of age. The two 'youth' categories have a significant effect on all forms of abstention, the effect being more pronounced in the case of Euro-and-national abstention (see Table 8.14). On the other hand, old age (being 81 or over) has no effect except in the case of circumstantial Euro-and-national absten-tion (this finding is taken up below). The effect of social class is limited to one form of abstention, albeit the most important form: having a manual occupation significantly increases the odds of being a vol-untary Euro-specific abstainer (by a factor of 1.23). At first sight, the effect of education appears to be quite limited. In the case of volun-

number of months since the last election as a proportion of the maximum term of office of the lower house of the legislature. It should also be noted that, in order to test the operationalization based on time until the next election, it has been necessary to use an estimate based on the average duration of inter-election periods for the Netherlands, as that country had not, at the time of writing, held a national election since the Euro-pean Parliament election of 1994.

[9] This is arguably the purest test of the electoral expectations hypothesis. When the elections coincide, the expectations variable is not, strictly speaking, measurable. If there is a concurrent national election, it is not that expectation of an election is at its maximum; rather, expectation has been replaced by actuality, a different matter altogether.

tary Euro-specific abstention, the educational effect is only significant with a probability of 0.095 and the factor by which the increase in education reduces this kind of abstention is only 0.93. If students, who by definition have moderate to high levels of education and who, as shown above, tend to have lower levels of turnout, are omitted from the analysis, the education variable becomes significant at 0.05 but the exponentiated coefficient is still only 0.92. Several considerations need to be borne in mind in assessing the performance of the education variable in the model, a performance that runs counter to the widely documented finding that education is a strong predictor of turnout in national elections. In the first place, one would not expect turnout in European Parliament elections to be as strongly affected by education. Secondly, the established educational effect on turnout may be partly indirect, i.e. education may function as an indicator of various attitudes, levels of political knowledge or political interest etc. Accordingly, the effect of education in the model may be limited partly because the model includes a substantial number of direct measures of such political orientations. Added to this, there are the difficulties with the measurement of educational levels in the Euro-barometer and with incorporating in a general model such particular effects as the tendency for those who completed their education at the age of 14 or under to have somewhat higher levels of participation than those who completed their education at 15 or 16 years of age.[10] In short, education has some effect on participation in European Parliament elections but, when a wide range of other variables are taken into account, the effect is, for understandable reasons, modest. The analysis confirms that degree of Judaeo-Christian religious practice affects three of the four forms of abstention considered. Finally, a personal characteristic that is not, strictly speaking, a socio-demographic characteristic has a marked effect on both forms of Euro-specific abstention: being registered at another address increases the odds of being a voluntary Euro-specific abstainer by a factor of 2 and increases the odds of being a circumstantial Euro-abstainer by a factor of 2.43. That the effect extends to voluntary Euro-specific abstention rather than being limited to the circumstantial variety suggests that the negative effect of practical obstacles to participation is wider than the reported levels of circumstantial abstention would indicate.

[10] See the discussion of both these aspects in the bivariate analysis of the relationship between participation and education above (pp. 211–13).

All of the variables measuring general political attitudes, second-order election perceptions, European attitudes, and experience of the campaign were included in the third stage of the analysis, using a stepwise variable selection procedure. As discussed above, the key issues here are the influence of attitudes to politics in general relative to the influence of European attitudes and the related question of the predictive power of the second-order election model.

Three national-level political variables—being attached to a party, being interested in politics, and being well informed about national politics significantly reduce the odds of each of the forms of abstention considered; the effects of party attachment and interest in politics are somewhat more pronounced in the case of combined Euro-and-national abstention. Moreover, the degree of left–right ideological alignment is a significant predictor of combined Euro-and-national abstention but has no effect on either form of Euro-specific abstention. What is equally, if not more, important, however, is the range of variables under this heading whose effects are so insignificant that they are not included by the variable selection procedure. This can be seen by comparing the list of variables in Table 8.11 with the variables that figure in the results in Table 8.13: being strongly dissatisfied with democracy in one's own country does not increase abstention; having a high party differential in national elections does not reduce abstention; the perception that the European Parliament has little or no power and the perception that it has less power than the national parliament do not increase the odds of any of the four forms of abstention. Moreover, three variables have effects opposite to those predicted by the prevailing theory: all other things being equal, having a high national party differential actually *increases* the odds of voluntary Euro-specific abstention; likewise, the perception that the Parliament has a fairly high degree of power *increases* rather than decreases the odds of circumstantial Euro-specific abstention; finally, the perception that there is less at stake in European Parliament elections than in national elections *reduces* rather than increases the odds of voluntary Euro-and-national abstention (see Tables 8.13 and 8.14). In short, several of the attitudes and perceptions that might indicate national political motivations for either participating or abstaining and all of those that are more or less directly related to a second-order conception of European Parliament elections either have no effect on turnout in European Parliament elections or have effects that are the opposite of those predicted by the theory.

The analysis confirms the expectation that one should not expect positive attitudes to European integration or to the Parliament or its election to have any particular effect on circumstantial abstention. Only two European attitude variables affect circumstantial Euro-specific abstention. The effect of the evaluative variable (support for rapid integration) is slight and, more importantly, is perverse—it increases the odds of abstention (see Table 8.13). The effect of the other variable makes more sense: EU involvement reduces the odds of circumstantial abstention, the effect being more pronounced in the case of circumstantial Euro-and-national abstention (see Table 8.14 below). Apart from these two minor effects, one can conclude that EU-related attitudes, preferences and orientations play no significant role in the explanation of circumstantial abstention in European Parliament elections. This finding underlines the importance of dealing directly with the causes of circumstantial abstention, a point which will be dealt with in Chapter 9. In more immediate research terms, it underlines the importance of distinguishing between circumstantial and voluntary abstention, in particular in tackling the problem of the effect of European attitudes on abstention.

In this regard, the results show that European attitudes affect the rate of *voluntary* abstention (of both kinds). Support for the EU as it is significantly reduces the odds of both voluntary Euro-specific and Euro-and-national abstention, the former somewhat more strongly. Support for rapid integration only affects Euro-specific abstention but a sense of EU involvement reduces both types of voluntary abstention. The index of EU knowledge also has a significant effect on voluntary Euro-and-national abstention; the effect is relatively slight—on the other hand, one should note that it occurs even when one has taken account of the effect of knowledge of national politics. Furthermore, all three of the attitudes that relate specifically to the Parliament or to the election (attitude to the reliability of the Parliament and perceived European party differentials and European candidate differentials) play significant roles in predicting both types of voluntary Euro abstention. For the reliability of the Parliament variable, the reference category is 'very low reliability'. Compared to this, even a don't know response reduces the odds of abstention. In the case of voluntary Euro-specific abstention, however, one must go to a very high evaluation of the reliability of the Parliament before one gets a further reduction in abstention. On the other hand, each increment in the perceived reliability of the Parliament has an effect, the effect in some cases being quite pronounced (see Table 8.13). In the case of European party differentials, the reference category is having a very low differential; compared to this base, any strengthening of the sense of having a party differential significantly reduces voluntary Euro-specific and voluntary Euro-and-national abstention. At very high levels of party differential, the odds are reduced by a factor of 0.40 in the case of Euro-specific abstention and 0.27 in the case of voluntary-and-national abstention. Each step up the candidate differential scale reduces Euro-specific abstention, whereas only the very highest level of candidate differential has a significant effect on Euro-and-national abstention. Taken as a whole, however, this evidence suggests that what is seen to be at stake in a European Parliament election has a significant effect on turnout whereas more subtle and complex calculations about the power of the Parliament or about its power relative to national parliaments or about there being less at stake in a European election as compared with a national election seem to be irrelevant. On this evidence, electors do not appear to abstain in European Parliament elections on the basis that they are second-order elections.

This brings us to the role of the campaign, a matter that, as emphasized, cannot, on the basis of the present evidence, be interpreted unambiguously as either an exclusively European or an exclusively national political influence. The first point to note about the campaign is that it has no effect on Euro-and-national abstention, either voluntary or circumstantial. This suggests that, allowing for all the other influences we have identified, the European election campaign does not directly mobilize those who are in most need of mobilization, namely those who have also abstained in their own national election. It must, of course, be acknowledged that exposure to the campaign could have indirect effects on the propensity of such people to vote by, for example, influencing their party or candidate differentials. A second and, perhaps, more important point is that passive campaign exposure has no direct effect on abstention of any shape or form. What is required is active exposure, that is reading about it or talking about it. Involvement in even one of these activities is associated with a reduction in the odds of voluntary Euro-specific abstention; involvement in both is required to achieve any reduction in the odds of circumstantial Euro-specific abstention.

Finally, there are the two particular effects included as the last items in the set of potential influences on abstention. Both effects are confirmed (see Table 8.13). Being Danish or French and being opposed to integration reduces the odds of being a voluntary Euro-abstainer by a factor of 0.72; being British and right-wing increases such odds by a factor of 2.12. The first effect is the more interesting of the two, because it has the potential to become more general. If European issues become more polarized and if parties and candidates articulate this polarization, then a higher level of electoral participation can be anticipated. In contrast, the second effect was particular in terms of time as well as place: it reflected the situation in Britain in mid-1994. It could of course arise elsewhere at any time but its incidence, being dependent on the domestic political situation, is difficult to predict. One might add that identification of this effect in Britain is the closest this analysis has come to finding a second-order effect on abstention. However, whereas the second-order model has tended to assume that the greater the degree of involvement in domestic politics the greater the probability of participation, this finding points to a case in which the reverse holds: more intense (right-wing) ideological commitment increases the odds of abstention.

In order to complete this survey of the sources of abstention in European Parliament elections, it only remains to review the relatively few factors that influence circumstantial Euro-and-national abstention (Table 8.14). Apart from compulsory voting, the dominant influences are age and being registered at another address. The youth effects that were evident in regard to the other forms of abstention are evident here also, but more strongly. For the first time, however, there is also evidence of an old-age effect that is quite powerful: being 81 or over increases the odds of circumstantial Euro-and-national abstention by a factor of 3.26. This suggests a correction to the conventional wisdom that says that abstention shows a curvilinear relationship to age: the relationship with circumstantial Euro-and-national abstention is curvilinear; the relationship with voluntary abstention (of either type) or with circumstantial Euro-specific abstention is not. The effect of being registered elsewhere is also more powerful in regard to this kind of abstention than in regard to the other types, suggesting that, for some people, the problem of registration at another address may be more than a very temporary problem. The attitudinal influences on circumstantial Euro-and-national abstention are few: party attachment, level of national political knowledge, and degree of involvement in the integration process. All three variables reflect a degree of political mobilization that, if it is present, assists in

TABLE 8.14. *Logistic regressions of voluntary and circumstantial Euro-and-national abstention*

Voluntary Euro-and-national abstention				Circumstantial Euro-and-national abstention			
Variable	B	S.E.	Exp(B)	Variable	B	S.E.	Exp(B)
Institutional and political context							
Compulsory	−2.675	0.314**	0.069	Compulsory	−0.964	0.261**	0.381
Weekday	0.572	0.155**	1.771	Weekday	0.116	0.208	1.123
Proportional	−0.002	0.011	0.998	Proportional	−0.053	0.014**	0.949
National E	1.242	0.627*	3.463	National E	0.997	0.508*	2.710
Regional E	−0.826	0.506	0.438	Regional E	−1.118	1.021	0.327
Time elapsed	−0.514	0.276	0.598	Time elapsed	−0.244	0.394	0.783
Personal characteristics							
Age 25<	1.378	0.191**	3.967	Age 25<	1.615	0.224**	5.029
Age 26–35	0.879	0.159**	2.408	Age 26–35	0.767	0.217**	2.153
Manual	0.237	0.148	1.267	Age 81>	1.227	0.460**	3.411
Education	−0.065	0.074	0.937	Education	−0.004	0.085	0.996
Relig pract	−0.355	0.059**	0.702	Relig pract	−0.163	0.079*	0.850
Other address	0.478	0.293	1.612	Other address	1.518	0.243**	4.563
General political attitudes and SOEM attitudes							
Party attach	−0.530	0.063**	0.588	Party attach	−0.489	0.075**	0.613
Interest-P	−0.385	0.100**	0.681	Info-national	−0.415	0.112**	0.661
Info-national	−0.197	0.094*	0.821				
Left–right	−0.249	0.080**	0.780				
Less at stake	0.186	0.076*	1.205				

Attitudes to the EU and EP					EU-involvement		
Pro-EU as it is	−0.194	0.077*	0.823		−0.303	0.105**	0.739
EU-involvement	−0.293	0.101**	0.746				
EU knowledge	−0.135	0.059*	0.874				
EP reliability		**					
Fairly low	−0.523	0.188***	0.593				
Don't know	−1.172	0.297**	0.310				
Fairly high	−0.940	0.227**	0.391				
Very high	−0.498	0.369	0.608				
Euro pty-diff		**					
Fairly low	−0.828	0.228**	0.437				
Fairly high	−1.122	0.235**	0.326				
Very high	−1.316	0.273**	0.268				
Euro cand-diff		*					
Fairly low	−0.227	0.236	0.797				
Fairly high	−0.433	0.234	0.649				
Very high	−0.675	0.259**	0.509				
Constant	2.297	0.976*			1.973	1.219	
Initial log likelihood function	2643.22				1467.60		
Improvement in fit	934.96				302.85		
Degrees of freedom	46				46		

* = 0.05; ** = 0.01; *** = 0.001.   *Source:* EB 41.1.

overcoming obstacles to participation and thus in reducing circumstantial abstention.

One can summarize the results of the multivariate analyses presented in this chapter quite briefly. First, some but not all of the contextual variables usually thought to affect abstention have a substantial impact (the ones that have an effect are compulsory voting, Sunday voting, and concurrent national and regional elections; those that do not are the proportionality of the (national) electoral system and the timing of the election relative to national elections). These effects vary according to the type of abstention: compulsory voting is less successful in reducing circumstantial abstention and the negative effect of weekday voting is more pronounced in regard to both types of Euro-specific abstention. Secondly, the evidence shows that the personal characteristic with the most consistent effect on abstention is age: substantial negative youth effects are found for all types of abstention; however, the popularly conceived curvilinear age effect applies only to circumstantial Euro-and-national abstention. The other very substantial inhibiting personal characteristic, or rather personal circumstance, is registration at another address. Social class effects appear to be quite limited and the effect of education appears to be, at best, modest, though one should note possible measurement problems in this area. Thirdly, and contrary to the findings of previous research, attitudes to the European Union have a significant impact on abstention: specifically, they affect both forms of voluntary abstention in European Parliament elections (the attitudinal influences on circumstantial abstention are minimal). Finally, the second-order explanation of abstention receives little or no support from the evidence. Some broad national political attitudes, mainly ones that reflect the individual's degree of general political involvement, have some effect on abstention but perceptions or calculations that indicate a presumed process of second-order reasoning do not help to predict voluntary Euro-specific abstention (which is the type to which the theory ought to apply) or any of the other kinds of abstention. This is in marked contrast to the impact on abstention of attitudes to the European Union and of attitudes and perceptions that relate to the European Parliament and to the European election itself. With this summary in mind, we can now turn to the conclusions that can be drawn from the evidence presented in this and the preceding chapters.

9

Conclusion: Participation, Democracy, and Legitimacy in the European Union

INTRODUCTION

In contemporary governance, more and more decisions are taken at an international or supranational level that is beyond the democratic control and accountability that can be achieved at the level of the individual state. There are many manifestations of this problem and they pose a major challenge to the process of representative democracy. The European Union presents both an acute instance of the problem and, especially through the European Parliament, a sustained attempt to deal directly with it. This book has been concerned with the relationship between people and parliament in the European Union, focusing in particular on participation and abstention in European Parliament elections, as a means of exploring this complex issue. An often unquestioned assumption has been that the legitimacy problems of the European Union stem in large part from the 'democratic deficit' of its institutions and, therefore, that an increase in the democratic content of these institutions would automatically increase legitimacy. Low levels of participation in European Parliament elections are presumed to both reflect and accentuate the problems of democracy and legitimacy in the Union. Yet the connection between participation, democracy, and legitimacy is not simple. One, and not necessarily the most important, indication of this is that the election of the European Parliament by direct universal suffrage did not ostensibly increase, to say the least, the legitimacy of the Union. Cynics might indeed suggest, with some obvious exaggeration but with a grain of truth, that the direct elections to the European Parliament increased rather than diminished the visibility, if not necessarily the reality, of its lack of legitimacy. Secondly, and more importantly, legitimacy itself is not monolithic: on the contrary, it can be expected to go up and down, to be concerned with several and perhaps many bodies at the same time, as well as to relate to specific fields or to be bounded rather than universal. The extent and breadth of the legitimacy of the Union has therefore to be explored, not whether that level of governance is or is not legitimate. Thirdly, democracy is a complex concept and the attempt to apply it at the supranational level multiplies this complexity. Fourthly, even the apparently obvious notion of participation has hidden pitfalls: both participation and abstention come in different forms and, in any event, as discussed in Chapter 1, if all of those who do participate were to behave according to the assumptions of the second-order election model that has been widely applied to European Parliament elections, participation in European Parliament elections would not add a jot to the legitimacy of the European Union. In short, it is not the case that more democracy would necessarily lead to more legitimacy; neither is it the case that more participation would necessarily mean more legitimacy. While low turnout may be a sign of a significant weakness in the process of democratic representation at the supranational level, the converse does not hold in all circumstances: more participation would not necessarily indicate a more representative political process at the European level; the effect would depend on the kind of participation involved.

What all this means is that understanding the connections between participation, democracy, and legitimacy at the European level depends on understanding the attitudes, perceptions, and behaviour of European citizens. This is why this book has devoted considerable space to analysing (1) attitudes to the EU, (2) attitudes to the European Parliament, and (3) the electors' perceptions of parties and candidates in and their experience of the campaign for the elections to the European Parliament in 1994. This concluding chapter summarizes the findings under each of these three headings. It then reviews the evidence regarding the connections between these attitudes and participation and abstention, taking into account also what abstainers themselves have told us about their reasons for not turning out to vote. This makes it possible to address the conundrums thrown up by previous research: is turnout in European Parliament elections idiosyncratic? Is it immune to the influence of attitudes to European integration? Is low turnout simply the inevitable consequence of the working of the second-order election model? Examination of these issues may throw some light also on the general problem of unequal electoral participation or what has been called 'democracy's unresolved dilemma' (Lijphart 1997). Finally, in addressing the question of how higher levels of participation might be facilitated or mobilized, the chapter concludes by examining the implications of our findings for the issues of institutional reform and the legitimacy of the European Union.

ATTITUDES TO THE UNION

Two conclusions emerge from the answers given to all the questions designed to assess the extent of support for the European Union among European citizens. The first is that this support is fairly widespread, though not as widespread as often assumed; the second is that it is fragile. Truly committed support for the Union does not seem to extend appreciably beyond a third of the respondents. On the other hand, outright opposition is markedly smaller, while there is in the middle a large group who, in regard to different aspects of integration, either find it difficult to adopt a clear line, are lukewarm, or are simply indifferent. These broad conclusions emerge from the separate and the combined analysis of a range of indicators of attitudes to integration that were used in this study, including both various standard Eurobarometer questions and questions added specifically for the purpose of the study.

For example, three in five think that their country's membership of the European Union is a good thing, only one-quarter are strongly in favour of efforts to unify Western Europe. The extent of apathy is indicated by responses to the 'dissolution' indicator: the proportion of those who say they would be 'relieved' if the Union were dissolved is only one in ten; the main 'sceptical' group, by far, is found among the substantial plurality (46 per cent) who declare, in one way or another, that they would be indifferent to a break-up of the Union. Lack of engagement with issues that are fundamental to the process of integration is confirmed by the fact that almost two in five either acknowledge that they have not thought about the appropriate scope of EU decision-making or give a don't know response to this question and that a further two in five respond to this matter on the basis of a 'general feeling' rather than having specific issues in mind. This suggests that the legitimacy of the scope of EU decision-making is limited not so much by opposition to EU involvement in particular areas, though both actual and potential opposition do exist, but by the lack of salience and awareness of the matter in the first place. When pushed by the question, people may express a preference as to whether a particular issue should be decided at EU or at national level but it is also clear that many people have only the most inchoate notion of the bounded character of the legitimacy of the European Union. Apathy is also indicated by the fact that the question of the democratic character of the Union does not agitate markedly the bulk of respondents and that the matter seems not to be for them of great moment.

Combined analysis of the entire set of EU indicators (in Chapter 8) suggested that there are three dimensions underlying attitudes to the EU: support for the EU as it is, support for rapid and far-reaching integration and degree of involvement in and engagement with the European integration process. The distinction between the first two dimensions is essential in assessing the extent of support for European integration. In regard to the third dimension, low levels of involvement and engagement are consistent with the final characteristic of people's orientations to the European Union that we examined: the distribution of knowledge of the European Union is heavily weighted towards the lower end of the scale, 28 per cent having virtually no knowledge at all, a further one-fifth having 'very little knowledge' and another one-fifth having 'some but not much' knowledge.

In short, the legitimacy of the European Union, understood as support among the mass public for this particular form of governance, is lower and more fragile than is often assumed; indifference, apathy, and ignorance are widespread and real commitment to integration is a minority pursuit. Perhaps the single most striking characteristic of European attitudes in the broad sense is lack of involvement. Integrationists may take heart from this on the grounds that it is better to have people uninvolved than opposed in that there remains scope to bring about greater involvement and increase the level of support for integration. However, such an outcome depends on the ability of the European institutions to elicit support and stimulate involvement and, in particular, on the ability of the Parliament to do so.

ATTITUDES TO THE PARLIAMENT

The European Parliament is certainly not seen by the public as a write-off either in itself or relative to national parliaments. Two in five see the European Parliament as being at least as powerful as their national parliament; the view that it is *substantially* less powerful is held by a minority of little more than one-quarter. Looked at in a future perspective, one-half of European citizens regard the likely impact of the European Parliament as equal to or greater than that of the national parliament and the view that its future impact will be substantially less than that of national parliaments shrinks to one in five. Given the different roles played by national parliaments in the various member states, it is not surprising that assessments of the relative power of the European Parliament vary across countries; more significantly, they vary also with levels of political knowledge: the higher the level of knowledge of politics (both European and national), the more likely it is that an individual will see the European Parliament as less powerful than the national parliament. This means that, while the Parliament may take some comfort from perceptions of its power, it should bear in mind that such perceptions are not always grounded in substantial political knowledge and experience. Like several other aspects of European attitudes, they are tenuous and may not be very effective in stimulating involvement or participation.

Among the various institutions of the European Union, the lowest reliability rating is accorded to the Commission and the Council of Ministers, but the Parliament is only marginally ahead of these two clearly unresponsive institutions: only two out of every five citizens see the European Parliament as even a fairly reliable means of ensuring responsive EU decision-making. To the extent that they believe in such responsiveness at all, European citizens look to national institutions, but no institution, European or national, is seen as a reliable instrument of responsive European governance by more than half of the citizens. A substantial part of the European Parliament's problem with its electorate lies in its image, or rather, in its lack of image. A plurality has no image of the Parliament, good or bad, and the proportion having either no image or a purely negative image of it amounts to a substantial majority (62 per cent). The bulk of the negative images of the Parliament refer to institutional aspects, some of these being criticisms made more in sorrow than in anger in the sense that they complain that the Parliament is not powerful enough. Given the preoccupation in some sections of the media with criticisms of the behaviour or of the salaries and expenses of MEPs, it is notable that only a small minority of European citizens share these concerns. A much more important problem for the Parliament is its failure to even begin to penetrate the consciousness of so many of its electors.

PARTIES, CANDIDATES, AND THE CAMPAIGN

More than half the European electorate has a *European party differential*, that is they attach a significant degree of importance to the matter of which parties win more or fewer seats in elections to the European Parliament. Party differentials in European Parliament elections are not only more widespread than might have been anticipated, more importantly, their distribution is not all that dissimilar to that of party differentials in national elections: more than half have an identical party differential in both elections and only a relatively small minority (18 per cent) see substantially less at stake in European elections. Furthermore, despite the fact that some of the electoral systems used in European Parliament elections put little or no emphasis on candidates, it also turns out that large numbers of European citizens have significant *European candidate differentials*. The proposition that 'there is less at stake' is one of the foundation stones of the prevailing approach to understanding European Parliament elections, namely the second-order election model. The evidence just summarized suggests that public perceptions stray quite far from what this model assumes.

European election campaigns vary markedly in form and in degree of penetration across the member states. While campaign exposure that involves some degree of activity on the part of the electors seems to have more of an effect on voters' perceptions and attitudes than does passive campaign exposure, the campaign as a whole could be faulted for not making a more decisive contribution to enhancing the perception of party and candidate differentials. Even in the absence of such an effect, however, the campaign may mobilize voters by simply bringing the election to their attention. This brings us to the question of how the campaign and the attitudes to parties, to candidates, to the Parliament, and to the Union, actually affect the probability of participating or abstaining in the European Parliament election.

SOURCES OF PARTICIPATION AND ABSTENTION

In approaching this problem this study draws on two modes of explanation. It begins with subjective explanations, i.e. with the obvious, though neglected, starting point of the reasons that abstainers themselves give for their non-participation. This enables one, first, to make a vital distinction between those who could not vote, irrespective of their interest in or commitment to European integration or of their political attitudes, and those who would not vote, because of something in their attitude to Europe or to parties or to politicians and candidates or to some other aspect of politics. There is an essential distinction between those who abstain in a European Parliament election for some *circumstantial* reason and those who can be described as *voluntary* abstainers. The second benefit of starting with abstainers' own explanations of their abstention is that they provide a preliminary but very significant insight into the range of reasons that lies behind these two forms of abstention.

Two-fifths of those who abstained in the European Parliament elections gave a purely circumstantial reason for doing so. The main inhibiting circumstances cited were work or time pressure, absence from home, illness or other disability, and registration or voting card problems. While some of these sources of abstention are, as it were, fixed quantities, it is also apparent that some of the circumstances that inhibit turnout are themselves affected by whether voting is on a Sunday or on a weekday, by the timing of the elections in mid-June, and by country-specific registration requirements and procedures. In particular, the analysis of circumstantial reasons for abstention brings out the point that, while Sunday voting tends on the whole to facilitate turnout, it also brings with it inhibiting factors of its own.

In the case of the majority of abstainers who explained their abstention in voluntary terms, lack of interest was the dominant voluntary reason given; this was followed by political distrust or dissatisfaction, feelings of not being adequately informed and dissatisfaction with the European Parliament electoral system. These reasons and the reasons given for circumstantial abstention are subjective and necessarily incomplete accounts. It is essential to probe beyond them. Doing so requires a systematic statistical analysis of the potential impact on turnout of a wide range of variables: institutional context, social and demographic characteristics, attitudes to national politics, parties, and elections, and attitudes to the European Union, to the European Parliament, and to the European election itself.

The relationship between each of these particular variables and abstention can be analysed in turn. This series of bivariate analyses suggests that attitudes to European integration do make a difference. For example, reported turnout in the European Parliament election of 1994 is 84 per cent among those who say that they would be very sorry if the EU were dissolved; it is 67 per cent among those who say they would be indifferent; and 62 per cent among those who would be very relieved. Turnout is also related to interest in European politics, to knowledge of the EU, to having a positive or even a mixed image of the European Parliament, and to regarding the Parliament as reliable in terms of ensuring the responsiveness of EU decision-making. Exposure to the campaign is also associated with higher turnout. The increments in turnout from one level of exposure to the next are not very large but, overall, there is a 22 percentage point difference in reported turnout between those with no campaign exposure and those with fully active exposure. Variations in turnout are also associated with whether or not the voter thinks it matters whether certain parties and candidates win more or fewer seats in the European Parliament election. In the shorthand terminology we have used, turnout is linked to European party and candidate differentials. It does not, however, appear to be determined by whether the voter sees *less at stake* in European as opposed to national elections. It also does not seem to be related to perceptions of the power of the European Parliament. In short, these findings suggest that turnout is related to attitudes to the European Union, to its parliament, and to the European election; at the same time, they raise question marks over the second-order election explanation of low turnout. Before confirming these indications, however, it is necessary to review the results of an analysis that takes all of the potential influences on turnout together and assesses their influence in a simultaneous or 'multivariate' fashion.

The multivariate analysis confirmed four important things. First, it confirmed the hunch that identification of the factors that affect abstention would be facilitated by breaking abstention down into its various components. Secondly, the analysis showed that turnout in

European Parliament elections is not simply influenced or not even mainly influenced by national political attitudes; European orientations play a significant role, among them being three distinct attitudinal syndromes—attitude to the European Union as it is, attitude to more far-reaching integration, and level of involvement in the integration process. Thirdly, it confirmed that electors who make adverse comparisons between the power of the European Parliament and their national parliament or between what is at stake in European elections and what is at stake in national elections are *not* any more likely to abstain in the European Parliament election. Whereas the variables that are central to the second-order election understanding of European Parliament elections do not play a significant role, other attitudes to the Parliament and the election—perception of the reliability of the Parliament, European party and candidate differentials, and exposure to the election campaign do significantly affect voluntary abstention in European Parliament elections. Fourthly, the analysis confirmed, though with a significant addendum, the influence of the core demographic variable, namely age. It also confirmed the obvious point that compulsory voting produces higher turnout. More importantly, it confirmed the negative weekday voting effect[1] but did not confirm the hypothesized effects of proportionality of the electoral system or of the timing of the European election in relation to national elections. It will be noted that several of these findings are in contrast with the results of much of the previous research in this area, which had concluded either that European attitudes make no difference and that proportionality and timing in the national election cycle are crucial or that it is more or less impossible to account for why some people turn out to vote and others do not. Also at variance with previous research are the indications that the second-order election model does not provide a persuasive account of the electorate's reasons for participating and abstaining in European Parliament elections.

This identification of the sources of low turnout gives some guidance on how to deal with the problem. There are two possible strategies that can be pursued in combating low turnout in European Parliament elections: those designed to *facilitate* voter participation and those designed to *mobilize* participation. The facilitation of voting is mainly a matter of the practical arrangements and rules that govern

---

[1] This has to be taken in conjunction with the negative effect of Sunday voting revealed by the open-ended question on reasons for abstention.

the conduct of the poll. The question of mobilization brings in larger institutional and political issues ranging from compulsory voting and concurrent elections to the formal and informal structures and processes that govern political decision-making and political competition in the arena in question. Accordingly, the task of teasing out the implications of the findings of this study for the appropriateness of alternative strategies of electoral mobilization at the European level will require a brief consideration of possible institutional developments in the European Union. First, however, it is necessary to deal with the issue of facilitating participation.

FACILITATING THE VOTERS

The practical arrangements for conducting the poll that have been shown to have a significant effect on turnout are, in ascending order of importance, the timing of the election in mid-June, the arrangements governing registration and the use of voting cards, and, finally, the day of voting. One-tenth of circumstantial abstention is directly attributable to being away on holiday. It is highly likely that this is an underestimate of the holiday factor as some significant but indeterminate proportion of those who simply cited 'being away from home' as their reason for not voting are likely to have been away on holidays. While June elections may fit the Euro-parliamentary calendar, they increase the likelihood of circumstantial abstention due to absence on holiday. The problem could be reduced by moving the election to another month, for example, to April.[2] Alternatively, it could be tackled by extending and facilitating access to postal voting, a measure that should be undertaken to deal with other forms of absence from home in any case. We have seen evidence to suggest that postal voting, where it exists, is more costly for the individual citizen; it is, therefore, not a totally satisfactory solution to the absence from home problem. Nonetheless, making it available to all voters in all member states in as simple and accessible a form as possible would facilitate participation.

As was pointed out in Chapter 2, problems related to registration have tended to be given markedly more prominence in the United

---

[2] The problem arising from the greater probability of *weekend* absences during June can be dealt with by addressing the problem of the day of voting as outlined below.

States than in Europe. Yet one form of registration problem—registration at another address—has been shown in the statistical analysis to have a substantial effect on circumstantial abstention, an effect that is confirmed by citizens' own accounts: these suggest that one-sixth of circumstantial abstention or, overall, about 5 per cent of all abstention can be traced to registration or voting card problems. Registration procedures should be simplified and made more efficient and voting card requirements clarified so as to remove these unnecessary impediments to participation. Britain, France, and Spain are the countries where the problems appear to be most prevalent.

Thirdly, and finally in terms of the practical arrangements for elections, a major change should be implemented with respect to the day of voting. It is clear that Euro-specific abstention (both circumstantial and voluntary) is significantly increased by weekday voting; but there is also substantial evidence of circumstantial inhibitions to participation arising from Sunday voting. This suggests two-day voting, as such a move would, in itself, increase the overall volume of turnout and would, at one and the same time, reduce the incidence of circumstantial abstention that occurs at present for different reasons and affects different groups in Sunday and weekday voting countries. The proposal is that the election would take place on both a Sunday and a Monday, a practice that had indeed been adopted in Italy for a long period for national and local elections. This change would have the added value of ensuring that voting occurred at the same time across the Union, while not constraining those citizens who are accustomed to voting either on a Sunday or on a weekday to forgo their usual or preferred practice. There would be the further advantage that the count would take place everywhere immediately after the close of the poll: one unfortunate consequence of the current arrangements would thereby be avoided, namely that which forces the citizens of the countries in which voting takes place on a weekday to wait for three days before being able to know the result of the election in their country, to the detriment of the experience of collective participation. In the interest of ensuring that electors are given the greatest opportunity to cast their ballot, the hours of voting should be made as extensive as possible during these two days. The major objection to this proposal is the additional administrative and financial burden that it would entail. However, these burdens must be assessed in the light of importance of facilitating voter participation. Remembering the point that voting is a low-cost, low-benefit activity and that, therefore, small reductions in the cost of voting may make all the difference in the overall balance of costs and benefits, every effort should be made to deal with any potential obstacles to participation that may be rooted in the prevailing practical arrangements for the poll. Voting on a single day may have suited a less mobile and less pressured society. Two-day voting, especially if it includes a weekend day and a weekday is more suited to contemporary society, in which the demands on people's time can be overwhelming. As a fledgling parliament that must be anxious about the level of participation in its elections, the European Parliament has a particular onus in this regard. Indeed, the European Parliament could, if it were to follow such a course of action, set an example that could be extended to national elections, thereby enhancing access to electoral participation at the national level as well.

MOBILIZING THE VOTERS

One way of mobilizing the voters would be to make voting compulsory. Compulsory voting works. The problem is that it is coercive and, as such, would neither be possible nor desirable for European Parliament elections. It would be impossible because it is manifestly unrealistic to expect to be able to introduce compulsory voting for European Parliament elections. If it were introduced for all elections, that would be different, but the prospects of such a development appear to be very remote (see p. 38 above). In any event, it would be undesirable for European Parliament elections because the real challenge is to provide the citizens with Europe-related reasons for participation; compulsory voting in itself would contribute nothing to this objective.

Evidence from the 1989 European Parliament election confirms the obvious point that voters can be more easily mobilized when European and national elections are concurrent. The problem is that it would be as impracticable to attempt to make European and national elections concurrent in all member states as it would be to introduce compulsory voting for European Parliament elections. One would either have to have European Parliament elections at different times in the various member states or one would have to introduce fixed terms for parliaments and governments and harmonize these with the term of the European Parliament. The first option would be a regression in integration; the second would be a leap forward that is at present inconceivable. The evidence of this study also shows, however, that participation increases when regional and European elections are concurrent. The relevance of this finding is that it might be regarded as more feasible to make regional or local elections concurrent with European Parliament elections. Such a measure should probably be considered in the long term, especially since a proliferation of elections may in itself reduce turnout. In the short to medium term, however, given the variety of forms and practices of regional and local government across the Union, this would be a mammoth undertaking. Even if it were possible, the issue remains as to whether, again in the short to medium term, it would be desirable. While it would increase participation, two problems would be greatly accentuated: that of participation being motivated by non-European considerations and that of any European message failing to be heard above the din of national and subnational politics. European elections need to establish their own identity before submerging themselves in the thick of local and regional politics. In summary, relying on sub-European forces to mobilize voters in European elections, while probably effective in the short term, would, in the short to medium term, be counter-productive in terms of improving the process of European representation.

The evidence presented above indicates that the proportionality of the electoral system has no discernible effect on participation and abstention. Accordingly, from the point of view of enhancing participation, the degree of proportionality of any proposed uniform electoral system for European Parliament elections would not appear to be an issue. However, the problem of abstention does add weight to the case for electoral reform at the European level and for a common electoral system. The evidence suggests that electoral reform is imperative but that the thrust of any effort to devise a uniform electoral system should be on making the system as transparent and as accessible to the voters as possible and on ensuring the presence of a significant candidate dimension to electoral choice. Discussions about a common electoral system need to take into account the fact that one-sixth of all voluntary abstainers referred to their dissatisfaction with some aspect of the electoral system as a reason for their abstention. In France, Germany, and Spain in particular, steps could be taken to bring Euro-parliamentarians closer to electors by dividing what has been up to 1994 a single district for the whole country into a number of constituencies. Apart from the need to bring elected representatives closer to those whom they represent, the prominence given to candidate choice by alternative electoral systems and the role that this could play in mobilizing voters should receive close attention.

As used in discussions of turnout in European Parliament elections, the term 'institutional' is frequently confined to reference to the practical aspects of the conduct of elections and to the particular institutional features of compulsory voting and the electoral system. There are, however, bigger institutional factors at work, in the sense of constitutional or quasi-constitutional features that define the context of elections and so affect the process of electoral mobilization. Consequently, while this is not the place to present a comprehensive analysis of either the present or the future institutional or constitutional shape of the European Union, some discussion of alternative institutional models is essential in order to tease out the implications of the results of this study for future strategies of electoral mobilization in the Union.

Such a discussion faces the problem that the relevant institutional models and concepts have all been developed on the basis of the experience of states, be they nation states or multinational states; at best they apply only by analogy to the European Union. The nature and limitations of the analogies involved can, however, be clarified by considering not the institutional models themselves but the fundamental attributes that define them. Lijphart has suggested that the basic distinction underlying all forms of democratic government is that between majoritarian and consensus models and has identified eight dimensions that define these fundamental forms.[3] This is a useful exercise but is too detailed and too tied to the historical experience of nation states to be directly applicable to the European Union. Instead, using Lijphart's model in a rather eclectic fashion, one can focus on just two dimensions that help to define alternative constitutional configurations in liberal democracies and that are particularly relevant to the European Union.

The first dimension is whether the style of decision-making tends to

---

[3] The eight dimensions are the degree of concentration of executive power, fusion versus separation of powers, asymmetric versus balanced bicameralism, two-party versus multiparty system, the dimensionality of the party system, a plurality versus proportional representation electoral system, unitary/centralized versus federal/decentralized government and, finally, an unwritten constitution with parliamentary sovereignty versus a written constitution with minority veto (Lijphart 1984: 36).

Concentration/dispersal of power

		Concentrated	Dispersed
Adversarial		Type I Britain	Type II The United States
Consensual		Type III The Netherlands	Type IV Switzerland

Style of decision-making

FIG. 9.1. Types of democratic governance

be adversarial or consensual. The former assumes a majority (single party or coalition) that governs while the opposition parties focus their efforts on seizing the levers of power at the next election. The latter involves various stages of involvement of most or all main parties and groups in the decision-making process; it presupposes a proportional representation electoral system and can take a neo-corporatist or a consociational form. The second dimension is whether power is concentrated or dispersed. Obviously, it is concentrated in unitary states and dispersed in federal systems. It is also concentrated in parliamentary systems with their fusion of legislative and executive power and it is dispersed in systems with a separation of powers. These distinctions are summarized in Figure 9.1. While the four abstract types defined in this way are not found in a pure form in any system, Britain can be regarded as an example of the concentration of power in an adversarial system and the United States as a system of adversarial politics substantially modified by federalism and the separation of power. The Netherlands, particularly during the heyday of consociationalism, is a case of highly consensual decision-making with a concentration of power and, finally, Switzerland combines consensual decision-making with federalism and the separation of powers.

The nature of electoral mobilization is quite different in each system. In the Westminster model (Type I) electoral mobilization aims at obtaining a governing mandate for a party or programme, the mandate being defined as holding a majority of seats on the basis of which an executive is elected and the mandate implemented. In the adversarial model in a separation of powers and, or, federal system (Type II), electoral mobilization produces various mandates (presidential and congressional at the federal level and gubernatorial and legislative at the state level). In such a system, the politics of the mandated majority are severely diluted. They are also diluted in consensual systems, even in those that have a strong concentration of power (Type III). Finally, mobilization on the basis of electoral mandates is at its most tenuous in systems, such as the Swiss, that are both consensual and involve the separation of powers and/or federal arrangements (Type IV).

As currently constituted, the European Union is an extreme variant of Type IV. In terms of the *first* dimension, the style of decision-making is clearly consensual rather than adversarial. This is so whether one considers the Commission, the Council, the Parliament, or the many ancillary bodies that make up the overall decision-making apparatus of the Union. Debates about the extension of qualified majority voting to wider areas and about the weighting of votes in the Council of Ministers only serve to highlight the centrality of consensual procedures. Beyond the borders of formal institutional procedures, the whole approach to and ethos of policy-making in the Union leads to the incorporation of groups representing a wide spectrum of interests in a way that is much more characteristic of neo-corporatist than of adversarial forms of governance. Turning to the *second* dimension, power in the European Union is quite clearly dispersed between the different levels of decision-making, as in a federal system, and between various institutions (Commission, Council, Parliament, and Court), as in a separation of powers system.[4]

Because, as argued above, electoral mobilization differs in different constitutional systems, any recommendations regarding strategies of electoral mobilization at the European level must take account of the

---

[4] The fact that one branch of the system—the Council of Ministers—tends to dominate the decision-making process does not mean that, in principle, the system is not closer to a separation of powers than to a fusion of powers system.

compatibility of the proposals with the present or possible future constitutional structure of the Union. Much of the discussion of the strengthening of representative democracy in the European Union focuses on the need to produce and implement a decisive electoral mandate. As Franklin, van der Eijk, and Marsh put it, 'until elections provide mandates to govern Europe in some particular fashion, the democratic deficit will continue to fuel the crisis of legitimacy that the European Union now faces' (Franklin et al. 1996*a*: 377). In some versions this requires that power be given to the Parliament either to elect the President of the Commission or the entire Commission or at least to direct or control its activities. Other proposals for bringing about an electoral mandate at the European level involve the intro-duction of an element of presidentialism into the system by means of the direct election by the European public of either an individual or collective presidency (Laver et al. 1996, Bogdanor 1989). The basic purpose of all proposals of this sort is to make the Commission adhere to the electoral mandate generated by a European election. In other words, they assume, implicitly or explicitly, that the legislature and executive in the Union should function along the lines of the Westminster model, or more like an adversarial presidential and separation of powers system, or, at a minimum, like a consensual system with a parliamentary system concentration of power. The evidence of this study suggests that, from the point of view of the political culture of European integration, such proposals are neither possible nor, for the purpose of mobilizing European voters, necessary.

To say that such proposals are not possible is, perhaps, an over-statement. In the long run and given a sufficient supply of those elusive commodities, political will and political leadership, all things may be possible. The point that emerges from the present study is that the creation of a strong electoral mandate at European Union level and the realization of the constitutional changes this would imply would face formidable obstacles in the political culture of Europe.[5] The obstacles are that the EU is a system of governance enjoying only limited and fragile legitimacy, that the legitimacy of the scope of EU governance is particularly underdeveloped, and that the awareness of its representative institutions, and especially of its Parliament, is very limited. Given this background, the project of producing and

---

[5] Other obstacles that the realization of such proposals might face are not con-sidered her.

implementing a strong electoral mandate faces a severe dilemma. On the one hand, the varied set of issues over which the Parliament has legislative competence or over which it might have such competence in the future does not have the potential to create clear and coherent alternatives to present to the Parliament's distant and disengaged electorate. On the other hand, the one issue that could create a majority and a minority in the Parliament and present clear alternatives to the electorate—the question of European integration itself— would risk breaking down the already fragile legitimacy of the system. Assuming that most European parliamentarians would wish to avoid the polarization and fragmentation that a campaign focusing on the issue of integration itself would involve,[6] they are then thrown back on the varied set of issues over which they can exercise some power and influence as the focus of the issue-appeal they make to the voters. In this respect, it must be borne in mind that both the Union and especially the Parliament are committed to the principle of subsidiarity. This inevitably provides the Parliament with a specialized and highly diversified agenda that is not reducible to simple alternatives that can be presented in an electoral campaign and that might be conducive to the construction of a straightforward electoral mandate. This problem is compounded by the evidence presented in this study to the effect that the public has only the haziest notion of the responsibilities of the Union and of the Parliament and little real appreciation of the implications of the principle of subsidiarity. In short, given the present state of European public opinion and given the current and foreseeable division of powers and responsibilities between the national and European levels, the mobilization of European voters on the basis of a mandate to govern Europe seems scarcely feasible.

If that is the bad news, the good news is that there are indications that electoral mobilization at the European level is possible without building everything on the shaky notion of a European electoral

---

6 This is not to suggest that the question of integration itself—how far and how fast it should go—should not be submitted to democratic approval. It is, however, to suggest that the best forum for doing so is the national forum with its more finely tuned and responsive political process. This may of course spill over into European Parliament elections as it does most obviously in Denmark. This is, however, very different from creating a pro-integration and an anti-integration platform at the European level with a view to making that the basis of voter choice and of the construction of a majority party or coalition in the Parliament.

mandate. The reason for the focus on an electoral mandate partly reflects the dominance of ways of thinking about elections that are based on national politics and partly, and more specifically, reflects the dominance of the second-order understanding of European Parliament elections. If low turnout were a function of the second-order status of the election in the minds of the voters, then it would appear that the only way to increase turnout is to make the European election more like a first-order election, i.e. more like a national election designed to produce a mandate and a government. This study has, however, provided both conceptual and empirical grounds for severely qualifying the second-order election account, at least in so far as the explanation of turnout is concerned. In particular, it has been shown that participation and abstention in European Parliament elections are not in fact affected by estimates of the power of the Parliament, nor by comparisons with the power of national parliaments, nor by calculations that there is less at stake than in national elections. Nor are they determined by general political attitudes, though these do play a role. In place of the second-order election conception of what goes on in the minds of the voters, the results presented here point to the influence of the campaign, of general attitudes to the European Union as it is, of attitudes to more rapid integration, of degree of involvement in the integration process, and of knowledge of the European Union. In terms of factors that are more directly within the control of the Parliament and of its members and aspiring members, attitudes to the reliability of the Parliament and to party and candidate differentials at the European level also influence the propensity to vote. In short, the evidence suggests that voters can be motivated by factors that are compatible with the present (and foreseeable) institutional structures and without resort to an unrealistic and unattainable notion of a European electoral mandate and the radical changes in European governance that creating and implementing such a mandate would require. It also means that the factors that increase or decrease turnout in European Parliament elections are, to some extent at least, subject to being influenced by the behaviour and the strategies of parties and politicians both during the campaign and in the period between elections.

Such a plea for what is in effect a modest approach to electoral mobilization and institutional engineering in the European Union is not based on 'minimalism' as far as the development of the European Union or the role of the European Parliament are concerned. It is in fact quite compatible with the fundamental objectives pursued by the Parliament since the initiation of direct elections, namely, the expansion of the competence of the Union in line with the principle of subsidiarity, the extension of qualified majority voting, and full co-decision with the Council on all legislation (Jacobs et al. 1995: 300–1). Far from reducing the role of the Parliament, this approach to mobilization and to the institutional shape of the Union has the effect of increasing it. This is so because there can be more give-and-take between European Parliament and Commission and between European Parliament and Council of Ministers in a context in which power is dispersed and decision-making is consensual. A consensual approach combined with the pronounced dispersal of power in the Union means that the Parliament would be able to look seriously and without strong external pressure from the 'executive' into legislative proposals and to amend or reject them on their merits. Given the granting of adequate legislative power to the Parliament in such a system, individual members of the European Parliament would be able to play a greater part in decision-making than their colleagues in many national parliaments in Western Europe. Such an emphasis on the role and freedom of action of individual members of Parliament has some precedents in the historical development of parliamentary politics and is also likely to resonate with European citizens who, as shown, are as concerned about which candidates win through to represent them as about which parties do so.

The process of electoral mobilization just outlined lacks the dramatic effect that would be attached to brandishing an electoral mandate. It is a slow, piecemeal process involving painstaking efforts to inform European citizens and to persuade them of the value of the process of European governance. It will also require strengthening of the image of the Parliament and improving citizens' perceptions of its reliability through greater activism by MEPs during inter-election periods. European election campaigning will need to be intensified, particularly in some member states, and this will have to be done in ways that will elicit active responses from the citizens. In terms of electoral choice, effective electoral mobilization will involve spelling out party differences across a wide range of complex issues that will not add up to simple alternative packages and will not be reducible to slogans and sound-bites. It will also, however, involve emphasizing the qualities and the achievements of individual candidates, be they incumbents or aspirants, a process that is not made easy by the electoral systems currently in place in several member states. The difficulties facing European electoral mobilization may be daunting; they are not, however, insurmountable and, in any event, they are rooted in the nature of European public opinion and in the nature of the integration process. Combined with the changes in the practical arrangements governing the elections advocated here and with a more transparent and more candidate-oriented electoral system, this modest but painstaking approach to European electoral mobilization should contribute to the enhancement of participation, democracy, and legitimacy in the European Union and to meeting the challenge to representative democracy that is posed by the emergence of internationalized governance.

APPENDIX

Questions in Eurobarometer 41.1 used in the analysis

Q.1. Are you . . . (NATIONALITY)?

a) (IF YES) Do you know whether your name appears in the Electoral Register (the register of people entitled to vote at the next General Election), under your present address, at another address, or does it appear at all?

- At present address
- At another address
- Don't know if registered
- Does not appear at all

Q.3. To what extent would you say you are interested in politics (READ OUT)

- A great deal
- To some extent
- Not much
- Not at all
- DK

Q.4. To what extent would you say you are interested in European politics, that is to say matters related to the European Union (European Community): a great deal, to some extent, not much or not at all?

- A great deal
- To some extent
- Not much
- Not at all
- DK

Q.5. In general, are you for or against efforts being made to unify Western Europe? Are you . . .?

- For - very much
- For - to some extent
- Against - to some extent
- Against - very much
- DK

Q.6. Generally speaking, do you think that (OUR COUNTRY'S) membership of the European Union (European Community) is . . . ?

- A good thing
- A bad thing
- Neither good nor bad
- DK

Q.7. Taking everything into consideration, would you say that (OUR COUNTRY) has on balance benefited or not from being a member of the European Union (European Community)?

- Benefited
- Not benefited
- DK

Q.8. Taking everything into consideration would you say that, in five years time, (OUR COUNTRY) will be on balance benefiting or not from being a member of the European Union (European Community)?

- Will be benefiting
- Won't be benefiting
- DK

Q.9. If you were told tomorrow that the European Union (European Community) had been scrapped, would you be very sorry about it, indifferent or very relieved?

- Very sorry
- Indifferent
- Very relieved
- DK

Q.10. On the whole are you very satisfied, fairly satisfied, not very satisfied or not at all satisfied with the way democracy works in (OUR COUNTRY)? Would you say that you are . . . ? (READ OUT)

- Very satisfied
- Fairly satisfied
- Not very satisfied
- Not at all satisfied
- DK

Q.11. And what about the way democracy works in the European Union (European Community)? Would you say that you are . . . ? (READ OUT)

- Very satisfied
- Fairly satisfied
- Not very satisfied
- Not at all satisfied
- DK

Q. 12. There has been a lot of discussion recently about the European Union (European Community). Some people say that too many issues are decided on by the European Union (European Community), others say that more issues should be decided on by the European Union (European Community). Which of the following statements comes closest to your view? (SHOW CARD**)

- Too many issues are decided on by the European Union (European Community)
- The number of issues decided on by the European Union (European Community) at present is about right
- More issues should be decided on by the European Union (European Community)
- On some issues there should be more European Union (European Community) decision making and on other issues there should be less (SPONTANEOUS)
- I have not really thought about it
- DK

Q.13. When you say (INSERT RESPONSE TO QUESTION 12), is this a general feeling that you have about the European Union (European Community), or have you specific issues in mind?

- General feeling
- Specific issues
- THE RESPONDENT DID NOT SPECIFY

What sort of issues?

(PROBE) Which other issues? (PROBE UNTIL THE RESPONDENT SAYS NONE)

Q.14. There was a European election on the (INSERT THE CORRECT WEEKDAY AND DATE FOR YOUR COUNTRY: Thursday, 9th June or Sunday, 12th June 1994). For one reason or another, many people in (OUR COUNTRY) did not vote in that election. Could you please think back to (INSERT THE CORRECT WEEKDAY AND DATE FOR YOUR COUNTRY: Thursday, 9th June or Sunday, 12th June 1994), did you yourself vote in the European election?

- Voted
- Did not vote
- Can't remember/refused

Q.19. (IF DID NOT VOTE: CODE 2 in Q.14) What was the main reason why you did NOT vote in that election?

(PROBE) Which other reasons? (PROBE UNTIL THE RESPONDENT SAYS NONE)

Q.20. Let us now look at some public figures.

Using this card, could you give me the name and letter of the individual who holds each of the jobs that I will read out? (SHOW CARD**)

- President of the European Commission
- European Commissioner appointed by (NATIONALITY) government
- (NATIONALITY) Minister of Finance
- (NATIONALITY) Minister of Foreign Affairs

CARD TO BE APPLIED - BUT NOT INSERTED IN THE FIELD QUESTIONNAIRE

A. (COUNTRY SPECIFIC NAME) (of a public figure, important in national or regional politics)
B. Jacques Delors
C. Perez de Cuellar
D. (NAME OF THE MOST SENIOR COMMISSIONER OF THE COUNTRY)
E. (COUNTRY SPECIFIC NAME)
F. (NAME OF THE NATIONAL MINISTER OF FINANCE)
G. (NAME OF THE HEAD OF THE NATIONAL GOVERNMENT)
H. (NAME OF THE NATIONAL MINISTER OF FOREIGN AFFAIRS)
I. Henry Kissinger
J. Bill Clinton

Q.25. Can you tell me which of the following countries are members of the European Union (European Community)? (SHOW CARD** - CODE IF YES)

- Denmark
- Spain
- Poland
- Switzerland
- Ireland
- Austria
- France
- Turkey
- Portugal
- Hungary
- Germany
- Norway
- None of these (SPONTANEOUS)
- DK

Q.26. In your opinion, how is the European Union, the European Unification advancing nowadays? Please look at these people (Show card**).
No. 1 is standing still, No. 7 is running as fast as possible. Choose the
one which best corresponds with your opinion of the European Union,
European Unification.

- 1
- 2
- 3
- 4
- 5
- 6
- 7
- DK

Q.27. And which corresponds best to what you would like? (SHOW SAME
CARD**)

- 1
- 2
- 3
- 4
- 5
- 6
- 7
- DK

Q.28. Are you for or against the formation, for the European Union, of a
European government responsible to the European Parliament?

- For
- Against
- DK

Q.31. As well as thinking of themselves as (NATIONALITY) or (ADD IF
APPROPRIATE (NATIONALITY) AND/OR SUBNATIONALITY), or whatever,
some people think of themselves ALSO as European. Others do not do
so. How about you? (SHOW CARD**) Please choose between the two
ends of the scale. If you fully agree with the opinion on the left hand
side, you give a score of 1. If you fully agree with the opinion on the
right hand side, you give a score of 10. The scores in between allow you
to say how close to either side you are.

NOT AT ALL, ALSO EUROPEAN									VERY MUCH, ALSO EUROPEAN	DK
1	2	3	4	5	6	7	8	9	10	11

Q.32. How much confidence do you have that the decisions made by the European Union (European Community) will be in the interest of (OUR COUNTRY)? (READ OUT)

- A great deal of confidence
- A fair amount of confidence
- Not very much of confidence
- No confidence at all
- DK

Q.33. Many important decisions are made by the European Union (European Community). They might be in the interest of people like yourself, or they might not.

To what extent do you feel you can rely on each of the following to make sure that these decisions are in the interest of people like yourself? (SHOW CARD**) Please use this scale. (READ OUT)

(a) First, to what extent do you feel you can rely on the European Commission?

(b) And what about the (NATIONALITY) government?

(c) And what about the European Court of Justice?

(d) And what about the Council of Ministers of the European Union (European Community), representing the national governments?

(e) And what about the (NATIONAL) (PARLIAMENT - OR - NAME OF THE LOWER HOUSE OF PARLIAMENT)

(f) And what about the European Parliament?

	CANNOT RELY ON IT AT ALL									CAN RELY ON IT COMPLETELY	DK
a) The European Commission	1	2	3	4	5	6	7	8	9	10	11
b) The (NATIONALITY) government	1	2	3	4	5	6	7	8	9	10	11
c) The European Court of Justice	1	2	3	4	5	6	7	8	9	10	11
d) The Council of Ministers of the European Union (European Community) representing the national governments	1	2	3	4	5	6	7	8	9	10	11
e) The (NATIONAL) (PARLIAMENT - OR - NAME OF THE LOWER HOUSE OF PARLIAMENT)	1	2	3	4	5	6	7	8	9	10	11
f) The European Parliament	1	2	3	4	5	6	7	8	9	10	11

Q.34.   We are interested in the good points and bad points about the European Parliament. First, is there anything in particular that you LIKE about the European Parliament?

What else? (PROBE UNTIL THE RESPONDENT SAYS NO)

Q.35.   And is there anything in particular that you DISLIKE about the European Parliament?

What else? (PROBE UNTIL THE RESPONDENT SAYS NO)

Q.36.   a) As it stands now, how much power do you think the European Parliament has? Please give me your opinion using this scale, on which 1 indicates no power at all and 10 indicates a great deal of power. (SHOW CARD)
b) And what about the (NATIONAL) (PARLIAMENT - OR - NAME OF THE LOWER HOUSE OF PARLIAMENT)?

	NO POWER AT ALL										A GREAT DEAL OF POWER	DK
a) The European Parliament	1		2	3	4	5	6	7	8	9	10	11
b) The (NATIONAL) (PARLIAMENT - OR - NAME OF THE LOWER HOUSE OF PARLIAMENT)	1		2	3	4	5	6	7	8	9	10	11

Q.37.   a) Thinking of the future, how much effect do you think what the European Parliament does will have on people like yourself? Please use this scale. (SHOW CARD**)
b) And how about the effect on people like yourself of what that (NATIONAL) (PARLIAMENT - OR - NAME OF THE LOWER HOUSE OF PARLIAMENT) does?

	NO EFFECT AT ALL										A VERY BIG EFFECT	DK
a) The European Parliament	1		2	3	4	5	6	7	8	9	10	11
b) The (NATIONAL) (PARLIAMENT - OR - NAME OF THE LOWER HOUSE OF PARLIAMENT)	1		2	3	4	5	6	7	8	9	10	11

Q.38.   a) Some people think that it would be a very good idea if the European Union (European Community) developed into a United States of

Europe. Others think it would be a very bad idea. Where would YOU
place YOURSELF on this new scale? (SHOW CARD**)

b) And where would you place the view of the (NATIONALITY)
government on this same scale?

	VERY BAD IDEA									VERY GOOD IDEA	DK
a) You, yourself	1	2	3	4	5	6	7	8	9	10	11
b) The (NATIONALITY) government	1	2	3	4	5	6	7	8	9	10	11

Q.39. At the European election we have just had, the parties and candidates
campaigned for votes. Did their campaigns come to your attention in
any of the following ways?
(READ OUT IN TURN - CODE IF YES)

- Party workers called to your home to ask for votes
- Election leaflets put in your letterbox or given to you on the street or
  in shopping centres etc
- Advertising on behalf of the candidates or parties
- Coverage of the campaign in the newspapers
- Coverage of the campaign on TV and radio
- Family or friends or acquaintances discussing the European election
- None of these (SPONTANEOUS)
- DK

Q.42. a) In an election, some parties win more seats and some parties win
fewer seats. Some say that it matters very little, other people say that it
matters a great deal. Thinking about a European election like the one
we have just had, where would you place your own view on this scale?
(SHOW CARD**)

b) And how about an election for the (NATIONAL) (PARLIAMENT - OR -
NAME OF THE LOWER HOUSE OF PARLIAMENT)

	IT DOESN'T MATTER AT ALL									IT MATTERS A GREAT DEAL	DK
a) A European election	1	2	3	4	5	6	7	8	9	10	11
b) An election for the (NATIONAL) (PARLIAMENT - OR - NAME OF THE LOWER HOUSE OF PARLIAMENT)	1	2	3	4	5	6	7	8	9	10	11

Q.43. a) Let us now focus on candidates rather than parties.
How much do you think it matters WHICH PARTICULAR CANDIDATES win seats in a European election like one we have just had? (SHOW CARD**)

b) And how about an election for the (NATIONAL) (PARLIAMENT - OR - NAME OF THE LOWER HOUSE OF PARLIAMENT)

	IT DOESN'T MATTER AT ALL									IT MATTERS A GREAT DEAL	DK
a) A European election	1	2	3	4	5	6	7	8	9	10	11
b) An election for the (NATIONAL) (PARLIAMENT- OR - NAME OF THE LOWER HOUSE OF PARLIAMENT)	1	2	3	4	5	6	7	8	9	10	11

DEMOGRAPHICS

D.1.   In political matters people talk of 'the left' and 'the right'. How would you place your views on this scale?
(SHOW CARD** - DO NOT PROMPT. IF CONTACT HESITATES, ASK TO TRY AGAIN)

LEFT									RIGHT
1	2	3	4	5	6	7	8	9	10

- Refusal
- DK

D.2.   Do you consider yourself close to any particular party?
a) (IF YES) Do you consider yourself to be very close to this party, fairly close, or merely a sympathizer?

- Very close
- Fairly close
- Merely a sympathizer
- Close to no particular party
- DK

b) (IF CODE 4 OR CODE 5 AT D.2.a)
Do you consider yourself a little closer to one of the political parties than the others?

- Yes
- No
- DK

D.5.A   The last general election took place in (INSERT MONTH AND YEAR OF LAST GENERAL ELECTION). For one reason or another, many people in (OUR COUNTRY) did not vote in that election.
Could you please think back to that election, the one in (INSERT MONTH AND YEAR OF LAST GENERAL ELECTION). Did you vote in that election or not?

- Voted
- Did not vote
- Can't remember/refused

D.6. a) Are you yourself a member of a trade union?
b) And is anyone else in your household a member of a trade union?

	YES	NO	DK
Respondent	1	2	3
Anyone else in household	1	2	3

D.7. Are you . . . ?

- Single
- Married
- Living as married
- Divorced
- Separated
- Widowed

D.8. How old were you when you stopped full-time education? (IF STILL STUDYING: CODE 00 - GO TO D.10)

D.10. Sex

- Male
- Female

D.11. How old are you?
YEARS OF AGE

D.15. a) What is your current occupation?
b) (IF NOT DOING ANY PAID WORK CURRENTLY - CODES 1 TO 4 in D.15.a). Did you do any paid work in the past? What was your last occupation?

	CURRENT OCCUPATION	LAST OCCUPATION
NON-ACTIVE		
Responsible for ordinary shopping and looking after the home, or without any current occupation, not working	1	—
Student	2	—
Unemployed or temporarily not working	3	—
Retired or unable to work through illness	4	—

	CURRENT OCCUPATION	LAST OCCUPATION
SELF-EMPLOYED		
Farmer	5	1
Fisherman	6	2
Professional (lawyer, medical practitioner, accountant, architect, . . .)	7	3
Owner of a shop, craftsmen, other self-employed person	8	4
Business proprietors, owner (full or partner) of a company	9	5
EMPLOYED		
Employed professional (employed doctor, lawyer, accountant, architect)	10	6
General management, director or top management (managing directors, director general, other director)	11	7
Middle management, other management (department head, junior manager, teacher, technician)	12	8
Employed position, mainly at a desk	13	9
Employed position, not at a desk but travelling (salesman, driver)	14	10
Employed position, not at a desk, but in a service job (hospital, restaurant, police, fireman, . . .)	15	11
Supervisor	16	12
Skilled manual worker	17	13
Other (unskilled) manual worker, servant	18	14
NEVER DID ANY PAID WORK	—	15

D.23. If you were asked to choose one of these five names for your social class, which would you say you belong to?

  • Middle class
  • Lower middle class
  • Working class
  • Upper class
  • Upper middle class
  • Refuses to be classified
  • Other
  • DK

D.26. Do you consider yourself as belonging to a particular religion? (IF YES) Which one?

- Roman Catholic
- Protestant
- Orthodox
- Jewish
- Muslim
- Buddhist
- Hindu
- Other
- None
- DK

D.27. (TO THOSE WITH CODE 1 TO 4 ON D.26)
Do you attend religious services several times a week, once a week, a few times a year, once a year or less or never? (ONE ANSWER ONLY)

- Several times a week
- Once a week
- A few times a year
- Once a year or less
- Never
- DK

REFERENCES

ALDRICH, J. H. (1993). 'Rational choice and turnout'. *American Journal of Political Science*, 37/1: 246–78.

—— and NELSON, F. D. (1984). *Linear Probability, Logit, and Probit Models*. Newbury Park, Calif.: A Sage University paper/Quantitative applications in the Social Sciences No. 45.

ANDUIZA, P. E. (1995). 'Looking for cross-national variation on the individual determinants of electoral participation'. Unpublished paper presented at the European Consortium for Political Research Joint Sessions, Bordeaux.

AUBERT, J. F. (1979). *Exposé des institutions politiques de la Suisse à partir de quelques affaires controversées*. Lausanne: Payot.

BARDI, L. (1996). 'Transnational trends in European parties and the 1994 elections of the European parliament'. *Party Politics*, 2/1.

BARRY, B. (1978). *Sociologists Economists and Democracy*. Chicago: University of Chicago Press.

BLAIS, A., and CARTY, R. K. (1990). 'Does proportional representation foster voter turnout?' *European Journal of Political Research*, 18/2: 167–81.

BLUMLER, J. G. (1984). 'European voters' response to the first Community elections', in K. Reif (ed.), *European Elections 1979/81 and 1984: Conclusion and Perspectives from Empirical Research*. Berlin: Quorum.

—— and FOX, A. D. (1982). *The European Voter: Popular Responses to the First Community Election*. London: Policy Studies Institute.

BOGDANOR, V. (1989). 'Direct elections, representative democracy and European integration'. *Electoral Studies*, 8/3: 205–16.

BORG, S. (1995). 'Electoral Participation', in J. van Deth and E. Scarbrough (eds.), *The Impact of Values*. Beliefs in Government Vol. 1. Oxford: Oxford University Press.

BRODY, R. A. (1978). 'The puzzle of political participation in America', in A. King (ed.), *The New American Political System*. Washington, DC: American Enterprise Institute.

BUDGE, I., and FARLIE, D. (1976). 'A comparative analysis of factors correlated with turnout and voting choice', in I. Budge, I. Crewe, and D. Farlie (eds.), *Party Identification and Beyond: Representations of Voting and Party Competition*. London: John Wiley & Sons.

—— CREWE, I., and FARLIE, D. (eds.) (1976). *Party Identification and Beyond: Representations of Voting and Party Competition*. London: John Wiley & Sons.

BURNHAM, W. D. (1979). 'The appearance and disappearance of the American voter', in W. D. Burnham (ed.), *The Disappearance of the American Voter*. Washington, DC: American Bar Association.

—— (1982). *The Current Crisis in American Politics*. New York: Oxford University Press.

CAMPBELL, A., CONVERSE, P. E., MILLER, W. E., and STOKES, D. E. (1960). *The American Voter*. Chicago: University of Chicago Press.

CONVERSE, P. E. (1970). 'Attitudes and non-attitudes: continuation of a dialogue', in E. R. Tufte (ed.), *The Quantitative Analysis of Social Problem*. Reading, Mass.: Addison Wesley.

CREPAZ, M. (1990). 'The impact of party polarisation and postmaterialism on voter turnout: a comparative study of 16 industrial democracies'. *European Journal of Political Research*, 18/2: 183–205.

CREWE, I. (1981). 'Electoral participation', in D. Butler et al. (eds.), *Democracy at the Polls: A Comparative Study of Competitive National Elections*. Washington, DC: American Enterprise Institute.

DANIELS, P. A. (1996). 'Italy', in J. Lodge (ed.), *The 1994 Elections to the European Parliament*. London: Pinter.

DENITCH, B. (ed.) (1979). *The Legitimation of Regimes*. London: Sage.

DIMITRAS, P. E. (1994). 'Greece'. *Electoral Studies*, 13/4: 343–6.

DITTRICH, K., and JOHANSEN, L. N. (1983). 'Voting turnout in Europe, 1945–78: myths and realities', in H. Daalder and P. Mair (eds.), *Western European Party Systems*. London: Sage.

DOWNS, A. (1957). *An Economic Theory of Democracy*. New York: Harper & Row.

DUCHESNE, S., and FROGNIER, A.-P. (1995). 'Is there a European identity?' in O. Niedermayer and R. Sinnott (eds.), *Public Opinion and Internationalized Governance*. Beliefs in Government 2. Oxford: Oxford University Press.

EASTON, D. (1965). *A Systems Analysis of Political Life*. New York: Wiley.

Eurobarometer (1993). *Eurobarometer 39*. Brussels: European Commission, June.

—— (1994). *Eurobarometer: Trends 1974–1993*. Brussels: European Commission, May.

Euromonitor (1993). European travel and tourism marketing directory. London: Euromonitor plc.

FEATHERSTONE, K. (1994). 'Jean Monnet and the "democratic deficit" in the European Union.' *Journal of Common Market Studies*, 32/2: 149–70.

FERRERO, G. (1945). *Power*. New York: Brentano.

FITZMAURICE, J. (1994). 'Belgium'. *Electoral Studies*, 13/4: 331–3.

FLICKINGER, R. S., and STUDLAR, D. T. (1992). 'The disappearing voters? Exploring declining turnout in Western European elections'. *Western European Politics*, 15: 1–16.

FONT, J. and VIRÓS, R. (1995). 'Catalan electoral abstention: a critical review', in J. Font and R. Virós (eds.), *Electoral Abstention in Europe*. Barcelona Institut de Ciències Polítiques i Sociales: 11–40.

FRANKLIN, M. (1996), 'Electoral participation', in L. LeDuc, R. G. Niemi, and P. Norris (eds.), *Elections and Voting in Global Perspective*. Thousand Oaks, Calif.: Sage.

—— VAN DER EIJK, C., and OPPENHUIS, E. (1994). 'One electorate or many? Accounting for electoral participation in Europe'. Unpublished manuscript.

———— and MARSH, M. (1996a). 'Conclusions: the electoral connection and the democratic deficit', in M. Franklin and C. van der Eijk (eds.), *Choosing Europe? The European Electorate and National Politics in the Face of Union*. Ann Arbor: University of Michigan Press.

———— and OPPENHUIS, E. (1996b). 'The institutional context: turnout', in M. Franklin and C. van der Eijk (eds.), *Choosing Europe? The European Electorate and National Politics in the Face of Union*. Ann Arbor: University of Michigan Press.

GAFFNEY, J. (1996). 'France', in J. Lodge (ed.), *The 1994 Elections to the European Parliament*. London: Pinter.

GOLDEY, D. B. (1994). 'Portugal'. *Electoral Studies*. 13/4: 359–62.

GOSNELL, H. G. (1930). *Why Europe Votes*. Chicago: Chicago University Press.

GRAFSTEIN, R. (1981a). 'The legitimacy of political institutions'. *Polity*, 14/1: 51–69.

—— (1981b). 'The failure of Weber's conception of legitimacy: its causes and implications'. *Journal of Politics*, 43: 456–72.

GRUNBERG, G. (1994). 'France'. *Electoral Studies*, 13/4: 336–8.

HEARL, D. (1994). 'Luxembourg'. *Electoral Studies*, 13/4: 349–57.

HELD, D. (1996). *Models of Democracy* (2nd edn.). Cambridge: Polity.

HERMAN, V., and LODGE, J. (1978). 'Democratic legitimacy and direct elections to the European Parliament'. *Western European Politics*, 1/2: 226–51.

HIRCZY, W. (1994). 'The impact of mandatory voting laws on turnout: a quasi-experimental approach'. *Electoral Studies*, 13: 64–76.

INGLEHART, R., and RABIER, J.-R. (1979). 'Europe elects a parliament: cognitive mobilization and pro-European attitudes as influences on voter turnout'. *Government and Opposition*, special issue 'After the European Elections', 14/4: 479–507.

IRWIN, G. (1994). 'The Netherlands'. *Electoral Studies*, 13/4: 357–9.

—— (1995). 'Second-order or third-rate? Issues in the campaign for the elections for the European Parliament 1994'. *Electoral Studies*, 14/2: 183–99.

JACKMAN, R. W. (1987). 'Political institutions and voter turnout in the industrial democracies'. *American Political Science Review*, 81/2: 405–23.

JACOBS, F., CORBETT, R., and SHACKLETON, M. (1995). *The European Parliament* (3rd edn.). London: Cartermill International Ltd.

KAASE, M., and NEWTON, K. (1995). *Beliefs in Government*. Beliefs in Government 5. Oxford: Oxford University Press.

KERR, H. H. (1987). 'The Swiss party system: steadfast and changing', in H. Daalder (ed.), *Party Systems in Denmark, Austria, Switzerland, the Netherlands, and Belgium*. London: Pinter.

KLINGEMANN, H.-D. (1994). 'Germany'. *Electoral Studies*, 13/4: 338–41.

LANCELOT, A. (1968). *L'Abstentionnisme électoral en France*. Paris: Fondation Nationale des Sciences Politiques, Armand Colin.

LANE, J. E., and ERSSON, S. (1990). 'Macro and micro understanding in political science: what explains electoral participation?' *European Journal of Political Research*, 18/4: 457–65.

LAVER, M., et al. (1995). *Electing the President of the Commission*. Trinity Blue Papers in Public Policy No. 1. Dublin: Trinity College.

LAZARSFELD, P. F., BERELSON, B., and GAUDET, H. (1948). *The People's Choice*. New York: Columbia University Press.

LEIGHLEY, J. E. (1994). 'Attitudes, opportunities, and incentives: a field essay on political participation'. *Political Research Quarterly*, 48/1: 181–209.

LIJPHART, A. (1977). *Democracy in Plural Societies*. New Haven: Yale University Press.

—— (1984). *Democracies: Patterns of Majoritarian and Consensus Government in Twenty-one Countries*. New Haven: Yale University Press.

—— (1997). 'Unequal participation: democracy's unresolved dilemma'. *American Political Science Review*, 91/1: 1–14.

LINDER, W. (1994). *Swiss Democracy*. New York: St Martin's Press.

LINZ, J. J. (1969). 'Ecological analysis and survey research', in M. Dogan and S. Rokkan (eds.), *Quantitative Ecological Analysis in the Social Sciences*. Cambridge, Mass.: MIT Press.

LODGE, J. (ed.) (1990). *The 1989 Election of the European Parliament*. London: Macmillan.

—— (1995). 'Democratic legitimacy and the EC: crossing the Rubicon'. *International Journal of Public Administration*, 18/10: 1595–637.

—— (1996). *The 1994 Election to the European Parliament*. London: Pinter.

MACKIE, T. T., and ROSE, R. (1991). *The International Almanac of Electoral History* (3rd edn.). London: Macmillan.

MADDALA, G. S. (1983). *Limited Dependent and Qualitative Variables in Econometrics*. Cambridge: Cambridge University Press.

MAGONE, J. M. (1996). 'Portugal', in J. Lodge (ed.), *The 1994 Elections to the European Parliament*. London: Pinter.

MARSH, M. (1991). 'Accident or design? Non-voting in Ireland'. *Irish Political Studies*, 6: 1–14.

—— (1994). 'The Republic of Ireland'. *Electoral Studies*, 13/4: 346–7.

MERRIAM, C. E., and GOSNELL, H. G. (1924). *Non Voting: Causes and Methods of Control*. Chicago: Chicago University Press.

MORTIMORE, R. (1994). 'Great Britain'. *Electoral Studies*, 13/4: 341–3.

MOXON-BROWNE, E. (1996). 'Republic of Ireland', in J. Lodge (ed.), *The 1994 Elections to the European Parliament*. London: Pinter.

NIEDERMAYER, O. (1990). 'Turnout in European Elections'. *Electoral Studies*, 9: 45–50.

—— (1995). 'Trends and contrasts', in O. Niedermayer and R. Sinnott (eds.), *Public Opinion and Internationalized Governance*. Beliefs in Government 2. Oxford: Oxford University Press.

—— and SINNOTT, R. (1995). 'Democratic legitimacy and the European Parliament', in O. Niedermayer and R. Sinnott (eds.), *Public Opinion and Internationalized Governance*. Beliefs in Government 2. Oxford: Oxford University Press.

NIELSEN, H. J. (1996). 'Denmark', in J. Lodge (ed.), *The 1994 Elections to the European Parliament*. London: Pinter.

NORUSIS, M. J. (1994). *SPSS Advanced Statistics*. Chicago: SPSS Inc.

OPPENHUIS, E. (1995). *Voting Behavior in Europe: A Comparative Analysis of Electoral Participation and Party Choice*. Amsterdam: Het Spinhuis Publishers.

PATERSON, W. E., LEES, C., and GREEN, S. (1996). 'The Federal Republic of Germany', in J. Lodge (ed.), *The 1994 Elections to the European Parliament*. London: Pinter.

PINDER, J. (1994). 'The European elections of 1994 and the future of the European Union'. *Government and Opposition*, 29/4: 494–514.

PIVEN, F. P., and CLOWARD, R. A. (1988). *Why Americans don't Vote*. New York: Pantheon Books.

POWELL, G. B. (1980). 'Voting turnout in thirty democracies', in R. Rose (ed.), *Electoral Participation*. London: Sage.

—— (1982). *Contemporary Democracies: Participation, Stability, and Violence*. Cambridge, Mass.: Harvard University Press.

—— (1986). 'Voter turnout in comparative perspective'. *American Political Science Review*, 80/1: 17–44.

RAGSDALE, L., and RUSK, J. G. (1993). 'Who are nonvoters? Profiles from the 1990 Senate elections'. *American Journal of Political Science*, 37/3: 721–46.

REIF, K. (1985). 'Ten second-order national elections', in K. Reif (ed.), *Ten European Elections*. London: Gower.

—— and SCHMITT, H. (1980). 'Nine second order elections: a conceptual framework for the analysis of European election results'. *European Journal of Political Research*, 8: 3–4.

ROSENSTONE, S. J., and HANSEN, J. M. (1993). *Mobilization, Participation and Democracy in America*. New York: Macmillan.

ROSENSTONE, S. J. and WOLFINGER, R. E. (1978). 'The effect of registration laws on voter turnout'. *American Political Science Review*, 72: 22–45.

SCHMITT, H., and MANNHEIMER, R. (1991). 'About voting and non-voting in the European elections of June 1989'. *European Journal of Political Research*, 19/1: 31–54.

SCHMITTER, P. C. (1996). 'Is it really possible to democratise the Europolity?' Revised version, unpublished document. San Francisco: Stanford University.

SIDJANSKI, D. (1979). 'Turnout, stability, and the left–right dimension', in H. R. Penniman (ed.), *Switzerland at the Polls*. Washington, DC: American Enterprise Institute.

SINNOTT, R. (1995*a*). 'Theory and the internationalisation of governance: bringing public opinion back in', in O. Niedermayer and R. Sinnott (eds.), *Public Opinion and Internationalized Governance*. Beliefs in Government 2. Oxford: Oxford University Press.

—— (1995*b*). 'Policy, subsidiarity, and legitimacy', in O. Niedermayer and R. Sinnott (eds.), *Public Opinion and Internationalized Governance*. Beliefs in Government 2. Oxford: Oxford University Press.

—— (1995*c*). *Irish Voters Decide: Voting Behaviour in Elections and Referendums since 1918*. Manchester: Manchester University Press.

—— (1997). *European Public Opinion and the European Union: The Knowledge Gap*. Institut de Ciències Polítiques i Socials Working Paper No. 126. Barcelona: Universitat Autònoma de Barcelona.

—— (1998). 'The measurement of party attachment in Eurobarometer data: an interpretation, a test and some implications'. *British Journal of Political Science*, 28/1 (forthcoming).

—— and WHELAN, B. J. (1992). 'Turnout in second order elections: the case of EP elections in Dublin 1984 and 1989'. *Economic and Social Review*, 23/2: 147–66.

STILLMAN, P. G. (1974). 'The concept of legitimacy'. *Polity*, 7/1: 32–56.

SULLIVAN, W. M. (1979). 'Shifting loyalties: critical theory and the problem of legitimacy'. *Polity*, 12/2: 253–72.

SWADDLE, K., and HEATH, A. (1989). 'Official and reported turnout in the British general elections of 1987'. *British Journal of Political Science*, 19: 537–51.

TINDEMANS, L. (1976). 'European Union'. *Bulletin of the European Communities, Supplement 1, No. 1*. Bull. EC 1–1976 Suppl. 1/76. Brussels: European Commission.

TINGSTEN, H. (1937). *Political Behavior: Studies in Election Statistics*. London: PS King.

TOPF, R. (1995). 'Electoral participation', in H.-D. Klingemann and D. Fuchs (eds.), *Citizens and the State*. Beliefs in Government 1. Oxford: Oxford University Press.

VALLÈS, J. M. (1994). 'Spain'. *Electoral Studies*, 13/4: 362–7.

VAN DEELEN, B. (1996). 'The Benelux', in J. Lodge (ed.), *The 1994 Elections to the European Parliament*. London: Pinter.

VAN DER EIJK, C., and OPPENHUIS, E. (1996). 'Appendix B: Variables Employed and Methods of Analysis', in M. Franklin and C. van der Eijk (eds.), *Choosing Europe? The European Electorate and National Politics in the Face of Union*. Ann Arbor: University of Michigan Press.

VERNEY, S., and FEATHERSTONE, K. (1996). 'Greece', in J. Lodge (ed.), *The 1994 Elections to the European Parliament*. London: Pinter.

VIDICH, A. J., and GLASSMAN, R. M. (eds.) (1979). *Conflict and Control: Challenge to Legitimacy in Modern Government*. London: Sage.

WEATHERFORD, M. S. (1987). 'How does government performance influence political support?' *Political Behavior*, 9: 5–28.

WEBER, M. (1947). *The Theory of Social and Economic Organisations*. New York: Free Press.

WEILER, J. H., with HALTERN, U., and Mayer, F. (1995). 'European democracy and its critique—five uneasy pieces.' Jean Monnet Working Paper 1/95 Harvard Law School. [http://www.law.harvard.edu/groups/jmpapers/jw1/index.html].

WESSELS, B. (1995a). 'Development of support: diffusion or demographic replacement?' in O. Niedermayer and R. Sinnott (eds.), *Public Opinion and Internationalized Governance*. Beliefs in Government 2. Oxford: Oxford University Press.

——(1995b). 'Evaluations of the EC: élite or mass-driven?' in O. Niedermayer and R. Sinnott (eds.), *Public Opinion and Internationalized Governance*. Beliefs in Government 2. Oxford: Oxford University Press.

WOLFINGER, R. E., and ROSENSTONE, S. J. (1980). *Who votes?* New Haven: Yale University Press.

INDEX

Note: European Parliament and European Union are abbreviated to EP and EU respectively.